Building for the Arts

A Guidebook for the Planning & Design of Cultural Facilities

Catherine R. Brown
William B. Fleissig
William R. Morrish

of CITYWEST

for the Western States Arts Foundation
and the National Endowment for the Arts

Western States Arts Foundation, Santa Fe, New Mexico

This publication was produced under a
cooperative agreement between the Western
States Arts Foundation and the Design Arts
Program of the National Endowment for the Arts.

Frank S.M. Hodsoll, Chairman
National Endowment for the Arts

Michael J. Pittas, Director
Design Arts Program

CITYWEST Project Director:
Catherine Brown

Editor: Cathy Curtis

Editorial Assistants: Laureen McGill,
Tom Hardy

Designer: Teri Hannigan

Cover and Cartoons: Lawrence E. Green

Technical Illustrator: William R. Morrish

Production Artist: June Winson

Typesetting: Novatype

Printing: Land O'Sun

National Endowment for the Arts
Editorial Director: Marcia Sartwell
Editorial Assistant: Phyllis Lehmann

Published by:
Western States Arts Foundation
141 East Palace Avenue
Santa Fe, New Mexico 87501

Authors' Acknowledgments

Because this guidebook encompasses the
fields of arts programming, finance, design,
management, real estate, and public policy,
and because we have sought the advice of
community groups and specialists in each
category, we are indebted to hundreds of
individuals whose insights and experience
have guided us in the preparation of this book.
To all of them we express our thanks.

    We particularly wish to thank certain
individuals whose contributions were essential
in the production of this handbook: Michael J.
Pittas of the National Endowment for the Arts,
for his vision in anticipating the need for this
book and his support and guidance in
producing it; Bill Jamison, Cheryl Alters and
Gerald Yoshitomi of the Western States Arts
Foundation, for their leadership and constant
support; Brian Arnott, author of *A Facility
Development Workbook* and *A Facility Design
Workbook;* Bradley G. Morison, President of
Arts Development Associates, for his
extensive knowledge of facility planning which
he generously shared; Cathy Curtis, for
coordinating manuscript preparation; and
Lawrence Green and Teri Hannigan for their
essential design contribution from the book's
earliest drafts.

Preface

The ability to respond to art—to be moved by it and enriched by it—is one of the most democratic of qualities. It is found in all segments of the population: young and old, schooled and unschooled, rich and poor, city folk and country folk, all races and creeds.

We have known for a long time, of course, that the artistic impulse respects no barriers—certainly not geographic, racial, or educational ones. But not until the "arts boom" of the last two decades did we understand how strong that artistic impulse is in the American people and how broad a segment of the population shares it.

In the last twenty years, the United States has experienced a cultural growth unequaled in its history. In 1965 about 1 million tickets were sold for dance performances, chiefly in New York City. Today there are more than 16 million ticket-buyers—and 90 percent of them live outside New York. Similarly, the audience for orchestral music has risen from 10 million to 23 million; and attendance at museums has gone from 22 million to more than 43 million. Last year performing arts centers around the country sponsored more than 47,000 performances for audiences of more than 40 million people. The "arts boom" has shown that the response to art—and, therefore, the *need* for art—is everywhere.

If the country is long on talent and enthusiasm for the arts, though, it is short on places to house them. Too often artists have had to "make do" with the facilities that were available—and this has meant performances in church basements, basketball courts, high school auditoriums.

Across the country community leaders, dedicated private groups, and planners have begun to respond to the demand for arts facilities that will meet the growing artistic needs of their communities. The movement is well enough underway to see that it has repeatedly run into two kinds of problems. The first is that arts groups often lack the political and economic expertise necessary to convince the community that the construction of an arts facility is not a frill but a need, not an extravagance but a catalyst for local economic development. The second is that too few arts administrators or architects know how to design a cultural facility that works well for the arts, the artists, and the audiences.

The Design Arts Program of the National Endowment for the Arts has long sought to promote design excellence in cultural facilities. The Program has funded more than 250 cultural facility plans and dozens of architectural design competitions. Yet the demand for assistance far exceeds the Program's available funds. Clearly there is a need for a guide in planning and designing an arts facility—a need that this book admirably fills.

The fact is—and this book makes the point emphatically—that as soon as an arts group becomes involved in a building project, the attention of the group must go beyond the arts world. From the beginning of the planning process, arts organizations must understand the role they play in the day-to-day functioning of local government and the sometimes conflicting patterns of needs in the community as a whole. CITYWEST, an architecture and urban design firm, was selected to write this handbook precisely because of the need to deal with facility design as part of a larger picture that includes public policy, real estate strategy, and other non-arts issues.

Produced under a cooperative agreement between the Western States Arts Foundation and the National Endowment for the Arts, this book has implications for both arts administrators and architects. For administrators, it demonstrates that the process of planning an arts facility is a complex but logical series of steps involving many sources of information and constant reevaluation of goals and means. For architects, it describes in detail the essential needs of both the visual and the performing arts, and sets design standards to ensure that the arts are presented under the best possible conditions.

We hope that this book will be a useful tool in helping artists, architects, arts administrators, and interested citizens build arts facilities, for these centers make an important contribution to the quality of a community's life and to its artistic vitality.

Michael J. Pittas
Director, Design Arts Program
National Endowment for the Arts

Foreword

Increasing population growth in the Western states and a proportionately greater demand for the arts have created a widespread need for improved cultural facilities. In recognition of this need, the Western States Arts Foundation, an alliance of ten state arts agencies, initiated a study of the existing status of facilities planning and design in order to assist local arts organizations.

The Design Arts Program of the National Endowment for the Arts recognized the far reaching implications of the project and provided generous funding for the initial research as well as for the actual production of *Building for the Arts*. The member state arts agencies and other organizations were able to provide important data and insights from staff experience with facilities development. The expertise of CITYWEST, an urban planning and design firm, was solicited to accurately collect that valuable information, explore the issues raised and then propose solutions.

While originally conceived to address the needs of Western arts organizations, artists, and their audiences, *Building for the Arts* provides expertise with universal application. Although every situation is unique, it is hoped that the proposed plans of action and supporting case studies from the Foundation's member states will provide assistance in the broadest range of circumstances. The detailed bibliography and resource lists help to make this guidebook the most complete single volume source of facilities information currently available. The content is a credit not only to the collective skills of CITYWEST's Catherine R. Brown, William B. Fleissig and William R. Morrish but also to the state arts agencies, arts organizations, artists and other individuals who participated in the project.

A final note of appreciation goes to Gerald D. Yoshitomi who oversaw *Building for the Arts* in its early development.

Cheryl Alters
Director of Special Projects

Bill Jamison
Executive Director
Western States Arts Foundation

Table of Contents

Appendix

Why You Need This Book & How to Use It

There are many reasons why an arts group or community organization might seek guidance in planning new housing for the arts. Do you recognize your situation here?

- You would like to see a new arts facility in your town but don't know where to start. How can you bring it about?
- You are dissatisfied with your present facility and interested in acquiring another building. The price is right, but the structure needs major renovation. Should you proceed?
- Arts groups are invited to participate in revitalization plans for the downtown area. How can you get what you want from the developer?
- Your community has voted down several bond issues for a cultural facility during the past decade. How can cultural groups organize a successful campaign?
- Your arts group does not have adequate quarters in which to present its work, but you cannot afford to build or renovate. What should you do?

If an improved arts facility is high on your priority list, this book is for you. It offers a step-by-step guide to help you determine whether you really need a new building, how to plan a building that meets your needs, how to fund it, how to generate community support for your plans, and finally how to get the building constructed to your satisfaction.

What This Book Can Do for You

Of course, no book can make you a self-sufficient expert in building an arts facility. You will still need help from people who have created facilities of their own, staff at local and state agencies, and consultants with specific expertise. But this book provides a link between the layman and the technical worlds of architectural design, politics, finance and real estate. Whether you are a performer or arts administrator, a patron of the arts, an activist in community affairs, or a local government employee, you will learn what kind of resources you need, where to look for them, and how to produce the building most suited to the needs of arts organizations, artists, and the community.

This book was written with the economy of the 1980s in mind. The chapters on funding and real estate in particular present business strategies to help arts organizations cope with reduced funding from the federal government and other traditional sources.

Organization of This Book

Not all material here will apply directly to your situation. What we have tried to present is an overall strategy based on numerous first-hand observations of the cultural facility building process and discussions with experts in various technical fields. Any group planning to build or remodel an arts facility should find useful information throughout. Where appropriate—as in Chapters 9 and 10, which deal with design standards for particular art forms—facilities for the visual arts are distinguished from buildings for the performing arts.

We have broken down this book and the facility development process into five steps:

1. **Exploring Ideas for a New Facility.** The first step is to set up a planning committee to collect information about your community and about the type of arts facility you want to build. Other areas to be considered are community and government support, funding, real estate, and professional consultants. You will explore many ideas and opportunities in order to define an idea or direction which can then be tested to determine its actual feasibility.

2. **Testing the Idea Through Feasibility Studies.** The next step is to gather concrete data on the resources available to you and on local arts needs. You will learn about financing, possible options for land acquisition, and ways in which various segments of the community may help or hinder your plans. You will also define your expectations for continued support for your new facility once it is built. To help you assess the overall picture, you will rely on consultants in specific fields. With their feasibility studies in hand, you will be able to judge whether the facility of your dreams is indeed a possibility.

3. **Making the Big Decision.** At this step, with feasibility studies in hand, you are likely to discover that some of your ideas won't work, and you will need to make some adjustments in your plans. You may find that the programming you want to present won't in itself support a new facility. Perhaps the building you envisioned is too large for the community, or the site you wanted is unaffordable. Be prepared to rethink the project—or even to accept the fact that the project is not feasible and could not be supported by the artists and audience you want to serve.

4. **Developing the Building Plan.** Once the parts of the puzzle fit together and you decide to proceed, you are ready to enter the design phase. In the building design, like the planning process, you will move from the general to the specific—from your first estimates

of the size of the workshop area you need to deciding exactly where the electrical outlets will go.

5. **Preparing for Opening Day.** Your final step and the reason for all the effort is the day when the doors of your new home for the arts open. From the very beginning and throughout the design process you will consider the critical issues of operations and management.

Of course, this neat outline is a simplification of a long and complex process. There will be many roadblocks along the way forcing you to turn back to earlier phases and to rework parts of the project that turn out not to be feasible.

But don't despair. Only through constant questioning of your goals and assumptions will you be able to figure out what you really need and can afford. The steps outlined in this book are designed to assure you that when you do break ground, you will be building a facility that works.

But It Sounds So Complicated!

Why not simply tell the architect what you want and have it drawn up into blueprints? For one thing, the design process is complex by nature. Also, an arts facility is more than just a building; it is an integral part of the community. The building you create will have more in common with the public library—responsible to a broad constituency—than with a downtown commercial building erected for the needs of office employees. The financing and construction of an arts facility can have a broad impact on the community, affecting the local tax base, the nature of a redevelopment area, the number of restaurants in the neighborhood, the quality of the educational system and the attitude of residents toward their town. If poorly conceived, it may become a burden rather than a delight.

Design drawings are powerful images. They can inspire people to devote their time to committee work, donate money or clear the path for political approvals. Before the architect starts drawing, however, you must be certain that both your needs and the needs of the community are accounted for. The design will be subject to considerable political pressure, and you don't want your theater's flyloft sacrificed because someone would rather spend money on chandeliers for the lobby. If features must be cut out for cost reasons, you must know beforehand what can be altered or eliminated with least effect on artistic programming.

By following the steps outlined in this book, your group will retain a strong position throughout the planning, design and construction process. The completed building will enhance the presentation of your artistic product and enrich the life of your community.

EXPLORE IDEAS

You're inspired by the dream of a new home for the arts in your community—and you've got an idea or two about how to create it. Now you must explore these ideas more fully with some basic groundwork. Organize a planning group and start to discuss:

- The need for a new facility
- Building local support
- Sources for funding
- Real estate options
- Consultants to help you

EXPLORE IDEAS

1. Getting Organized to Explore

your group will have to lay some important groundwork before you can actually go after a piece of real estate, raise money, or hire an architect. In this chapter, you will learn how to form a planning committee, keep it afloat during the crucial early stages and monitor the pulse of the community you must depend on for support.

A TIME TO TRY OUT YOUR IDEAS

If you've discussed the idea of a new facility with other members of your organization or like-minded people in the community, the time has come to begin testing your ideas.

Before your dreams get out of hand, consider why you want to build a new facility or remodel your old one. Do you have a specific need (more space), or has an opportunity arisen (a bequest or a chance to be part of a new commercial development) that someone is reluctant to pass up? It is deceptively easy to confuse opportunity and need.

The primary issue to keep in mind is the proposed use of the facility. What will the new building permit you to do that you cannot do now?

Who Builds Arts Facilities?

Groups that initiate the arts facility planning process tend to fall into one of four categories. Each group goes through the same planning steps, but with a slightly different approach.

The first category is the **single arts group**, which will be the major tenant of a building created to its own specifications. Generally, the group already has a facility that it has outgrown or that no longer suits its needs. The arts group has probably built up a loyal following and is funded by earned income and private donations, possibly in combination with government funding. Fully aware of its own needs, such a group is generally in a strong position to plan a new facility.

In other cases, **several arts organizations** join forces to acquire permanent quarters they can share. Financial support is generally broader in this situation, with funding coming from more public sources, including for example the local arts council. Success depends on harmony among the groups involved. Certain requirements of one group may be in conflict with those of another, but compromise must not jeopardize the functional design of the facility.

Still other arts facilities are the product of **municipal** efforts. Frequently the impetus for the project is a specific opportunity—the availability of Economic Development Administration or urban renewal money or commercial development, such as construction of a convention center. Initial support comes from such groups as the Chamber of Commerce, the local arts council and major arts groups. The mayor may form a commission to study the need for an arts facility. Civic pride and "boosterism" are often driving forces in the process; the new facility might be seen as a way of putting the town on the map or making the area more hospitable to relocating industry. Whatever the type of facility—symphony hall, municipal auditorium, art center, multipurpose arena—public projects of this nature are bondable through general obligation or revenue bonds or other tax revenues. "Mixed use" facilities, involving participation by the city, a private developer and arts groups, are the most sophisticated type of municipal arts project created in conjunction with commercial uses.

The fourth category is the **nonarts group**, generally a civic-minded organization interested in saving a historic building or in providing an educational experience for local residents. Its task is to find the right arts group or groups to make the project a success. In some cases, the tenants of the building may be a mixture of arts and nonarts groups, as in the Home of the Good Shepherd (a former home for wayward girls in Seattle, Washington), which now houses arts and social service groups in its spacious, rambling quarters.

Where Do You Fit In?

Your group must determine where it fits among the categories described above. Your answer will determine how much public involvement you should expect, the degree to which you need to analyze your requirements, the type of funding you can expect, the duration of the project, and the way in which the facility will operate once the doors open. Obviously, public involvement is greatest when the facility is a municipal effort and much less important if it is initiated by a single arts group. A municipally sponsored plan will also require more extensive research into community attendance patterns. A single arts group will already know what it needs in the way of a new facility, while a nonarts organization planning a facility for arts groups will have very little idea of what is needed.

Funding will vary from predominantly private money for the single arts group to tax dollars for a municipal facility. The nonarts group may be able to draw on public monies in addition to private donations. The more groups and agencies involved in the project, the longer it will take to plan and build. And, of course, management for the new facility also will vary depending on the degree of municipal control involved. Certain types of facilities report to a branch of city government; others are entirely private.

Finally, a word of caution for arts groups invited to participate in a project originated by someone else. Before agreeing to move to new quarters or to build an addition, consider carefully how the plan fits in with your own priorities.

Opportunity or Need: What to Do with a Gift Horse

Being given the chance to occupy a new building or be part of a new development can be a great opportunity—but only if it ties in with your organization's overall plans. Accepting a "gift horse" without analyzing your needs may result in an unusable facility that you would be better off without. Opportunity may knock when:

- A donor offers his collection to a museum with the stipulation that a special wing or facility be built to house it.
- An arts group receives a generous bequest, either open-ended or tied to the building of a new facility.
- A landmark building is about to be demolished and an arts group wants to take it over to save it from destruction.
- A developer offers local arts groups rented space in his shopping center.
- The city treasurer's office, parks department or school board offers an arts group unused property or land unsuited for other public use.
- As a result of local boosterism, the city plans a downtown revitalization that may include a convention center and arts complex.
- The cafeteria in the new school building may be able to accommodate the needs of a performing arts group on a shared basis with school functions.

Community support is extremely important, and your group doesn't want to turn down what appears to be a golden opportunity. But what good is a new facility if it won't accommodate your programs? If you can't find the money to maintain the building? If no one wants to set foot in that part of town?

ASSEMBLING A COMMITTEE

Get other people involved in the project early. If it is a brand new venture, expand the initial support group to include more people with specific expertise. Look for demonstrated support for the arts in your community. If you are an already functioning arts group, pinpoint the board members and staff who really make things work. If you are hard put to find people for your planning committee, you should have second thoughts about embarking on the project.

The exact composition of the planning committee will vary according to the scope of the project.

Planning a major, full-scale arts facility requires the skills and experience of a diverse group of people: practicing artists; arts managers; representatives from local government and other community leaders in the know about civic matters; someone familiar with banking and real estate development; and an expert in architecture, design or construction.

If yours is an already established organization, your board of directors should be represented. Be sure to include at least one committee member with experience in organizing a similar building campaign. People with skills in public-speaking and fundraising are also assets to a planning committee.

Don't be afraid to ask people whose opinions you respect whom they recommend for your committee.

Organizing the Committee

There are no hard and fast rules about committee size. A mere handful of people will "burn out" faster because each individual will carry heavy responsibility. Conversely, too large a group will contain people who have very little to offer. Good committee management, wise delegation of tasks, and careful attention to individual points of view are more important than having a specific number of members.

Appoint only *one* chairperson with decision making power, even if it seems politically wise to appoint an honorary chairperson to share leadership. The chairperson should delegate specific tasks to subcommittees or members with the most appropriate background.

Be sure to make an agenda for each meeting and keep records of your decisions. This back-up material will be valuable when you present your case to potential donors or the public and when you want to bring consultants up to date on the project.

Funding the Committee

Although members of the core committee will be donating their time, certain aspects of the planning process do cost money. Postage, duplicating and telephone costs add up no matter how modest the campaign. But it is often possible to cut costs by appealing to the community for help. In lieu of a rented office, for example, you may be able to operate out of a committee member's living room, or someone might be persuaded to donate office space. Sometimes a group can get a city department to donate office equipment or staff time. A typewriter may be rented or borrowed, and a committee member might be able to provide duplicating facilities. When you order special letterhead, a local printer might be willing to donate the stationery.

In-kind donations won't cover everything however, so expect to raise money for the planning effort. Typically, money comes from committee members themselves, as well as from friends and associates.

Filing for Nonprofit Status

In order to be able to offer a tax deduction to potential contributors and apply for grants, your group must file for nonprofit, tax-exempt status. There are two kinds of nonprofit foundations: private and public. You will need a lawyer to advise you on the status most appropriate for your organization and to help draft literature explaining the tax benefits of various types of donations.

TAKE STOCK OF WHAT YOU'VE GOT

One of the first activities of your committee should be to clearly define your purpose. If you can describe who you are and what you need, you are that much closer to getting funding that will help test your ideas within the community.

An Inventory

Once your committee is able to answer the questions below, your group will be in a solid position to continue the project. In the process, you will create the basis of a prospectus you can use as a fundraising tool. The answers to these questions will, in fact, be a compilation of all the facts, figures, trends and philosophies involved in your decision to create a new facility. By forcing yourselves to document your reasons for becoming involved in the project, you may come up with information you didn't know you had—and you will be ready to answer the toughest question a potential funder can ask.

First, take stock of your organization and community.

1. What is your organization's philosophy in regard to:
   - Arts programming
   - Artistic direction
2. Describe your organization's:
   - Audience composition and attendance
   - Community image and support
   - Strength of management/governing structure
   - Current level of activities
3. Describe your organization's economic assets and liabilities currently and for the past three years (see Appendix A):
   - Expenses
     - personnel
     - administrative (other)
     - facility rental/utilities
     - debt service/taxes
   - Revenues (include sources)
     - earned
     - grants from public sources
     - private grants

□ other
□ possible future sources of revenue

4. Describe other arts facilities in the community and their locations. Why are these facilities not acceptable for your use?
5. What other building fund drives are currently under way?
6. Describe the current facility your organization is using in terms of:
   - overall condition
   - level of technical equipment for your needs
   - physical location (assets and liabilities)
   - community image
   - biggest asset
   - biggest liability
   - budget deficits
   - suitability for your needs

Now clarify the kinds of changes you have in mind and the assistance you can draw upon in making these changes.

1. Do you want to make changes at this time in your organization's:
   - programming (level or kind of change)
   - management
   - community image/support
   - funding base
2. What type of facility changes do you want to make?
   - new facility
   - major renovation (be specific)
   - minor addition(s) or interior alterations
   - technical improvements
   - correction of a previous "improvement"
3. What are the space needs of your organization and any other organizations involved?
4. Are there other local arts or community organizations in need of space who might be potential users/renters? What are their needs and use requirements?
5. Will the facility changes require alterations in your:
   - programming
   - management structure
   - community support
   - financing
   - operating costs
6. Who will benefit from the new facility?
   - arts lovers (the already-committed)
   - the local community in general (how?)
   - a 100-mile radius (how?)
   - the region (how?)
   - business—retail, hotel, restaurant
   - industry (by attracting new employees)
7. What kind and degree of support (broken down into capital construction funds, operating funds and political assistance, see Appendix A) can you expect from:

- city/county departments (building/school/planning) and local officials
- community organizations/neighborhood groups
- other arts groups
- corporate and financial leaders in the community, including local merchants

8. Why do you believe this support is forthcoming?

Evaluating Your Answers

Think about your findings, and ask yourselves some tough questions:

- Will your present committee be able to handle the task ahead? (If this seems like a great deal of work so early in the game, remember that potential funders—private individuals as well as foundations—will be asking you the same questions.)
- Who are your supporters? (Include the backgrounds of the committee and key community people who are enthusiastic about your project and can offer concrete assistance.)
- Is your committee sufficiently equipped and broadranging enough to deal with the arts facility issue? (The following chapters will clarify what areas of technical expertise you will need.)
- Do the audiences/artistic resources/community needs justify the changes you are advocating? What evidence substantiates this?
- Do you need to commission a feasibility study at this time to better answer the questions above?
- Do you feel ready to establish yourselves as a public group, publicize your plan in a formal way, and incorporate yourselves into an ongoing committee? In order to do this in a professional way, you need to know exactly what you are advocating—not just that you want to build a museum, but precisely what kind of museum it will be. You must be able to articulate what you want and justify it to consultants, potential funders, people in control of local politics, and community leaders. The real test is to be able to talk someone into spending money on your project—and to do that, you have to make it sound like a winner.

Should You Go Ahead or Not?

After completing the inventory and answering the questions above, consider very seriously whether the idea of a new or renovated facility makes sense at all. If, for example, you have little money and are unable to locate the necessary funding from other sources, it is inadvisable to proceed. At minimum, your group must now be able to afford modest publicity, possibly the services of a consultant, and office help.

Similarly, if you are unable to drum up local interest in the project, or if the activities of local arts groups are just getting off the ground, maybe this is not the time to proceed. It may be necessary to wait a few years for the community's artistic maturity to catch up with your facility dreams.

COMMITTEE OUTREACH

If you still feel that the outlook for a new facility is positive, one of the first things you must do is survey local opinion. Talk to all kinds of people about your plans. Publicize your activities and seek the views and services of a broad range of local residents. The important thing is to plant the existence of your project in the minds of a large number of people.

Research Other Facilities
Talk to other groups that have been through the same process. Get names of arts organizations in your field from the state arts council, and find out which of these has recently redesigned or built an arts facility. Chances are that someone has already made many of the mistakes that could plague your group.

Were the other groups successful in their building campaigns? If so, why? If not, why not? In what ways did the community and local government rally around the project or throw roadblocks in its path? How was the architect chosen? Did the committee work harmoniously with the architectural firm? What kinds of consultants were used in planning the project, and how valuable were their recommendations? How much research did the group do before choosing a site? Does the facility currently serve the purpose for which it was designed? Are there features of the building which the managers would now like to change?

If you are planning a performing arts facility, for example, speak to the people who book events at your local college. What have they learned about the preferences of the community? How many seats does their facility have, and what percentage of those seats are generally filled? What have their experiences been in maintaining and staffing their facility?

Visit as many arts facilities in your field as possible to get an idea of what others have done. Be sure to figure out *why* you like a facility. See it "in action" during an exhibit or a performance and take a tour of the support or backstage facilities.

Don't be afraid to ask questions. Talk to the people who run the facility, from the artistic director to the scenery shop manager, from the lighting crew to the ushers. In a visual art facility, talk to the director, a curator, a preparator, the museum shop manager and a volunteer or two. Poke around and find out how the place works from the point of view of performers, technical people, audience members or gallery visitors.

Talk with Local Artists
Speak with the directors of local theater groups and other performing arts organizations. What are their needs in terms of rehearsal and performance space? How have local performing groups kept afloat financially and artistically?

If you are planning a facility for the visual arts, speak to local gallery owners and artists, who can give you an idea of the type of art the community has responded to in the past and information about the kind of facility suited to displaying various kinds of art. If there is a local museum, speak to the director about the advantages and drawbacks of running an arts facility in your community. What kinds of shows are best attended? What kind of community outreach has the museum initiated to date?

Go Beyond the Arts Community
Seek the opinions of people not directly involved in the arts—industry leaders, merchants, social and service club leaders, local benefactors, city government officials, amateur arts buffs, and others active in community affairs. How do they view the role of the arts in their community? In their own lives? Are they already committed to another "cause" or might they be helpful to yours? Do they see a connection between arts activity and a more lively economy?

Plan a Public Workshop
One way of heightening community involvement in the early planning stage is to schedule a series of public meetings.

Workshops that allow for an exchange of ideas may be particularly advisable when a community is dealing with an "opportunity" for new arts space. In San Francisco, for example, the developer of a large redevelopment project had a mandate from the city council to set aside an area solely for arts use. Public workshops provided a forum for arts organizations to express their opinions and discuss their diverse needs in terms of the square footage available. During many months of these meetings, committees were formed to deal with such issues as financing, arts programming, image, and design.

Even for a small-scale project, in which you may be gathering information on arts groups and audiences in a more informal way, a workshop can be a good idea. Assembling a group of interested people gives your project a concrete identity. In return, the planning committee benefits from hearing different points of view.

Every public workshop should have a clear agenda. People you invite should have the opportunity to do their "homework" before they arrive, which means that your group has to produce some pertinent reading material about the project. If possible, hire a neutral party to act as moderator so that all points of view receive equal airing. For more information on workshops and how to conduct them, contact Partners for Livable Spaces or VOLUNTEER: The National Center for Citizen Involvement (see Appendix E).

What If Your Town Has No Current Arts Activity?

If there are no arts "experts" to consult, seek the opinions of such people as the town librarian and those who give to social service charities. Identify the local "movers and shakers"—professional people, politicians, business people, the newspaper editor—and find out what they think about creating a cultural facility.

In a "company town," try out your idea on the corporate community affairs department or on a high-placed company officer if someone on your committee has a contact.

But be sure that your town really needs an arts facility at this point in its growth. If there is little arts activity, needs may be met by using schools, churches, grange halls, or community centers. A new facility will not necessarily make the arts thrive.

What To Do While the Planning Process Continues

While your committee works on the details outlined in the following chapters, you must keep your organization in the public eye. In Mesa, Arizona, a savvy consultant suggested that the new children's museum could gain public exposure by setting up temporary quarters in a shopping center owned by a member of the organization's board of directors. With seed money from private donors and a local foundation, the museum hired a director and began developing programs. Next the city offered use of a building scheduled for demolition in several years. Meanwhile, the fundraising campaign for a permanent structure proceeded at full steam, aided by the museum's visibility in the community. Every group should start early to publicize the planned use of a new facility. Schedule ad hoc art exhibits or stage theatrical productions in the town park or shopping mall—anything to get your name and your product before the public.

Study the Whole Process

As you read through this book, try to keep the whole planning process in perspective. Take note of what is involved in maintaining community and government relations, raising money, and putting together a feasibility study. Learn the design requirements of your art form and study the design and construction process. Even though your group may delegate the details of building and renovating to a separate committee, you will still want to keep tabs on the entire effort.

Study the other planning guides listed in Further Reading for additional information and points of view. The best book on planning an arts facility is Joe Golden's *Olympus on Main Street* (Syracuse University Press, 1980), the saga of the Civic Center of Onondaga County in Syracuse, New York. Another useful source is *A Facility Development Workbook* (Brian Arnott

Associates, for Arts Division, Ministry of Culture and Recreation, Ontario, Canada).

You need to strike a delicate balance—maintaining the momentum of the project without pushing too hard for results. The early planning process may take well over a year, during which there will be times when things proceed rapidly and times when progress seems at a standstill. Remember that a group which loses its momentum is in danger of losing valuable people. But above all, avoid the impulse to proceed so quickly that you skip important steps along the way. There are no shortcuts in planning and building an arts facility.

EXPLORE IDEAS

2. Community & Government Support

Generating community support means selling your idea to the people whose opinions, money, donated materials, votes, and permissions you need in order to carry out your project. We can't emphasize enough the importance of building local support as early as possible.

Once you have documentation of your plans, you are ready to discuss them with other members of the community. Some people will be excited; others might actively seek to keep you from completing the project. Many local residents might even be indifferent to your cherished goals. But if you have plotted a strategy for attracting the backing you need, you will be in a better position to deal with negative opinion and to tap a wide range of potential supporters.

THE THREE KINDS OF SUPPORT

At each stage of the planning process, you need to identify the types of support you are seeking: **financial** (money and materials); **physical** (man-hours of work that get the job done); or **political** (agreement that your project is a worthy one). First, figure out where you can look for each type of support. Then identify allies who will help you deal with local bureaucracy and other arts groups and civic organizations; identify and contact potential funding sources; and create a positive image for your group in the community.

WHAT YOU WILL NEED AT VARIOUS STAGES

Initial Exploration

In the early planning stage, consider the various types of political support and approvals you will need to create a new facility. Seek funding for the work of the planning committee and volunteers to handle specific tasks.

Feasibility

At the feasibility stage, when the merits of your plan are being tested, you must keep the public up to date on the committee's progress and determine which political approvals are most crucial to your success. Members of your group will coordinate the work of consultants you hire, while seeking funding and volunteers to help in the data-gathering process.

Project Implementation

As soon as your committee has settled on a specific course, you need to convince key people to commit time, money, and political support to your campaign. The three-pronged fundraising process (discussed in Chapters 3 and 7) for planning, construction, and operation of the finished facility should be in full swing. Large-scale projects now require approvals from various city or county departments and officials, including the mayor, city council, and city planning agencies. Your project will also benefit from the support of the school board, professional and industry leaders, the media, and church leaders. Be sure to involve your town's cultural activists—the people who support the library, community theater, and the horticultural society. A volunteer corps is important at this stage for getting out the word about your plans and keeping the administrative process running smoothly.

Ongoing Public Support

During the lengthy design and building process, don't let the public forget about your group. If yours is an ongoing arts organization, try to keep your programs running at a temporary location. The fundraising campaign will still be running strong with the help of volunteers, and the core group will be evaluating the work of consultants. At this point, the people who met back in the early stages may have stepped aside in favor of individuals with greater expertise in working with architects and a fresher perspective on the project. But throughout it is imperative to keep the project in the public eye.

When the facility is completed, day-to-day operation will be turned over to a director or manager, under the guidance of a board of directors. But always the number one priority will be public support—in the form of both dollars and attendance.

BUILDING SUPPORT

Start with a Strong, Influential Committee

Community support starts with the composition of your own planning committee or board of directors. Every committee needs members who can roll up their sleeves and produce results by means of well-placed connections, personal qualities such as tact and diplomacy, and strong dedication to the project. Some members should have acquaintances with power to help you get what you need from the community.

You will also want people who have demonstrated their abilities on specific projects—persuading the library not to reduce its hours, perhaps, or launching a campaign for a stop sign at a dangerous intersection. Still others should function as direct pipelines to city government, the financial community, and the social leadership of the area.

Plot Your Strategy

Once you have assembled your committee or board, you need to map out a specific strategy for community support. Whom do you need to convince or ask for money? Where are they located in the social and political structure of your community? What will you do now, in six months, and two years from now to ensure their continued support?

Make three lists: key allies and supporters, neutral parties, and the "opposition". What other support can the allies and neutrals help you gain for your side? Who can the opposition enlist against you? In general, opponents will include those who are against the spending of public money and those who have plans of their own for the building or location you want.

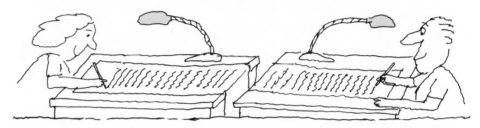

Strategy Memos—For Your Eyes Only

Two kinds of strategy are crucial to the planning process. One concerns your dealings with people; the other, the means by which you hope to obtain funding, materials, and labor. The first step then is to prepare a political strategy memo—for internal use ONLY—that outlines how you intend to handle community relations.

Every member of the group should compile a set of lists divided into "allies," "neutrals," and "the opposition". From these will evolve a master list including city and county agencies, community organizations such as the historical preservation group, business leaders, foundations, and influential individuals like the mayor or newspaper editor. Be sure to identify any groups or individuals capable of stopping your project, such as fiscal conservatives in local government, preservationists, neighborhood groups, the city planning department, or another arts group.

On your "allies" list, note the kind and degree of support that you might expect from each source. Remember that support comes in many forms—useful advice, liaison with other helpful people, or the ability to help form others' opinions.

Follow up on your lists. Assign committee members to contact your allies and to ask them for suggestions on how to improve your facility proposal.

The second strategy memo will outline sources of tangible aid for your project. First, draw up an inventory stating your needs in terms of dollars, leadership, volunteers, building materials, and other categories. Identify sources of public assistance—city, county, state, and federal agencies and various quasi-public groups—as well as potential supporters in the private sector—service and arts organizations, professional clubs, businesses, neighborhood and church groups, and key individuals in the community. To locate these resources, consult the Chamber of Commerce, the planning department, the Yellow Pages, and members of your own group.

Once you have drawn up your lists, consider the motivating factors that would convince these groups to support your plans. What will your project do for them? In what kinds of projects are they usually interested? What is the overriding philosophy of the group?

After you have matched resources to your needs, draw up an implementation strategy. Discuss how to approach each potential resource. Who is the best person in your group to initiate contact, and what should your "angle" be? Perhaps you can enlist other individuals who are better placed to sound out interest in your project. Carefully plan the timing of your approach to each group—you want to present your plans at the time of the year or even the day of the week when the group will be most receptive to your ideas. Determine what supporting materials you will need for the meeting. Should you take a proposal? A list of potential benefits to that group or individual? Letters from influential backers of your plans? Your organization's financial statement? After you have approached each contact, be sure to follow up any sign of interest with letters or phone calls, and keep careful records of who has done what. When the building is completed, you will want to thank your supporters publicly, unless they specifically request anonymity.

Choose a "Power King"

Among the first people your group should talk to is the powerful individual or group in town whose negative impression of the project could be a severe liability. By meeting with the opposition, you can learn the precise reason for their disapproval and possibly defuse their concern. Nearly as important is the publisher of the local newspaper; projects that have an ally in the media often are able to sway public opinion.

Make a point of asking politicians where they stand. Is the current mayor against your project? In Portland, Oregon, even though the mayor lacked interest in the Performing Arts Center campaign and kept his friends from supporting it, the Center was able to attract enough supporters to make a bond vote successful. It may seem that the powers behind a convention center can't be talked into including an arts facility, but with the right support, you can change their minds. Again, in Portland, the convention center planners discovered they would need to build the theater they had previously opposed in order to justify the one-cent tax they wished to institute.

Try Out Your Ideas

Talk to acquaintances with expertise in the areas where you need help. If you know a retired mortgage broker, describe your idea about taking over the old vaudeville house and find out if your reasoning is faulty. Friends can act as devil's advocates, poking holes in your ideas before you actually go public with them.

Be selective about informing outsiders. Speak first with people likely to respond favorably. The snowball effect ("Everybody's behind it—I guess I should be too") is a well-known fundraising procedure. But to make this technique work, you must be sure to approach people in the right "pecking order".

Get Your Ideas in Writing

The more tangible evidence of planning that you can submit to the community, the more seriously your project will be taken. A completed feasibility study demonstrates the care and thought that has gone into the planning process. Architectural sketches can provide tangible evidence of the direction your project will take.

Be Aware of Your Image

The tone and energy of your media campaign will be vital to the success of your project. If you are planning a big campaign to promote your project, find a public relations consultant to help you tell your story to the community. In smaller building projects, the temptation is to project a "just folks," impression in promotion materials—partly in order to save money and partly to keep things on a cozy level. But this seat-of-the-pants approach may backfire if it makes your project look poorly managed or unimportant. Consider asking an image-maker in the community—a "star" sports figure, for example—to promote the project. Planning groups working with a nationally renowned architectural firm can use the firm's blue-chip credentials to build confidence among potential backers.

A Political Support Campaign Requires a Major Effort

Getting political support for a bond campaign is a major undertaking. A large number of volunteers will be needed to ring doorbells, collect petition signatures downtown and in the shopping malls, operate telephone banks, and perform other tasks. These people need to be organized by capable leaders who understand how to get the most from volunteers while maintaining a good "espirit de corps". At the top, you need as a consultant a campaign strategist who knows how to reach the greatest number of probable "yes" votes.

If you need to obtain signatures on a petition to get the facility issue on the ballot, plan where to look for supporters and how to present your case. Volunteers in Portland, Oregon, for example, talked up the Civic Auditorium bond package at every cultural event during the six weeks before the election.

Is there a way to strengthen your case? Will your plans be more acceptable once your group has chosen a specific site? Will a major corporate donor bring more money your way? Don't be afraid of making an early decision that can help establish your group's identity.

Should You Play It Close to the Chest?

The chief advantage of publicizing your work is that it inspires trust on a broad level. But a back-room approach may be necessary in certain cases.

Early announcement of an arts facility project for example, can sometimes drive up land values beyond what arts groups can afford. Prejudicial editorials in the local newspaper may nip facility planning efforts in the bud. Your group will have to weigh the advantages of playing it close to the chest vs. full disclosure of your plans. No matter which route you take, you still must talk to key people to seek both political and financial support.

MAINTAINING A BROAD SUPPORT BASE

Stay in Touch with the Public

Keep people informed throughout the process. The community should get the word via announcements you make to the media of major breakthroughs in the campaign. Keep special supporters up to date with a newsletter or some regular written communication. Very special people deserve personal phone calls at appropriate intervals.

Establish a schedule to make sure you actually do these things. Once your people get wrapped up in the project, they may forget to keep up the contacts so eagerly sought in the beginning.

Good Timing Is the Key

Choose the right time to make your appeals. If your town is experiencing a rise in unemployment or if people have recently voted on a big bond issue, the time is not right to launch another major campaign.

Good public relations also means making the most of your supporters. Find your corporate and other big-league backers early to give your campaign a strong kick-off. Make sure you have carefully prepared the people in charge of granting the permissions you may need. In Roseburg, Oregon, the Umpqua Arts Center became a reality when the arts groups began attending city council meetings and briefing key people about their record of activities and the public involvement they fostered. The group clinched its case with testimony from a similar visual arts organization that worked out a rental arrangement with its town government.

Keep the Home Fires Burning

Don't forget that you are an arts group! Use this time to build audiences through a residence program in the schools or by participating in a local festival. Keep up your concert activities wherever you can find a temporary home. If you sell out, blow your horn about it: "We sold out at the high school gym—think what we could do at a new hall!" If your program is in the visual arts, make your presence known via temporary exhibits in non-art spaces around town. In Los Angeles, the permanent home of the Museum of Contemporary Art is still on the drawing board, but the exhibition schedule has already begun at The Temporary Contemporary, two warehouses that were slated for demolition.

Nothing can replace the support you can generate through your own creative efforts. Sample arts programming while the building is underway can create a definite image for your group in the community. Equally important, it helps you explore your producing capabilities, build audiences, and test audience response to your efforts.

3. Funding Sources & Strategies

Recent changes in tax laws and federal funding for the arts have altered the pattern of support to which arts organizations were accustomed for more than a decade. The Economic Development Administration (EDA), a traditional source of capital construction funds, may no longer be an option. There is less Housing and Urban Development (HUD) money. Reductions in National Endowment for the Arts grants will also have an impact on the arts in the 1980s. In this era of shrinking federal support, the most reliable sources of public money will now be the city and county, through local bonding issues paid for by tax monies.

Private support will continue to come from individuals, foundations, and corporations. With the recent changes in tax laws, however, your group will need a sophisticated strategy in order to attract these donors.

THE THREE KINDS OF MONEY

There are essentially three types of money needed to finance the planning, design, construction, and maintenance of an arts facility. The money for each one can be obtained from different sources.

1. **Seed money.** This is what gets your planning group to the point of starting actual construction on the building. The money keeps the committee afloat day-to-day and finances the fundraising necessary to support feasibility studies, manage a bond campaign, and get word of your plans to the public. These funds may also pay for design work needed to prepare a prospectus for use as a fundraising tool. During the seed money phase, your group is looking for relatively small sums, versus the "big bucks" required for design and construction. Your success in attracting seed money and your growing knowledge of other funding sources will guide you in deciding whether to go ahead with the highly expensive second phase of the project.

2. **Capital support.** This funding is earmarked for design, land acquisition, "bricks and mortar" construction, permanent equipment, and furnishings for the facility. The money will come from private sources if yours is a single arts group; public, multi-group projects will be eligible for public support, augmented by private donations.
3. **Operational Funding.** No form of support is easy to come by, but funds to keep a facility running after it is built are unquestionably the most difficult to raise. For that reason, you must devote part of your energies during the capital campaign to securing the money that will permit the new building to keep its doors open. The momentum generated by the capital drive provides a needed boost for the operating fund campaign.

As you seek money for each category, be sure to keep your basic purpose in mind. Any funding strategies you select should not cause you to change your original direction.

Seed Money for Planning

Some seed money is available from various sources in the form of one-time grants ranging from $15,000 to $25,000. But this money is not there just for the asking. You need to prepare studies that inventory existing cultural spaces and demonstrate a need for your proposed facility. You must have in mind a specific location or strategy, such as renovating an abandoned movie theater.

Putting your case into the form a legislator or city council member wants to see may take more than a year of preliminary planning.

How will your group stay afloat during this time and while funding applications are being considered? Generally, the committee itself contributes at least one third of the private sector donations, which means that you must have on your board of directors or planning committee people with significant financial resources. With money in hand from your own ranks, it is much easier to approach potential donors on the outside: "We already have commitments of $5,000 from . . ." is a very effective fundraiser.

Federal/State Sources

Federal and state agencies award certain one-time grants by competition on a regular schedule. Frequently, the arts organization must match the grant funds with donations raised at the local level. The details of government grant programs change frequently, so be sure you have the latest information and application forms.

Modest amounts of money are available from the **National Endowment for the Arts** to fund the planning stage. When applying, you will be in competition with many other arts organizations. The better your group's track record and the more urgent your facility need, the greater your chance of success. Try to single out the aspects of your project that make it unique.

Other common sources of federal and state seed money are **state arts councils** (amount of assistance and information available varies from state to state); **state economic development agencies**; and **state historical societies**.

Local Government Sources

One-time grants from city departments, such as parks and recreation, public schools, and social service agencies, may tide your group through this period. Success in obtaining these funds depends on how you couch your request. The school board planning a new high school might be talked into funding a feasibility study for a theater your group could share with the students. Allying with social service groups interested in joint use of a building is another way of financing this part of the project.

In one town, the arts facility happened to be on the boundary of an area slated for redevelopment by means of industrial revenue redevelopment bonds, so the arts group was able to "cash in" on a lucky coincidence. To find out potential funding sources of this kind, seek out people in local government departments who have some interest in the arts.

Private Sources

Foundations may provide seed money, but not all that give to the arts are interested in this type of funding. Check national foundation guides for those that permit seed money donations to arts groups. Depending on foundation policy, these grants may be awarded on a set schedule or on a flexible, year-round basis.

Private **community organizations**, like the Rotary Club, are a possible source of funding, but you will need to be extremely organized and businesslike in stating your case. Discuss specifically how your plan will boost the local economy. Will your facility, for example, attract more potential shoppers to the downtown area?

Local **corporations** may be interested in funding your group, but again, presentation is all important. Find out if the corporation has a *gift-matching program,* in which an employee's gift to a tax exempt organization is matched by the company, or a special *volunteer program* that provides donations up to a set limit to organizations in which an employee has been actively involved for a stated length of time. A firm's community relations office can tell you whether such programs exist.

Corporations are just beginning to organize their giving along these lines. But if you are lucky enough to deal with one of the pioneers in this field, be precise about why you need the money, and be sure to bone up on materials provided by the firm before you apply to the program or go for an interview.

Redevelopment agencies—and special private downtown development corporations—might be willing to put up money for consultants if your group is thinking about moving into an area earmarked for improvement.

Services-In-Kind

Donations of staff time, office space, equipment, and supplies may be available from the community resources department in your town. Determine your most pressing needs and find out what policy governs these services.

The **local arts council** may also help you find equipment and supplies, as well as low cost printers for your stationery, arts-loving office help, access to master lists of local arts patrons, odd-jobbers, and consultants.

Capital Funding for Construction

When you begin to plan for capital funding, you will rely in large part on the strategies and financial sources suggested in the funding feasibility study you have commissioned. Your group will have documented the need for a new or renovated facility, and you will know how much the building should cost. Some facilities are built almost entirely with either public or private funds, but a combination of funding is far more common. The capital funding source charts in Appendix A will help you plot your own strategy.

Public Sources

Public bond funding is a common way of financing arts facilities that serve a broad public purpose. Several types of bonds can be used for capital funding. One is *general obligation bonds*, which require voter approval. You might persuade voters to pass a bond by arguing that the new facility would create additional jobs, increase retail sales and tax revenues, boost the local economy in general, and, of course, bring cultural benefit to the entire community. Each city has a "bonding limit," generally set by legal charter or statute and tied to city assets. Money is usually generated by levying a property tax increase; therefore, repayment of the bond involves the entire community.

Revenue bonds, which may or may not require voter approval, have a higher interest rate than general obligation bonds. Pledged revenues come from specific sources, such as facility operations or taxes on hotel rooms, food served at restaurants, ticket sales, liquor sales, or coin-operated games. Frequently, a municipal parking garage is built with revenue bonds, and the parking revenues are then pledged to pay off the bond.

Industrial development revenue bonds are a special category of bonds established by the U.S. Treasury to promote economic and job development. They are used to build industrial plants, parking garages—and, rarely, cultural projects. These bonds may support parking structures or roads that are related to an arts facility if local powers can be convinced that culture is a means toward economic development.

Industrial development revenue bonds are paid off by income produced by the new entities they finance, in addition to taxes pledged toward the city's repayment obligation. They do not require voter approval. To find out if your group is eligible for this form of assistance, contact the community development or planning department. They will refer you to the appropriate city office, generally that of the city manager or economic development department. You will no doubt have to present your case convincingly to the mayor's chief financial assistant, who generally holds the purse strings for projects of this nature.

Tax increment financing is another type of bond available only in certain states. Under this arrangement, a specified area of a city becomes a separate taxing district, and all future tax monies from that area go to a special agency. Bonds are floated and paid off from the revenue coming from this development district. The city gets only so much of the pot for its ongoing costs; the remainder of the money goes to subsidize the redevelopment project.

Although little money comes in at first, taxes on the new construction give the project increased leverage in ten to fifteen years. After about twenty years, the special district is eliminated and all tax income goes to the city. This type of financing has the best chance of success when the city has a healthy tax income and does not need an instant revenue source. The advantage is that it can finance several facilities built by a city agency or subsidize a developer with a substantial loan. To determine whether this might be feasible for your area, talk to the planning department and the mayor's office.

Line items in the general budget of a municipality may include money for a specific project. Your project might qualify if you are requesting support for a small building or renovation program that can be completed in one budget year. You will need substantial evidence of local support and skill in presenting your case convincingly to city officials.

Categorical grants of public monies allotted for a specific purpose might finance part of your capital costs. One type of stipend comes from city departments. Parks and Recreation, for example, might allocate money if your facility will occupy land or buildings under its control. Another possibility is revenue sharing—U.S. Treasury funds allocated quarterly to your state and local government—for projects that are community priorities. There are no restrictions on these funds; the total amount is based on population and income formulas. Ask your local planning department or community redevelopment agency about the availability of such grants.

Special state allocations are another possible source of funding for one-time programs. The Bicentennial in 1976 provided many opportunities of this nature.

Specific tax monies may provide a nest egg for your facility. In boom-industry areas, oil drilling taxes based on the amount of coal removed from the ore head are earmarked for specific community uses. Cultural organizations may receive a certain percentage of these funds. Or, a portion of local hotel and motel taxes may go into a general arts fund, to be divided among various groups. Some cities have "Percentage for Art" ordinances that require one or one and a half percent of the total construction cost of government sponsored projects to be set aside for the acquisition of art or for the construction of facilities to house the arts. Check with city hall to see whether your community benefits from any of these taxes.

Mandated joint or mixed use provisions may be in force where land costs are high and the land in question is held by the municipality. Generally, development is under the jurisdiction of a redevelopment agency or a downtown development corporation. Under these provisions, a certain portion of the property to be developed may be reserved for nonprofit use.

Challenge Grants from the National Endowment for the Arts have helped numerous arts organizations finance capital costs. Obtain the current guidelines from the NEA well in advance of the application due date; you will need to make a very solid case for the stability and artistic worth of your organization to receive one of the comparatively few grants awarded.

Private Sources

To determine which corporations and foundations might help your capital fund drive, you need to research their philanthropic policies. (This information is available from *Funding Sources for Cultural Facilities: Private and Federal Support for Capital Projects*, published by the Design Arts Program, National Endowment for the Arts and the Oregon Arts Commission, March, 1980.) Annual corporate reports also will give you an idea of previously funded projects. See Further Reading for more funding sourcebooks.

Obtaining individual donations from the community requires a pyramid approach: an initial campaign focusing on a select group of potential major donors, followed by a broad-based appeal to the public. Even though raising money from the general public is only slightly less expensive than taking out a bank loan, individual donations demonstrate public support. Your project wins points with public donors who always like to see evidence of wide-ranging community support.

It is most important to keep detailed records of individual donations. You should be able to see at a glance the donor's past record of support, notations about each formal contact, the donor's pertinent interests, and other resources he or she might contribute to the building campaign.

In return for their generosity, most donors will want special privileges, public recognition, and the feeling that their contribution will improve the local business climate and general welfare of the community. Inscribed bricks and nameplated seats are common ways of honoring major givers. In fact, your group can "sell" the entire building, including offices, meeting rooms, galleries, or dressing rooms.

Check Further Reading for sources on fundraising procedures. Remember: four years before the opening of a major facility is not too soon to start the funding campaign machinery rolling.

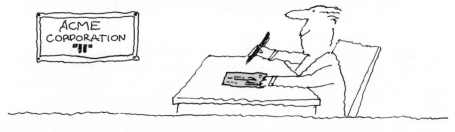

The Arts Group As Developer

The model for this new funding strategy is the Museum of Modern Art in New York. The condominiums the Museum is building above its facility will yield income to fund expansion of the exhibition and office space. (See Chapter 4 for more information on this and other innovative means of generating capital development funding and acquiring real estate from a private party. Also see Appendix A for charts on which you can plot estimated "hard" and "soft" capital costs and list the source and amount of potential funding.)

Operational Funding: Running the Facility

It is exciting to help create a new building, but no one clamors to pay for electricity bills or cleaning services once it is built. For that reason, you must go after operating funds at the same time you launch the capital campaign. Money to pay the day-to-day costs of running your new facility will come from a variety of sources.

Earned Income

This is money raised from ticket sales, festival profits, souvenir sales, rentals to outside groups, liquor and food concessions, and similar ventures. Total earned income may cover anywhere from 25 percent to 75 percent of operating costs. Traditionally, visual arts facilities earn a much smaller percentage of their expenses than do performing arts facilities.

Contributed Income

Annual giving, generally through memberships that offer certain privileges in return, helps pay some operating costs. But an **endowment fund**—consisting of long-range gifts and bequests invested in stocks, bonds, and money market funds—is a major source of ongoing income and must be a crucial part of your fundraising efforts.

A portion of the money you raise for operating costs during the capital fund drive should be earmarked for an endowment. Over the years, this pool of "money that makes money" will be extremely important. With a $9 million endowment as the condition of university approval, Harvard University's Fogg Art Museum raised money to build a $10.2 million new facility.

Public Support

Public support may come in the form of a **line item in the city budget**. Aid may range from in-kind services—maintenance of the grounds by the city parks department, interior maintenance courtesy of the school board, if your group uses school facilities— to actual budget allocations. **Specific program support** may also help with daily maintenance. If you receive a foundation or corporation grant for a particular exhibition or a series of concerts, certain overhead costs will probably be included within the grant guidelines. (The charts in Appendix A will help you plot your own strategy for ongoing support by calculating estimated revenues and expenses.)

Development Dividends

The innovative models of **mixed use development** and **cultural organization-as-developer** (see pages 44-47) may also yield bonuses for operational funding. In a mixed use development, you might request that a portion of retail earnings accrue to the cultural facility that helps draw shoppers to the area.

DEVELOP A FUNDING MASTER PLAN

Basic Funding Models

The funding decisions you make will have a major impact on the image of your facility. The following models will give you an idea of the diversity of the funding picture and should help you determine what combination may work best in your particular situation.

Traditional Funding Model for a Cultural Facility

The facility is a free standing, single use building—a "monument in the park". Funding includes heavy support from the institution's board of directors and other private sources. Ongoing support is provided by the city, which may own the structure. Large deficits are offset by private or public monies.

Example: The Seattle Art Museum, located in Volunteer Park, was built by private individuals and given to the city in 1933. The museum is indebted to the city for maintenance and utilities.

Joint Public/Private Funding

The facility is generally located in or near a central business district or urban renewal area and is surrounded by retail, commercial, and financial buildings. Some of the capital costs are borne by the city, which typically owns the land and is involved in renovating the building.

Example: The Capitol Theater in Yakima, Washington—built in 1920 as a touring house—was acquired by the city in 1975 with federal revenue sharing money and a land trade deal. The city also matched local contributions after a fire severely damaged the building. A portion of the operating budget comes from city and county funds, and the city is responsible for maintenance.

New structures are funded through a bond issue or with urban renewal money. Often the result is a multi use complex that is expected to "put the town on the map." A hotel or convention center may be part of the package.

Example: In Eugene, Oregon, the Performing Arts and Conference Center complex was financed by a bond issue and fundraising campaign organized by the Eugene Arts Foundation. Operating costs will come in part from hotel room tax proceeds; other taxes are under consideration. Located in an urban development area, the Center, with adjoining hotel and "parkade," is conceived as a major economic boost for the greater metropolitan area.

Combined Use and Shared Costs

The facility is owned by a university or municipality which shares both capital and ongoing costs with the arts organization. When the other tenants are social service organizations or university departments, the arts organization may derive certain benefits. A theater sharing its quarters with a child care center, for example, may get free access ramps for the handicapped as part of the city's obligation to the center. An arts organization located on campus may receive university maintenance services.

Example: The Morrison Art Center in Boise, Idaho, enjoys both community and Boise State University support. Construction and operation funds came from both sources, with the state contributing approximately 40 percent of the capital costs and more than 50 percent of the operating expenses. A scheduling agreement ensures equitable use by university and community groups, as well as touring companies.

Civic Owned and Funded Model
This is the community center created to serve both civic and cultural needs. Financed by a major city bond and supported by city revenues, the facility generally receives some private money for capital costs. (See *Olympus on Main Street*, by Joe Golden, which deals in depth with the creation of the Civic Center of Onondaga County, New York.)

Example: The Elko, Nevada, Civic Auditorium and Convention Center was financed by a bond issue, and operating costs are met largely by city room tax revenues. Sports and commercial events will augment cultural uses. Residents hope the cowboy town image will attract a large number of convention visitors.

Private Entrepreneurial Model
Located in an urban mixed use complex or a shopping center, this is either a new structure or a rehabilitated old one where culture and commerce co-exist. The cultural facility helps bring in people during the evening hours and creates an atmosphere attractive to retail clientele. Revenue-producing segments in turn help offset capital and operating costs of the cultural facility. Contributions from the developer are also part of the funding package.

Arts groups thinking of relocating to a mixed use complex must consider the potential impact of a commercial ambience on their operations. They will want to retain control over programming but at the same time must consider ways to attract visitors who might otherwise not be inclined to sample their art.

Example: The Bellevue, Washington, Art Museum was offered space virtually rent free in a shopping mall owned by a long-time museum board member. The move will mean no loss of control over programming and no major operational changes, except possible admission charges and longer hours. A $400,000 capital campaign will pay for moving expenses, adaptation costs, and the first year's operating expense.

User-Financed Facility
Generally a renovated store or warehouse intended for single use by a cultural group, this facility is financed largely by private lenders and individual donations. A bank might be induced to provide an affordable capital fund loan. But the arts group is left to search on its own for operating

funds, which typically come from a mix of earned income and private donations. This model provides the greatest independence for an arts organization but also involves an ongoing financial burden.

Example: In Cheyenne, Wyoming, the Little Theater Players negotiated a 100 percent bank loan for a structure on the National Register of Historic Buildings. Renovation funds came from a match-required grant from the National Trust for Historic Preservation, the Union Pacific Railroad (which donated twice as much as was requested), and local businesses.

Funding Strategy

Devising a funding strategy and fundraising are two separate processes, involving two different consultants. The overall funding strategy set forth in your feasibility study will assure a steady cash flow from many sources for the different segments of your project. This type of planning takes advantage of the latest information on real estate, tax legislation, arts management, and any other pertinent area. You will need the services of people with expertise in all these fields.

Fundraising

A fundraising consultant, on the other hand, is brought in after the feasibility of the project has been established. His or her job involves three basic steps: identifying potential sources of funding, selecting sources key to your project, and following through with a campaign to solicit the money. The consultant should have experience in organizing a door-to-door fund drive, identifying potential private donors, and writing a grant proposal. On a major project, a strong grasp of public relations is also important. There are pros and cons to choosing either a local consultant or an "outside" professional. A local expert may be familiar with your community but may lack wide-ranging experience with arts projects. On the other hand, an outsider may have innovative ideas but won't "know the territory". (See Chapter 5 for advice on how to locate and work with a fundraising professional.)

Whether or not you hire a fundraising consultant—you may be able to manage without one if your project is small and someone on your board or committee has experience in this area—there are typical fundraising mistakes of which you should be aware.

Some Fundraising Pitfalls

Inadequate planning is at the top of the list. Draw up timetables for work expected from individuals as well as for awaited donations. Insufficient manpower also bedevils many a fundraising committee. Without a carefully briefed team of volunteers, your project probably won't get off the ground. Remember that fundraising is a slow and painstaking process. Some people will take months or even years to make a commitment, but when they do respond, your periodic tactful contact may be repaid many-fold. Prompt acknowledgment of every donation is mandatory.

Fundraising campaigns also flounder because goals were set too high. If community support has not been fostered, if you are competing with many other fund drives, or if your area has been hit by economic depression, even the most dedicated committees cannot work miracles. Seek advice from other local fundraising committees. How did they achieve their goals? Whom did they ask for help? And be sure to time your campaign wisely. There might be ways you can "piggyback" onto other fund drives rather than compete for the same dollars.

The Impact of Tax Law Changes for the Arts

The Economic Recovery Act of 1981 brought about major changes in the tax laws that have made private donations more difficult to secure. On the other hand, certain provisions may actually spur business giving and development of facilities for the arts.

A lower tax bracket ceiling—down from 70 percent to 50 percent—means that a wealthy person has less incentive to donate part of his or her income to a nonprofit organization as a tax write-off. A new **ceiling of $10,000 on untaxed gifts** will also work against private fundraising. A potential donor may now prefer to give a smaller sum to a relative rather than a generous amount to your building campaign. As a result of increased tax credits for scientific research, but not for research in the humanities or social sciences, some individuals and organizations that formerly gave to the arts may now change the focus of their philanthropy. Other tax shelters—especially real estate and oil—have also become increasingly profitable and are likely to offer strong competition for the arts dollar.

On the other hand, **lower corporate tax rates** may be a spur to business giving. The maximum deductible amount for charitable purposes has increased from five percent to ten percent, and larger contributions can be carried forward with no penalty for a five year period. **Accelerated depreciation of property**—down from forty to fifteen years—should encourage developers who own or plan to create an arts or mixed-use complex. The developer can now shelter greater amounts of revenue. **Increased tax credits on property** is another positive aspect of the new tax laws. Structures 30 to 39 years old qualify for a 15 percent credit; owners of buildings more than 40 years old receive 20 percent; and "certified historic structures" are allowed a 25 percent credit. This provision may encourage sale/leaseback arrangements, under which the building owner receives the depreciation benefits for which the nonprofit group is ineligible and the arts group works out a lease setting forth its priorities and rights.

Now that you have some background on the types and sources of funding you will need, you are ready to plot out your own strategy. Make lists of all possible sources for each pool of funds. How much is available from each one? What stipulations might apply to the money? Realize that you need a master plan. You need to figure out how to "package" the money coming in at different times from different donors and how to locate private "matches" for public funds. Keep in mind your overall schedule, funding deadlines imposed by foundations, and restrictions on the use of certain grant money. Be savvy about whom you approach first. The large donor starts the ball rolling and helps to get others on the bandwagon. Solicitations from the general public—while indispensible to the campaign— always come last. Remember that money tends to be given where its effects will be most visible or most pertinent to the donor. A corporation may extend its largess only in towns where it has factories or stores.

Consider the impact of various funding strategies on future arts programming. But remember to think in business terms, too. The huge amounts of money involved in a building campaign make it mandatory for an arts organization to act in a professional, businesslike manner.

EXPLORE IDEAS

4. Real Estate

Your choice of location will affect virtually every aspect of your new arts facility. Your capital fundraising campaign cannot credibly get off the ground until a site is selected. Tax issues and budgetary decisions will vary according to the manner in which you acquire property. Finally, the site chosen will have a long-range impact on operating costs and arts programming.

In real estate matters, you will probably be in a position of reacting to the current market situation. However, there are alternative methods of acquiring real estate that you should consider—including sale/leaseback arrangements, joint use arrangements and obtaining publicly owned property. These are discussed later in this chapter.

BRING IN AN EXPERT

No matter what type of real estate arrangement best suits your needs, you must have an expert on board to help your group make the best decision. Your architect, whose design skills are central to the success of the project, cannot be expected to serve as a real estate expert. The planning committee should include someone with experience as a **mortgage broker** (middleman between the party that needs the loan and the bank that offers it), **real estate broker** (middleman between buyer and seller of property) or **real estate developer** (coordinator of a project from original concept through construction). The complexity of property tax laws also makes it essential to have a **tax lawyer** experienced in dealing with donations, trusts, and other issues. If you can locate a real estate broker or lawyer who is involved in the arts, perhaps as a board member of an arts organization, he or she may be especially sympathetic. But be certain that your project poses no conflict of interest for your advisors.

On a large project, it makes sense to delegate real estate negotiations to a small subcommittee. Sometimes, one individual reporting to a committee can handle this task. But don't allow your general manager or museum director to be in charge of these dealings; you need him or her to provide constant leadership in the day-to-day business of your organization.

RESEARCH POSSIBLE SITES AND BUILDINGS

The search for an appropriate site proceeds in stages. During early planning sessions, your group will determine which land parcels and buildings may be available. By the time feasibility studies have been completed, you will be considering perhaps three or four sites that are most attractive to your potential audience. The site and building-study portion of the feasibility package will give you the information you need to rank the final choices. By the time your group decides to build or renovate, you will have likely selected the one site that best fits your needs and your pocketbook. But try to keep your options open as long as possible to provide insurance against unexpected roadblocks.

Never grab a piece of property without checking around first. Bone up on the market and look at as many possible sites or buildings as you can before making up your minds.

Should You Build or Renovate?

Despite popular opinion to the contrary, renovation is not always cheaper than new construction. You have to consider ongoing maintenance costs as well as the one-time expense of building or renovating. Your architect might be able to incorporate money-saving features into a new structure that you won't find in an older building.

If you are considering renovating, get a mechanical engineer to walk through the proposed building and give you informal advice on probable upkeep costs and pitfalls.

As you search for a site, remember the adage: the three most important things about real estate are location, location and location. If a new facility would have to be on the outskirts of town, it might make more sense to renovate a downtown building where you could attract more passers-by.

In an area being uprooted for freeway rights-of-way or redevelopment, there may be buildings you could purchase and move to a better site. Find out from city hall whether there are empty fire stations or schools for rent or purchase.

Above all, don't begin the search before you know exactly what kind of programs you want to present. Then keep your programming requirements paramount.

Remember that the purpose of an arts organization is to present art, not to preserve buildings. If your planned use is not compatible with the design of the building you are considering, it is not the building for you.

Look over the chapter that deals with building program requirements for your art form. Consider whether building codes will allow you to use the building to best advantage. And always check into future maintenance costs (see Chapter 13). Two useful guides to renovation for arts groups are *Reusing Space for the Arts: A Planning Assistance Kit* (Educational Facilities Laboratories) and *Will It Make a Theater?* (Off Off-Broadway Alliance).

Looking for a Site

Be sure to consider any site in a city- or county-wide context. Think about future growth patterns, zoning, availability and cost of land, other land uses within the area and how these fit in with your arts programming.

Site Accessibility

Transportation is a major issue. How accessible is the proposed site by car? By public transportation? Is there paved parking nearby? If parking space is unavailable, will you be permitted to construct some or use existing street parking without upsetting adjacent business owners or residents? Is the site located near major thoroughfares or highways? Or is it in the heart of the downtown area? If your facility is hard to reach, your group will have a doubly hard time attracting an audience.

Will It Convey Your Image?

Image is another major consideration. How visible do you want your organization to be? Is it important that the facility be a single building with a distinctive profile, or might it be part of a larger complex? It might be worth sacrificing a portion of your image to present a "united front" of arts organizations.

What's going on next door to the site? Compatability of your facility with other building uses in the area is an aspect often insufficiently researched by arts groups. A nearby restaurant may be welcomed by performing arts audiences. A shopping center draws diverse groups of people who might not otherwise be attracted to your museum. On the other hand, a noisy freeway or nearby airport can be a serious drawback.

Your facility may upgrade and enliven a rundown area, but think carefully about safety before moving to "the wrong side of the tracks." Your patrons may be fearful of attending performances at night or even unwilling to visit during the day. You must deal not only with the documented crime rate in the area, but also with people's perceptions of the neighborhood.

Land Use Regulations

Zoning regulations may have a significant impact on the facility you propose to build or renovate. Government restrictions on the use of the land or building may conflict with your plans. Height restrictions may limit the flyloft of the theater you want to build, thereby dashing your ambitious plans for presenting touring companies. Setback requirements that stipulate certain distances between the planned building and surrounding structures or requirements for truck and fire access and parking may also stymie your initial plans. In some areas, solar zoning codes outline requirements for access to the sun's rays and specific building materials that reduce glare and heat loads.

In historic areas you might have to abide by design guidelines established to preserve the character and style of a bygone period. These guidelines usually include a design review process.

If your group is eyeing undeveloped land, you may have to produce an environmental impact report (EIR), routinely required by the government for ecologically or historically sensitive sites. Citizen groups worried about the impact of your facility on the neighborhood may also call for an EIR. These reports can be very costly in terms of consultant time, because they must address such details as soil types, natural vegetation, the impact of the proposed facility on historic structures, the existence of endangered species on the land, and the impact of the proposed art facility on the pedestrian or vehicular traffic patterns of the surrounding neighborhood.

You can be required to submit an EIR on demand of a government agency, but when faced with planning and/or building code restrictions, you do have a recourse: you can apply for a variance. First determine why your proposed use is illegal. Then find out exactly how the approval process works in your town. Speak informally with officials in the city planning or building department and tell them your needs. They may give you possible solutions that fall within the law. If you informed city agencies of your plans at the outset of the project, you may get a more sympathetic hearing now. If your request for a variance is still denied, try again.

Sources of Information

By studying information available at the city or county planning department or the local board of realtors, your group can learn of important developments in local growth patterns and land costs. You might hear of "revitalization" areas, where land costs may be cheaper, or locations on the outskirts of town where a facility might capitalize on urban growth. Large municipal, corporate, or shopping center developments currently on the drawing board may also be of interest to your group.

Likewise, local sources can inform you of decaying areas where it might be *unwise* to locate. Knowledge of zoning regulations and permitted uses in particular neighborhoods may also help your group to narrow down its choice of site. While doing research, you should note requirements for submitting information to local agencies. Knowing their policies at the outset may keep their intervention in your plans to a minimum and help you secure approvals more quickly.

The Site Visit

Armed with information you have gleaned from the planning department, someone in your group should visit each available site and make notes on its suitability. Document key facts about each piece of real estate to help you make decisions later. But make certain your information comes from unbiased sources and does not represent only the perspective of a real estate broker attempting to make a sale.

Following is a checklist to complete for each site you investigate:

1. Specific location (address)
2. Date you checked the property

3. Whom you spoke with
4. Asking price of land/building(s) and terms of lease or sale
5. Contingencies in acquiring property (special liens or mortgage provisions)
6. Possible special arrangements that could be worked out to your organization's benefit
7. Size of parcel
8. Utility services (will they be adequate for your needs?)
9. Condition of existing structures on the property and whether buildings to be renovated are structurally sound; nature of repairs to be made
10. Utility easements and rights-of-way through surrounding property—important for auto access and parking; you can learn these from the department of public works, property deed covenants, or city hall utility planning maps
11. Adjacent land uses (and economic impact of locating arts facility in this area)
12. Image projected by site/building
13. Accessibility by car and public transportation

Dealing with Key "Actors" in the Real Estate World

These are certain key people and departments who can give you advice and warnings before you make a commitment to a specific site.

The **city or county planning department** can provide an overview of the real estate situation in your community. Typically, the department has neighborhood planners for each district and area-wide planners who deal with broader zoning issues. Planning departments also have free documents, updated every five years or so, containing economic and social data about specific areas.

Visit the planning department to discuss your ideas before they are fully developed. Department members may be able to direct you to the real estate source who has property your group can use.

The **tax assessor** can check on land values and who owns the surrounding property. Does a single owner control many properties in the area? Might he want to build high-rises on his holdings some day?

The **city attorney** can advise your group whether there are any restrictions on public property you are considering.

A **real estate broker** can check on parcels for sale in the area you have singled out. He or she can advise you about the asking price of the land and what kinds of uses are planned for the district. It is wise to have the real estate expert on your committee talk to the broker. Remember that the broker works on a commission and will only spend time with you if you are a serious buyer. Be sure to ask all the questions on your mind to get information that the broker won't offer directly. And don't jump at an "emergency purchase," even if you are told the property will be snapped up within two weeks. There are very few great deals in property, and you need time to check out all the angles.

A **developer** who has approached your group or who is working on a project in an area you are considering also needs to be handled carefully. Take your time discussing terms. If you are renting, get as long a rental period as you can. As a cultural organization, you have something unique to offer the developer of a retail/commercial area. So keep your cool—and let your real estate expert do the talking.

A **banker/investor** will be interested only in a professional presentation from your organization, so have a financial plan drawn up (see Chapter 3). Put your best foot forward, but don't exaggerate the fiscal health of your organization. Your group will be fully checked out before an investor puts up any money.

There are various routes your group can take to secure a bank loan. One is to have board members personally co-sign the loan, a demonstration of firm belief in the project. Another method is to use the building as collateral. Or, you can guarantee the loan against future funding pledges in addition to the building. If a consortium of arts groups is to run the facility, you will need letters of intent from each group indicating their commitment to the plan.

Find out about the bank's Community Reinvestment Act provisions, which can be found in the bank's annual report. According to the CRA, a certain portion of the bank's capital must be available to community-oriented projects. Once you have presented your plans to the banker, ask if they fall within the current CRA guidelines, which are updated every six months.

Purchase, Lease or Rental—Benefits and Drawbacks
The decision to purchase, lease, or rent depends on the nature of your organization, the arts programs you intend to offer, and the stability of your group (see Figure 4-1).

Purchase
Owning a building involves serious responsibilities. It may be desirable to have equity in the structure, and certainly, it is reassuring to know that no one can force you to move. But your group is responsible for improvements, and you need ongoing revenue to pay the mortgage, maintenance costs, and property taxes.

The key question is whether you will have enough cash to stay in business. The money you are spending to buy a facility might otherwise be used for programming. On the other hand, it may be easier to acquire the down payment from a fund drive than to ask the community for program support. Run a cost analysis for the structure you are planning to build or buy. What will it cost one or two years after completion? Five years later? Ten years later? Look at the price tag for maintenance, repairs, and mortgage costs, and consider how these figures will be altered by inflation. Factor in the amount of equity that will go into purchasing the building or acquiring the land and paying for construction. Before you decide to buy, make sure you will still have a reserve fund for emergency use.

Lease

If you lease the facility, you are protected against sudden rent changes, although the lease will usually include an annual inflationary adjustment for utility costs. Typically the tenant is responsible for interior improvement costs. The lease should run for a minimum of three years; five years is more appropriate. Over five or ten years, your organization should be able to amortize the cost of improvements you make.

Rental

As a renter, you have the least control and the least financial risk. Rental terms are usually set for one year. When the year is up, the landlord may greatly increase the rent or decide to convert the building to a different use. On the other hand, many arts organizations have fairly harmonious, long-standing relationships with their landlords.

Figure 4-1   Comparative advantages of owning, leasing and renting.

	Ownership	Lease	Rental
Capital	Your capital is tied up in the building.	Your capital is committed only for the duration of the lease	Your capital is not tied up at all because you pay monthly.
Taxes	Tax advantages are available if private investors participate in the deal (see Figure 4-2 Sale/Leaseback) If you sell the building, you may realize appreciated values. (However, it is unlikely that your group will take advantage of this benefit.)	Your nonprofit group can amortize improvements you make as an operating expense. You may be able to arrange a lease-option with payments going toward future purchase.	You receive no tax advantages.
Costs	You have fixed costs as the building landlord.	You have fixed costs per year, with a built-in rate of increase.	Your costs of occupancy are not fixed—rent can be increased.
Property Control	You have control of the property and can make additions and changes.	You have long-term control of the property limited by the duration of the lease.	You do not have control.
Maintenance	You are responsible for all maintenance, repair, and improvements.	You might or might not be responsible for maintenance and repair, depending on the terms of the lease.	You are typically not responsible for maintenance and operating expenses (except for utility fees).

Optioning a Property

If you are thinking of acquiring private property, your group may be one of a number of competing interests. Purchasing an option to buy guarantees you time—generally 90 to 120 days—during which you have exclusive purchase rights. Options are not possible on city-owned property, but you can obtain an exclusive negotiating agreement.

Buy your option as soon as possible after you have run your feasibility analyses and evaluated the land or building in question. You can then begin fundraising, secure in the knowledge that the site won't be snatched from your hands. The price of the option will vary from a token $1 to a small percentage of the purchase price, depending on the property owner. The fee will apply to the sales price, should you decide to buy.

CREATIVE ALTERNATIVES IN REAL ESTATE ACQUISITION

Because of limited federal funding for the arts, increasing construction costs, and new tax laws, arts organizations are exploring new ways to acquire property and construct facilities. The following are some of the more innovative options available.

Donated Private Property

An individual may donate up to 30 percent of his or her annual income, tax free under current tax laws. The ceiling for corporations was recently raised to 10 percent in 1982. In certain tax brackets, it may be more beneficial to donate property to a nonprofit group than to sell it and pay capital gains tax. With a property donation of this kind, the arts group receives a facility with few strings attached, and the donor can write off a sum equal to the market value of the property.

Similarly, a developer may keep a building and depreciate it over 15 years. When this benefit has been exhausted, the developer can get one final tax advantage by donating the facility to a nonprofit group.

Charitable Remainder Trust

This is an attractive arrangement for people who bequeath stocks, bonds, or property to a nonprofit organization. During the donor's lifetime, he or she can receive income from the trust while the principal or the building remains the property of the arts group. Upon the donor's death, the trust income reverts to the arts organization. The details of a trust can be established by your attorney.

Donations of property can be very tempting to the financially pressed arts group, but don't feel obliged to accept a site or building that won't accommodate your plans. Retain the right to sell the property at a later date, should you discover that you cannot use it effectively.

Acquiring Public or Government-Owned Property

This scenario involves a direct transfer from one public group to another or an arrangement by which an arts group leases the facility from the city or county. The building in question may be an unused school, hospital or federal building. If the building remains public property, the arts group will not need to pay property tax and may get maintenance from the city. A city strapped for funds, however, will want to make money from the sale of the property. For an arts group to be successful in this venture, it must head off the owner from putting it up for sale on the open market. Political strategy is crucial.

Property in Tax Arrears

Property that has been foreclosed for nonpayment of mortgage or tax can be considered for a facility site. Such property is acquired by the city and sold to the highest bidder. If the property hasn't sold after a year or two, the city and banks will want to get rid of it as quickly as possible. Of course, anything that doesn't sell quickly probably will be in a poor location or badly dilapidated.

This kind of deal is for the intrepid only! Interested parties must offer sealed bids for the amount they are prepared to pay, and ten to twenty percent of this figure is required as a deposit. The winning bidder has 30 to 45 days to come up with the remainder of the money. If your group is unable to raise this sum, the deposit will be forfeited and the land or building lost. Up to the moment of the actual closing the owner can still reclaim the property by coming up with the money to pay the taxes or mortgage due.

Sale/Leaseback Arrangements

This scenario can work if you already own a building or land or are receiving donated property. You sell your holdings to a developer at market value. The buyer receives special tax benefits that are not available to the nonprofit organization. You pocket the capital from the sale, and as a nonprofit group, escape paying capital gains tax. The purchaser then leases the property back to you for a period of 15 years or more. After the tax benefits have been exhausted the developer may wish to donate the property to your arts group as a tax deductible gift.

Figure 4-2 spells out the benefits to each participant in the sale/leaseback arrangement.

Figure 4-2   Sale/Leaseback agreements, benefit to participants.

Original Landowner (if other than arts group)	Arts Group	Developer
Receives a tax deduction on the appreciated value of the donated property.	Receives capital from the fully appreciated property.	Receives depreciation and other tax benefits (including investment tax credit for construction of the building).
	Negotiates a favorable lease arrangement.	May later receive appreciated land value if a portion of the land is sold for another use.
		After the tax benefits have been used up, may later donate building to the arts group as a tax deductible gift.

The historic Schubert Theater in New Haven, Connecticut, is being renovated with the help of a sale/leaseback plan. Partly financed by the city, an Economic Development Act grant, and the state legislature, the project is also supported by a $3 million tax-shelter syndication to private investors. The city sells the property to a private developer who, in turn, sells it to individuals looking for a tax break. The city then leases the property back from the developer and sets up a nonprofit corporation to run the theater. After 40 years, ownership of the theater will revert to the city. Investors also benefit from a 25 percent investment tax credit for helping to rehabilitate a National Landmark building.

In Oakland, California, the city will rehabilitate its Civic Center Auditorium—a $10 million project—on a nonexistent budget by selling to an investment syndicate the as yet unrehabilitated structure along with the city-owned Oakland Museum building. The city, which retains land ownership, will issue a municipal improvement bond for the auditorium's renovation on the strength of the syndicate's promissory note. Oakland will lease back each of the buildings from the new owner for a 30 year lease term. At the end of this period the city can: repurchase the building at fair market value, lease them for an additional period, or abandon them.

Other Alternatives for the Arts

Cultural Facilities in Commercial Centers

If a municipal government controls the site, terms of the sale may require the developer to set aside a portion of the property for cultural uses. The rationale is that a cultural facility can be the distinguishing feature of a commercial center—the "draw" that makes it different from the competition. The developer may be willing to pay maintenance costs in the early years, freeing some of your funding for artistic programs. In San Francisco, for example, the Yerba Buena Center developer is committed by the land disposition agreement to set aside 50,000 square feet of land for cultural purposes. Arts task forces held public meetings to draw up a list of spaces they wanted and a plan of operation for the cultural complex.

Joint Use Possibilities

In some cases, sharing your facility with another group or locating in a mixed use center can be the answer to the real estate dilemma. Here are five ways this can work:

1. **Joint use of an office building.** Joint use does not mean hanging an exhibition in an office lobby never designed to accommodate art. Cultural uses should be programmed into the plans of the office building from the outset—an idea that can be marketed as an employee benefit or a way of boosting the image of commercial occupants.

    Arts group should realize that the space they are allotted might not accommodate all the projects they have in mind. Or, commercial interests may restrict certain kinds of programming in order to maintain a businesslike climate. But the opportunity to exhibit art or put on a noontime performance in a frequently traveled area may make up for some of the drawbacks. (Be sure to check Chapters 9 through 11 for minimum facility design standards.)

Have someone on your board with connections in the business community check with his or her acquaintances about local joint use possibilities. Of course, an arts group that has already established a good reputation stands a better chance of being considered a "draw" by the business community.

The Whitney Museum of American Art at Philip Morris Inc. is a blue-chip example of the way this kind of partnership between business and art can work. Scheduled to open at the company's new world headquarters building in New York, the structure includes a street level pedestrian plaza with a sculpture court in addition to a 1,100 square foot gallery. The Whitney project came about because of a city policy which encourages developers to provide public space on the ground floor in exchange for a variance permitting the construction of an extra floor in the building.

2. **Locating in a shopping center.** To an arts organization offered space in a retail complex, location is of prime importance. If art is really considered a "draw" by the developer, it should be right up front where the action is—on the first floor or near a large department store. If you are offered space on an upper floor, ask for kiosks or other displays at ground level to advertise your presence.

Advantages of a shopping center location include support from commercial tenants and readily available parking. However, the identity of the arts organization does merge to some degree with that of the center. On a practical level, standard ceiling heights and interior finishes are not optimum for an arts facility. If you do decide to move into a shopping center, be sure to clarify your particular specifications at the beginning.

The Bellevue Art Museum in Bellevue, Washington has recently moved to a new space in a shopping center in the central business district and museum visits have increased threefold. In return for their third floor location, the museum pays $1 per year in rent and all leasehold costs.

The Rouse Company has taken the lead in this marriage of commercial and arts interests. The development firm, which owns or manages over 50 shopping centers, instituted its Art in the Marketplace program in 1957. Currently nine museums and two art centers have been given exhibition space and program funding at shopping centers in their geographic areas. Among the best known of these are Harborplace in Baltimore and Faneuil Hall Marketplace in Boston. It is the Rouse Company's policy to allocate $100,000 annually to visual and performing arts programming, an amount that is increased by 10 percent each year and augmented by funding from public agencies and the private sector.

3. **Sharing a space with another user.** A hotel with an auditorium or unstructured open space may suit your needs; school auditoriums may be used at night; churches often have spaces suitable for rehearsals or performances. Your group might share a space of this kind to gain public visibility until you can afford a facility of your own. You will, of course, have to establish a schedule with the other users, and liability insurance will probably be necessary.

The arrangement has advantages for the other tenants as well. Allowing you to use their facility helps to fulfill their community service obligations, and your presence during times when the building would ordinarily be closed will prevent vandalism. The ideal situation is to work out an agreement with the other tenants before the building is constructed, so your group can lobby for architectural features essential to your art form.

If a school, convention hall, or other public building is being planned in your community, ask the decision-making body about the possibility of joint use. If the answer is positive, ask that the initial pool of funds be disbursed at the outset. With your portion, you can hire a consultant to determine the feasibility of constructing an auditorium or gallery for your specific needs.

4. **Multiuse by several arts groups.** When several arts groups share space, they generally have a fundraising advantage and can share expensive technical equipment and the costs of maintaining a building. Disadvantages include some loss of your group's identity and possible difficulties in agreeing on design and scheduling. Never assume that things will automatically work out equitably. Make your organization's needs clearly known at the beginning of negotiations.

Private Enterprise: The Arts Group As Developer

Mixed use projects combining revenue producing units with an arts facility are probably the most exciting of all the real estate innovations affecting cultural organizations. Revenue-producing segments of the project help to offset both capital and operating costs of the arts facility. However, such arrangements involve complex financial decisions and some adjustments in an arts organization's legal status. The sizeable risks and the need to weigh tax advantages carefully make it imperative that the arts group work with economic research and development firms, tax lawyers and investment consultants in formulating a successful strategy.

For example, when the Yale Center for British Art began in 1977 renting ground floor space in its four story downtown New Haven building to shops and a restaurant, it meant that a traditionally nonprofit, educational institution was engaged in a profit-making venture. As a result, Yale now must pay the city the equivalent of property tax on the profit-making space and the federal government tax on the rental income.

The situation at the Museum of Modern Art in New York is even more complex. To raise funds for an expansion project, the museum sold its air rights to a private developer, who is building a 44 story condominium tower on top of the new six story west wing of the museum. If the museum were to have negotiated this arrangement directly, it would have had to pay taxes on "unrelated business income" represented by the income from this development. Fortunately MOMA is able to benefit from the Trust for Cultural Resources, a public benefit corporation established via the New York City Cultural Resources Act of 1976. The trust is able to undertake combined use development on behalf of New York state institutions that meet its specifications.

Since the property the condominiums occupy is owned by the museum and therefore not subject to taxation, real estate tax equivalency payments (similar to property tax) will be paid annually by the condominium owners to the museum. These payments will be used to pay the debt service on the museum expansion bond.

Most arts groups tend to think in traditional terms about how to acquire a building or site. In the changing real estate world of the 1980s, however, it pays to be creative and adventurous in your planning. So be sure to obtain the best advice and explore all options until you have found the situation that best suits your needs and your pocketbook.

EXPLORE IDEAS

5. Professional Consultants

Creating an arts facility is measurably different from building a house or office, and few, if any, members of your committee will have had prior experience in this special planning process—good reasons not to rely solely on your own judgment. Specialists can provide:

- Experience in an area in which your group is deficient
- Familiarity with workable and nonworkable solutions in similar projects
- Cost-effective, efficient solutions to problems
- Credibility in the community and with government agencies
- Credibility with potential funders (by means of reports issued at different stages of the project)
- Evaluation by an outside source able to see the project from a nonbiased perspective

If the idea of spending a few thousand dollars "just for advice" seems exorbitant, keep in mind that construction costs will be far higher. Professional advice can mean the difference between building a facility you can use and being stuck with one you cannot.

What Can't Consultants Do?

Consultants can't read minds; they need the response of a committee that has done its homework. However, they might help you define your questions or identify a particular problem, as well as suggest workable solutions. Be sure to provide the consultant with a full summary of the project goals you prepared during the planning phase of the project.

Your consultants can't make final decisions for you or be expected to take full responsibility for the outcome of the project. While they have certain expertise, only your group can know what programs you will run, the needs of your staff, the habits of your audience, and other information unique to your situation. Your contact with consultants must involve give and take, with ample opportunity to explain your perspective, make suggestions, and disagree when necessary. Do your part by reviewing the information presented by your consultant and staying on top of each phase of the planning process.

The key to success is to do your "homework" and be an informed client. The better you are able to prepare your consultants, the easier it is for them to put their expertise to work for you.

WHAT KINDS OF CONSULTANTS ARE THERE?

There are six areas in which you might need to seek professional help: arts planning and administration, facility development, facility operations and management, design and architecture, funding, and real estate. A single consultant, however, may combine varying degrees of expertise in a broad range of fields. For example, a former facility manager may be familiar with both operations and technicalities of the art form. Or a funding expert may also be knowledgeable about real estate. It will be up to your committee to judge the breadth of knowledge of any potential consultant.

On large, complex projects, you must have a high level of expertise in each area. And no matter what the size of your project, someone who has actively been involved in a particular field will always be preferable to a consultant who "knows something about it" but lacks demonstrated experience. The following descriptions will help you develop performance criteria regarding a consultant's skills and the tasks with which he or she can help.

Arts Planning and Administration
Here you need hands-on knowledge of the art form—familiarity with the kinds of exhibits that will work in a given architectural space or knowledge of the behind-the-scenes functioning of the theater as well as the demands of particular types of performances. This consultant must have years of managerial or technical experience, preferably in several situations.

Facility Development
Someone who has been involved in the planning and construction of an arts facility, either as a facility manager or director or as a consultant to other projects could be invaluable to your committee. This person should be familiar with the dynamics of committee/consultant collaboration, building community support, and the overall design and construction process. Ability to deal with various groups and individuals, understanding of the time frame and the pitfalls involved in facility development, and proven ability to see a project through are hallmarks of the experience you require.

Facility Operations and Management

Familiarity with the day-to-day running of an arts facility, viable methods of cutting costs, and ways of coping with emergencies that arise are all part of operations expertise. A former manager or administrative director is the person you are looking for. If you are planning a civic arts facility, your expert should be familiar with operations that involve the municipal government.

Design and Architecture

These areas will virtually always be the province of an architect, who incorporates the technical specifications into the overall design of the building. Whether or not the architect has designed an arts facility before, he or she will need to work with specialists familiar with the requirements of the art form.

Funding

Funding strategy involves assessing potential support from all funding sources, developing a realistic cash-flow projection, and mapping out a campaign for obtaining both capital and operating funds. Frequently, funding know-how is closely tied with a knowledge of real estate and tax law

Real Estate

Your group will need expert advice on the local real estate market, current strategies for acquiring property, and methods of financing your purchase.

WHEN SHOULD YOU HIRE CONSULTANTS?

Initial Exploration

At the early planning stage, you will probably need only one consultant with general knowledge of the arts and experience with the facility planning process. This person may be an **arts generalist**, a person with a feel for the kinds of activities that go on in the arts and the way they are scheduled and otherwise accommodated in an arts facility. The generalist will have had experience in working with organizations.

Hands-on experience in long range planning, arts programming and scheduling, audience or patron development, staff requirements, and organizational structure should all be part of the generalist's background. Be wary of someone with only a degree in arts management and no practical experience; you need more than book knowledge. Be careful also to choose someone whose personality is compatible with your committee.

"Arts generalist" is not a conventionally defined term like "architect". You won't find a listing for it in the phone book. These experts tend to have backgrounds as museum directors, heads of nonprofit arts service groups, or managers of performing arts complexes.

During the early planning stage, you may also wish to call briefly on the services of a specialist—possibly someone with expertise in your art form or someone with a background in real estate transactions. It will probably be sufficient to hire the specialist consultant for only a day or two to make sure your initial plans are on the right course.

Feasibility and After

During the feasibility stage, you will still be working closely with the arts generalist, but specialists such as a **design team**, **funding strategist**, and **real estate expert** will begin to be more important to you.

Between the feasibility and the start of the design process, you will need expert advice on funding and organizing your fundraising drives. If you are planning a bond campaign, you need to bring in a **bond strategist** now. And you will require the services of a **public relations consultant** and a **graphic designer** to get your message to potential donors and foster community goodwill.

Design

Your generalist will now step back and serve almost as an additional member of your committee in reacting to the advice of more specialized professionals. Your **architect** and a number of specialists retained by the architect will be working closely with you at this point. The **facility manager** of a performing arts facility or director-to-be of an art museum should now be hired on a part time consultant basis. The committee that hires the director/manager at least a year before the completion of construction gains invaluable expertise and avoids costly mistakes.

A **theater or museum consultant** can help make sure you are considering every factor that goes into presenting or exhibiting your art form. The museum consultant can advise you on whether a particular design is appropriate for the exhibitions you have in mind. He or she can work with the architect to determine the number and size of the galleries and the relationships of the gallery space to support areas. The museum consultant will also be familiar with such specifics as environmental controls, security systems, and lighting design.

The coordinating theater consultant will work with the architect to plan the arrangement of spaces and to reconcile the sometimes conflicting demands placed on a hall by the various performing arts. He or she should have hands-on experience in several areas of theater production and be concerned with the quality of the performing experience for the performer, individual spectator, and the audience as a whole.

HOW TO FIND THE RIGHT CONSULTANT

First, know what you need, and be as clear as possible about the kind of assistance you want. You can't hire the right person for the job if your can't define the job.

Sources

Check the listings of consultant organizations (see Appendix E) for names of prospects to interview. Sources of help include the National Endowment for the Arts, state arts agencies, the International Association of Auditorium Managers (IAAM), The Art Museum Association of America, U.S. Institute for Theatre Technology (USITT), and regional organizations such as the Western States Arts Foundation.

Ask managers of completed facilities in your area for names of consultants they used. Were they happy with the quality of the work? Was the person's style suited to the task? Did the consultant communicate well with the group? Was the work completed on time?

RFQs and RFPs

Your first communication with the firms or individuals that seem most appropriate will take the form of either a **request for qualifications (RFQ)** or a **request for proposal (RFP)**. The RFQ may be simply a form letter asking for basic information about the consultant and a sample of past projects he or she has done. After the consultant is chosen, the planning group and consultant work out a scope of services outlining exactly what the consultant will provide.

What to Look For

The basic information a potential consultant should provide includes the date the firm was established, resumes of key staff members, references from former clients, fee schedules, and a list of similar projects completed in recent years. This list should state the size of each project, innovative approaches on the part of the consultant, and the names of subconsultants used for services not directly provided by the firm answering the RFQ. A proposed timeline for completing your project should also be included in the package.

The RFP includes a request for all of the above plus a statement about the goals of the project and specific information already assembled. The consultant is then asked to submit a proposal describing how he or she would tackle the project and an outline of fees that would be charged. (See page 68 for a sample RFP.) In order to issue an RFP, the planning group has to have gathered enough data to give the consultant a sufficient basis on which to create a proposal.

Making Your Decision

Hiring a consultant is much like hiring an employee. *Never take someone's credentials on face value.* Some "experts" coast on an outdated reputation. Others may present slick, "canned" materials unsuited to your needs.

Thoroughly review the capabilities of the people who respond to your RFP or RFQ, and be sure to check their experience in working on a project similar to yours.

Check references, particularly from those organizations similar to your own, and ask for a frank appraisal of the consultant's services.

The Interview

When you have winnowed down the list, request a preliminary meeting with the people you are considering. In this face-to-face encounter you can get a feel for the consultant's personal style and working methods. (In a large project, prospective consultants should be told in advance who will be on the selection committee so they can tailor their presentation to the appropriate technical level.) Normally, the consultant will request reimbursement for expenses involved in coming for an interview but should not bill your group for time spent. However, you should not expect to get substantial free advice at this meeting.

This is your opportunity to weigh your personal impressions of the consultant against the person's professional background and the way he or she begins to address your group's situation. Don't be impressed by smartly packaged materials that are not suited to your needs. It is essential that the consultant demonstrate an understanding of your project and how to approach it.

Be Thorough

Always talk to more than one consultant, even if the first person seems adequate for the job. If your project sounds especially interesting, you may be lobbied by consultants who want the job, but don't make a commitment until all the evidence is in. And avoid people with an ax to grind; a balanced, viewpoint is essential. If you hire a local person, take special care to uncover all possible sources of personal bias.

AFTER THE CONSULTANT IS SELECTED

The Contract

Always draw up a written agreement clearly stating your expectations. A contract should include:

- Specific tasks with schedules for completion.
- Mutually agreed-upon goals, including dates for interim progress reports.
- Fee and billing procedures. (Always tie a payment to a specific piece of work due on that date. Retain about five percent of the fee for the final payment, to be paid upon completion of the consultant's work.)
- Evaluation and follow-up procedures, including the role of the consultant in monitoring the way his or her work is included in the design process.

After the contract is signed, the consultant is paid a retainer—usually 15 percent of the total amount—to begin the work.

Make sure who will actually be doing the work, especially if you hire a large firm. If you think you'll be getting the wisdom and experience of Famous Arts Consultant, and it turns out he or she has delegated the project to a young assistant, the results may not be what you expected.

Establish Clearly Who Is in Charge

Particularly in civic projects, the consultant must know whether to report to a municipal government department or to the nonprofit organization in charge of the project. But even in a small planning group, there should be one person to whom the consultant will be responsible.

Stay in Touch

The planning group must allot time for briefing sessions with the consultant throughout the contract period. Your group will also need to meet privately to discuss material submitted by the consultant. Don't be pushed by the schedule the consultant proposes; insist that the job be done in a complete and orderly way. On the other hand, try not to pressure the consultant to produce material too quickly.

Know the Limits of Your Power

Never approve a major design issue before checking with your major sources of funding and community support. If the committee is not in a position to make the final decision, as in a civic project, it should still make a recommendation to whomever is in charge.

Participate actively in the shaping of your facility. Don't sit back and accept what you are told, and never agree to any move you cannot understand. If you feel misunderstood or you don't like the consultant's suggestions, speak up!

THE COST FACTOR

Consultants have different ways of setting their fees. Often they will charge by the hour during the early phases of the planning process. An "average" daily fee may range from $300 to $800, depending somewhat on the number of days the consultant is engaged.

What you get for your money depends in part on the amount of time the consultant takes to learn about your situation. An expert hired for a day will have only a superficial familiarity with your project and will offer advice based mostly on past experience. Such quick guidance may be just what your group needs to get out of the doldrums or be reassured that things are proceeding well. But if you are looking for more than an educated response to your plans, a consultant will need a longer period of time to become familiar with your community and the background of the project.

Starting with the feasibility study phase of the project, a consultant may combine hourly charges with an "upset"—or maximum charge for the whole project. (If the upset is, say, $8000, the consultant may end up charging $7800, but he or she cannot bill you for $8100, no matter how many hours it takes to do the job.)

Obviously, the planning committee must be sure there is money available to pay the consultant. Should someone be willing to donate consulting time, don't be too quick to jump at the opportunity. Remember that you will have less control over scheduling and the quality of work done as a "favor".

As a rule, money is well spent on a good consultant. Saving money by getting the cheapest advice or shortening a consultant's contract period may prove false economy when key elements of the facility turn out to have been poorly conceived.

THE ARCHITECTURAL DESIGN TEAM: ADDITIONAL CONSIDERATIONS

The architect is the central expert with whom you will be working after the feasibility studies have been completed and you have decided to proceed with the project. It is the architect's job to incorporate the specifications of each technical specialist into the overall design of the building.

For a large-scale project, you may be tempted to hire a nationally known architectural firm with proven experience in designing arts facilities. You should realize, however, that you will be buying a particular style, along with the firm's experience, skill, and imprimatur. At the other end of the scale, an arts group in a smaller community may be tempted to hire a local architect with little or no experience in creating an arts facility. This decision may be penny-wise and pound-foolish because the architect will, in effect, be using your project as a learning experience.

One solution to the local versus out-of-town dilemma is a team architect approach. Your group can save money on the lower fees of the local group, while benefiting from the expertise of a big-name firm. You also gain the checks and balances of having professionals with different perspectives contribute to the project. Remember that a team approach will require considerable effort by the planning group to maintain good working relations and a realistic division of the work load.

Whatever approach you choose, never entrust the design of your building to anyone other than a professional architect. And be sure to hire the firm or firms most likely to create the image you want to project. Architects should always "speak your language," no matter how impressive their credentials.

Sometimes, an architect is hired at the outset of the project to prepare the site and building portion of the feasibility study, but there is no obligation to give the same firm the entire design package. It is possible to hire one firm to run the feasibility study and another to produce the design drawings. Actual design work on the building must wait until your planning group knows exactly what it wants in the facility—that is, after you have developed the written preliminary building program described in Chapter 8.

Three Options for Selecting the Architect

There are three standard ways to locate an architect. One is to have the **building subcommittee** compile a list of architectural firms whose past projects suggest they might be likely candidates. The firms are then invited to submit a proposal or statement of qualifications along with work samples. The planning group invites a selected few of the applicants for meetings and discussions before a final selection is made. This option works on the premise that the only architects the group would want to consider are those currently recognized as "name" firms.

Another method is to hold a **design competition** to locate the candidate whose design best fits your needs and pocketbook. You may either invite specific firms to compete or announce your specifications for an open competition. (See Appendix B for specific details on design competitions.) A design competition may be a good way of publicizing your project in the local or national media. It also provides a greater opportunity for unknown firms to prove their worth.

The third method of architect selection is to place a **request for written proposal** in leading architectural publications. Interested firms then respond with a proposal and statement of qualifications to be evaluated by the committee. This option allows the design process to be as open as possible while demanding that prospective candidates address themselves directly to your needs. Your group may wish to hire a professional advisor (typically an architect) to help prepare the RFP, evaluate the proposals, and select the design team. After the team is chosen, you might consider retaining the advisor to help manage the design phase of the project.

Regardless of how you choose the architect, your contract with the firm should be structured in two parts. While the project is in the feasibility and schematic design phases, the contract should cover time and materials on an hourly basis, with an "upset" or maximum, fee permitted. After the project is fully funded and construction is about to begin, the contract can be budgeted in more detail. You can negotiate either a straight fee based on hourly costs or one based on a percentage of the construction budget.

Consultants to the Architect

During the design phase, the architect will be working with a number of technical experts. In a theater project, these might include specialists in stage design, theatrical rigging, lighting, stage flooring, stage machinery, audio-visual equipment, audience seating, and acoustics.

The **acoustician** is a particularly important member of this team. During the early design discussions, he or she must work closely with the architect to ensure adequate planning for the quality of sound in a facility. In a symphony hall project, the acoustician is often selected before the architect and frequently reports to the committee rather than to the architect.

In a museum or art center project, the architect will need the advice of experts in exhibition design, lighting, and conservation. A **building lighting consultant**, for example, can advise on the layout of lighting fixtures in the gallery. A **conservation consultant** will make suggestions concerning facilities for repair, continuing maintenance, and storage of art objects.

Other consultants include **structural engineers** and **mechanical engineers** (who assist the architect in the choice and installation of heating, ventilation, air conditioning, and plumbing components). General lighting, electrical power, and wiring are the province of **electrical engineers**. The **interior designer** is responsible for finishes and colors inside the facility. The **landscape architect** assures that the structure conforms to the site and determines the design of plantings and other outdoor ornamentation, such as fountains and terraces.

Typically, the architect's fee is sufficient for him or her to pay all of these consultants directly. Another consultant who works closely with the architect but who may be directly responsible to the planning committee is the **construction cost estimator**. His or her job is to figure the time and costs involved in building the facility and to serve as a watchdog over the contractors, keeping cost overruns to a minimum.

The planning group may also wish to hire a **construction manager** to act as its agent during the construction process. This consultant coordinates the work of all subcontractors and takes the place of a general contractor.

Remember—before you hire a consultant at any stage of the project, know exactly what type of expertise you need. Look first within your own ranks for available advice, particularly in areas like real estate or tax law. Check with local nonprofit agencies for consultant help. And be sure you have allocated a sufficient budget for consultant expenses.

During the selection process, talk to more than one consultant in each area and get samples of previous work done for projects similar to yours. A good consultant will look for your point of view, not try to impose another opinion on the project.

After you've hired the consultants, prepare adequately for meetings with them and keep on top of the entire planning process. Never agree to a move you don't understand. And, as always, be prepared to hear that cherished portions of the project may not be workable.

TEST YOUR IDEA

You've explored your ideas and found one that is worth pursuing. Now, you are ready to test that idea. Three separate points of view will help with the examination:

- Is there an audience for your planned program?
- Can the proposed building sites accommodate your plans?
- How much will the building and operations cost, and where will the money come from?

TEST YOUR IDEA

6. Feasibility Studies

Now comes the point when you must collect the facts that will help you finally decide whether you need a new facility, whether renovation or new construction is the best way to meet your needs, and how the project can be funded. You need experts in arts programming, funding, real estate, and design with proven abilities in collecting information and suggesting realistic goals.

Each consultant will gather information in his or her area and at some point mesh their individual findings with the scope of the entire project. Or, you may first commission a program feasibility study, then—based on the results—find someone to look into available real estate, and finally hire a funding expert to advise you whether the project outlined so far can be financed. At the end of these studies, your group should have a firm grasp of how available resources for building or renovating fit in with your arts needs, as well as a plan for implementing the project. Any feasibility study should identify the next steps in the process so that you can move smoothly into design and construction.

TAILOR YOUR STUDIES TO YOUR NEEDS

The extent of the feasibility phase depends on the type of project you are planning. A large civic project that will involve public money and a broad constituency requires the most detailed study. Need for the facility must be clearly established; arts groups must be consulted to determine potential usage. You will also have to justify civic projects to a number of public and private bodies, including the mayor's office, various government departments, and organizations such as the Rotary Club. Your detailed feasibility studies will provide much of the ammunition.

On the other hand, a project initiated by a single arts organization requires much less documentation. You wouldn't have embarked on the project if you hadn't outgrown your present location. So your study should focus on locating suitable property and analyzing available funding. Things will get more complicated if, as a result of the feasibility studies, you decide you cannot go it alone. Once you involve another group, you will have to modify your studies.

This chapter contains hypothetical feasibility studies at both ends of the spectrum—for a large performing arts facility to serve both local and touring groups; and for a single tenant museum. The next chapter explains what your committee should do with the studies once the consultants leave and you enter the "commitment" phase of the project.

THE COMPONENTS OF A FEASIBILITY STUDY

There are several stages in the evolution of a feasibility package. From your planning sessions you have developed a prospectus for the facility that may exist either as a formal document or only as minutes of your informal meetings. Whatever you proposed will now have to be tested against three factors: the arts programs you plan to run and the features of the building needed to house them; the tasks of acquiring land or a building; and financial considerations (see Figure 6-1).

Testing the Arts Program
The first step is to develop a report on your planned arts program. Who will be on your stage? What type of art will be on your walls? What type of patronage can you expect? Who will be walking through your doors?

Consider the nature of your planned programming. If you are building a performing arts facility, are you thinking of an auditorium for local needs? For several groups or for one tenant? Or do you expect to bring in touring shows? Is the facility primarily for symphonic music? Or will you be hosting the road companies of Broadway shows? The design of the building you need will be intimately linked to the scope and type of arts programming you intend to present.

For visual arts facility, design requirements vary according to whether you will bring in traveling exhibits packaged elsewhere, whether you plan to design your own exhibits, or whether the facility will be devoted solely to the display of an existing, permanent collection.

You must then survey the local arts picture. Are performances/exhibits currently being presented in other community facilities? Who attends these programs? How large is the audience? How often do segments of that audience return during the course of a year? Are these other facilities being adequately used? For example, a performing arts building that stands idle most nights should give your group pause. What went wrong? How will your facility improve the situation?

You should also survey the community at large. What are the current demographic projections for the area? Who is moving in? Transient workers? Professionals? Retired people? Or is your community losing a significant portion of its population? What about neighboring towns? Will you benefit from widespread patronage?

Testing Possible Locations
With a clear picture of the programming that will go into the facility, your

consultant can advise you about the strengths and drawbacks of each possible site. This aspect of the feasibility process is directly tied to the physical needs of each art form. (See Chapters 9 and 10.)

You want maximum allowable flexibility in arts programming, rather than being locked into, say, exhibits that contain no large works or road shows that have only minimal sets. You will also be concerned with the *image* the site projects. Will a warehouse district location keep your patrons away?

How the site will affect day-to-day operations is another important consideration. Is the building structurally sound? Is it hard to insulate? Will the proportions of the rooms accommodate your plans for them? What kind of support services—dining, shops, parking, lodging for out-of-towners—are available in the surrounding area? Will you need nearby lodging for touring company members or sources of equipment parts, printing services, and so forth?

Your group should also investigate the impact on the immediate neighborhood. In a public project, proof of a positive economic impact may greatly enhance acceptance by the community. On the other hand, your group may be involved in lengthy political battles if your plan threatens to disrupt a residential neighborhood, by increasing traffic noise at night, for example. Finally, you must consider the costs of preparing the site to meet your needs.

Testing the Project Economics

The final portion of the feasibility package will determine whether you can afford the project. Your consultant will give you figures on capital costs (price tag for the building) as well as a projected operating budget and deficit. The cost of the building will include outlays for planning studies, acquisition and development of the site, fees to building and capital development specialists, the actual cost of construction, the costs of different types of spaces within the facility, equipment and furnishing costs, utility services, and allocations for project financing.

Capital Financing Study

The consultant determines the availability of funding and presents suggested financing strategies. He or she also establishes a cash flow projection to ensure that your group will have the right amounts of money at the right times and outlines the approach to be made to lending institutions, as well as the basic design of the funding campaign. Also included is a discussion of the potential economic impact of the facility on the surrounding area.

Projected Operating Budget

Another aspect of the project that must be carefully planned from the outset is how you will provide for the day after you cut the ribbon—and for future years. On the debit side will be staff salaries, janitorial services, insurance costs, fees for performers or costs of bringing in traveling arts exhibits, and the yearly cost of preserving the works of art in a permanent collection. Income will depend on such factors as the ticket prices, admission fees and memberships, the number of seats in the auditorium, and the yearly total of exhibitions or performances. Donations, bequests and grants, and projected revenues from a bar, restaurant or gift shop also must be considered. The consultant will balance these debits and credits against the financial health of the community as a whole. (Study the financial feasibility charts in Appendix A for an outline of the data you will need to assemble in your own study.)

Figure 6-1   The Three Components of a Feasibility Study

Arts Program Feasibility Study
Survey of the market to determine what will be on stage and who will be the audience, taking into account:
- intended programming
- needs of organizations in community
- use of existing facilities
- community audience survey
- audience attendance patterns

Site/Building Feasibility Study
Analysis of possible sites and buildings for their ability to accommodate desired arts programming within available budget. Alternative sites are analyzed in terms of:
- fulfilling artistic programming needs
- location
- support available from surrounding area to meet needs of patrons, production, and touring companies
- accessibility
- image
- operations and management implications
- land costs, availability, and financing
- project phasing and implementation

Financial Feasibility Study
Analysis of all costs for facility operations, planning, and construction. The operating budget includes projections for:
- earned income (admissions, sales, rentals, memberships, etc.)
- contributed income (private and public)
- operating expenses (salaries, overhead, maintenance, etc.)
- special programming costs

Capital Construction estimates for facility planning and construction include:
- consultant fees
- site acquisition and development
- construction costs
- equipment and furnishings
- project financing

Capital Financing Study includes:
- capital dollars available for construction
- financing strategies
- cash flow projections
- economic impact of facility on the community

Synthesizing the Findings

The final step involves pulling together the findings of each of your consultants—or, if a single consultant is handling the whole study—making the essential connections among the three areas the study covers. Your committee must then evaluate the conclusions and decide how—or whether—to move ahead with the project. The next chapter will help you through this decision process.

Keep in mind that the feasibility studies are not supposed to merely rubber stamp your initial plans. Rather, they should clarify your needs and identify resources that are actually available. Remember that the project may not, in fact, be feasible the way you have envisioned it. Maybe you need to scale down your building program, or perhaps you will want to change your focus from new construction to renovation. At worst, your group may decide that timing is wrong for any kind of change, and the whole project may have to be scrapped or tabled indefinitely.

If you aren't willing to consider "quitting while you're ahead", you are wasting your time and money in commissioning the feasibility studies. One nationally known theater consultant will not take on a project feasibility job unless the group that hires him is willing to be told the facility should not be built.

INVOLVE THE COMMUNITY

Whatever the scope of your project, you need to involve the outside community (see Chapter 2). Even if your town depends heavily on tourist traffic, local people will be the ongoing users of the facility; asking for information and opinions now will help you to market the facility later. The community is also your source of political and financial support. Regular patronage donations and general revenue funds will all depend on the attitudes of local people toward your project.

However, the degree of community involvement in the feasibility process will depend on the type of project and how well the consultant understands your town's cultural profile. The feasibility studies for a major city project will involve direct communication with the mayor's office, the planning department, and other community leaders and groups. Public workshops are one means of seeking the views of arts organizations, defusing opposition to your plans, and publicizing support for the facility. (See Chapter 1 for a discussion of open workshops.)

On the other hand, a single arts group planning a move to larger quarters will be concerned mostly with identifying sources of cash and in-kind donations in the community. The group should also publicize the advantages that the move will bring to faithful patrons.

WORKING WITH THE FEASIBILITY CONSULTANT TEAM

A successful client-consultant relationship depends on each side doing its share of the work. The planning committee must do the thinking and research necessary to ask the right questions. Consultants must have the expertise to ferret out the answers and the analytical skills to come up with suggested ways of organizing the project.

Schedule frequent meetings to review the progress of your consultants. Study progress reports and interim memos; they will reveal problem areas to be discussed. Mid-point reviews are important ways of dealing with any "red flags" that crop up in the feasibility process. Whatever you do, don't simply allow the consultant to work privately and bring you only the final results.

To help you get a feel for the client-consultant relationship, look carefully at the information you gathered from other arts groups before hiring consultants (see Chapter 5). Obtain copies of their contracts and ask about the price tags for the study. What groundwork did the other planning groups do before hiring consultants? How pleased were they with the studies? How were their ultimate decisions influenced by the information in the studies?

DESIGNING YOUR STUDIES

The mere presence of charts and graphs and pages of analysis does not insure that your needs were fully considered. A County Cultural Needs and Resources Study, produced for a small town in the Southwest, is an example of analysis gone astray. The consultant was asked to document cultural facilities in the county, when in reality, the issue centered on whether to locate a performing arts facility downtown or on the community college campus. The report not only contained much useless information on the needs of the whole county; it also based conclusions on responses of less than a quarter of the existing organizations countywide. The report's conclusion? That "the town needs a performing arts center." *A true feasibility package should provide a full implementation plan, not just a yes-or-no answer.*

The simplest feasibility study can be done by calling selected individuals and assessing community need from the planning committee's perspective. At the other end of the scale, a thorough survey for a major project will involve the use of detailed questionnaires sent to arts groups and others interested in the arts. But no matter how basic the study, it should still include artistic needs and programming; design features required; real estate considerations; funding sources; and plans for managing the structure.

A planning group that cannot fund a professional feasibility study should not despair. One option is to hire graduate students in urban planning and arts administration. Or, you may be able to assemble enough skills in your own group to produce a study. However, if you do the study yourselves, you must try to reach the broadest possible segment of the community with any interest in the arts. A project that merely reinforces your wishes is worse than no feasibility study at all, and it might call your group's credibility into question.

TWO SAMPLE FEASIBILITY STUDIES

The following studies, based on real-life examples, should give you a better idea of the work involved for (1.) a small community museum and (2.) a large scale, municipal performing arts facility. Although your own needs may fall somewhere in the middle, the samples will convey the rationale for assembling information in each area of the feasibility study.

The Edna A. Campion Community Museum

For more than thirty-five years, the Edna A. Campion Community Museum maintained a collection of painting and sculpture bequeathed by a well-known local patron of the arts. Operated with the proceeds of a small endowment and located in the former Campion mansion, the museum had failed to keep pace with the cultural needs of the growing town. Specialized industries were moving to the area, bringing an influx of well-educated personnel used to the amenities of big city living.

Impetus for change occurred when a developer made known his desire to purchase the museum site for a mixed use development including office space, a hotel, and possibly a cultural facility. The museum's board of directors could either negotiate to become part of the development or use the developer's cash payment for the site to find another location, perhaps in the suburbs, where the population center had shifted.

Defining the Problem
The chairman of the board felt the museum should find out more about local arts' needs and the interests of the community. Several board members were suspicious of any changes in museum traditions, but these individuals were outvoted, and a request for proposals was issued, outlining the situation in terms of the choice of a new location and ways in which the museum might become more responsive to community needs.

Organizing a Consultant Team
The board chose as consultant a former museum administrator joint-venturing with an architectural firm experienced in alternative site evaluation.

The consultant's first step was to spend two days with the museum director, staff, and members of the board to get a good overview of the museum's history and the opinions of people currently associated with the museum. Part of the consultant's task was to help achieve a consensus among board and staff on the image the museum should present.

Survey of Community Needs
As a former museum director, the consultant was already familiar with budgeting for a small museum, as well as with the costs of developing exhibits and displaying traveling shows. Focusing his research on the community, he arranged interviews with similar small arts organizations

to determine whether there were unmet needs in arts education, how the museum might better serve the public school system, and whether certain programs, such as the photography club's annual exhibition, might be incorporated in the museum's plans. He spoke with representatives from the local college, community service organizations, and government agencies to learn about their activities. He sought opinions from outside the arts community on the effectiveness of the art museum and the need for expanded programming.

A detailed questionnaire solicited more specific information from local arts groups on the frequency of performances, financial resources, space needs, and audience composition. Aware that the museum might increase its effectiveness and become more economically viable by merging with another arts group, the consultant was interested in exploring possible joint arrangements.

His investigation yielded two good leads. The chamber orchestra group, which presented summer outdoor concerts, might be interested in using the museum if it were located in suitable surroundings. Also, the photography group was looking for space for its exhibits as well as for small classes in beginning photographic technique. In the opinion of the consultant, both uses were compatible with each other and with the general focus of the museum.

Survey of Audience Interests and Desires

The next step was a direct market survey—by telephone, mail and interviews with downtown business people and shoppers—to explore how a new facility might affect attendance at the museum. The consultant asked whether a suburban location, as opposed to a new site downtown, would change people's likelihood of visiting the museum. He sampled interest in art studio classes, a film program, and a special introduction to art class for children. How much would people pay for such activities? Would they want to attend on a regular basis? Did they have any other ideas for new museum programs? The answers encouraged the board to plan for a range of special programs. Activities for school children proved a popular choice, and there was a great deal of interest in moving the museum to a suburban area closer to the younger population.

Exploring Possible Locations

In the meantime, the board of directors had been discussing whether to work out an arrangement with the developer to remain on the same site, even though it would mean accepting less square footage than the present museum occupied. However, a majority of the board members realized that reduced space ran counter to their desire to expand the museum's activities. The decision was to look for a new location, either in the same downtown area or in the suburbs. New construction was one alternative; renovating a former car showroom near the present museum was suggested by one board member.

At this point, the architects began to work with the consultant in determining the merits of each suggested site.

In addition to the car showroom, they considered a site near an interstate highway and another near a shopping center in the suburban area where most of the questionnaire respondents lived. Each site was analyzed in terms of its ability to accommodate the museum's planned programming and its community image; accessibility to patrons; land acquisition costs; building costs; and implications for continued maintenance. The consultants continually weighed pros and cons in terms of design, financing, and political ramifications.

Review of Financial Implications

The board of directors meanwhile considered how to finance the project. Income from the endowment would have to be supplemented with private donations and a bank loan. The board agreed that the projected programs for schoolchildren provided a strong basis for public support and decided to ask the city to make a line item allocation for the programs.

The consultant reviewed the museum's current operating budget and projected a future budget that reflected a more extensive exhibition program and additional community activities. Final details would be filled in when one site was chosen.

The Synthesis: Making the Decision

Presented with the pros and cons of each site, the board spoke with community leaders and members of the arts community with whom they had a special rapport. Finally, they decided to build the museum in the suburban location where land was cheaper and where they could design a building to their specifications. (The car dealership would have posed numerous design problems.) The cash settlement from the developer covered part of the cost of the land; the rest was paid with a bank loan granted at favorable interest rates because of the museum's long history in the community and strong fiscal management.

The feasibility process demonstrated to the planning group that their ideas were sound and helped them decide which direction to pursue. Now the board was ready for the next step—the actual design of the building. Because they had built up such a close working relationship with the architect who served as feasibility consultant, they were seriously considering hiring the firm to proceed with the design of the project.

The Hillsdale Performing Arts Center

The planning committee was appointed by the mayor of Hillsdale in response to pressure from influential members of the arts community in this medium-size city. After meeting for several months, representatives from local arts organizations and civic and business leaders came up with certain "givens" for the project. The facility should be located in the downtown redevelopment area. Economically, it would attract businesses serving theater patrons to the currently run-down area. As an architectural focal point, it would revive the area in a more general way, lessen vandalism, and increase property values.

The theater would be equipped to serve local groups, such as a professional regional repertory theater company, dance companies, and jazz groups, as well as host touring attractions. Information gathered from the arts community gave the planners confidence that there were enough potential local users of a new theater. The planning committee decided that they wanted a top quality management team to run the facility, which would have to be supported by funds beyond earned income. Because design was also judged to be of chief importance, the committee proposed a "charette-style" design competition to determine the form of the new facility (see Appendix B for a discussion of design competitions).

Funding for the feasibility study came from the National Endowment for the Arts and matching private contributions and in-kind donations from the state arts commission and the city.

Finding a Consultant

Requests for Proposal

The committee contacted five consulting firms, asking each to respond with a scope of services, a time line, and a budget for investigating the following areas:

- Artistic needs and programming
- Audience size and interests
- Possible sites within the downtown area
- Architecture (form and size of the theater)
- Funding support (public, corporate and private—for building, operations, and creation of an endowment)
- Management structure

Obviously, every planning group will have a different set of "givens." The important thing is to set realistic parameters for the feasibility study. If you are too specific, the study may not be far-ranging enough to head your group in the right direction. On the other hand, too vague a directive may result in an inconclusive study.

The Winning Team's Response

From the four consultants who responded to the request, the committee selected the team that seemed most qualified to work on the project. This team proposed to survey local performing arts groups about their current productions and financial resources, as well as determine the size of the potential audience for such productions at the new facility. When "supply" and "demand" had been investigated, the consultants would examine potential sites in terms of cost and suitability for the arts and test available funding resources against the costs of various types of arts programming and real estate options. Finally, the results of each separate study would be incorporated into an overall plan.

After the planning committee approved this scope of services and details of the time line and budget, a contract was signed with the consultant team. (Your group may be working with individual consultants, rather than a firm with experts in each area. However, the mechanics of organizing the feasibility studies remain the same; you would simply deal with a separate scope of services for each area of investigation.)

Arts Program Feasibility

Who Will Be Onstage?

The first task was to identify the performing arts organizations in town, their space needs, and what use they would make of the planned facility. Outside arts groups with an interest in performing in Hillsdale were also included in this survey.

To gather this information, the consultant team called every performing arts organization in the Hillsdale area, using a standardized inventory form (Figure 6-2) designed to take up only about 15 minutes of telephone time. (*Note:* For help in conducting such a survey, check the standard data collection system developed by the National Information Systems Project (NISP) and described in the publication, *All in Order: Information Systems for the Arts.* (Also see Joe Golden's *Olympus on Main Street* for further pointers.)

Figure 6-2   Telephone Survey Form

Basic information
- Name and address of the facility.
- Name and title of person answering the questionnaire.
- Founding date of the organization.
- Existence of a particular ethnic focus.
- Status of the facility as producer of events, presenter, or both. If both, the dominant activity.
- Classes offered by the facility, if any.
- (For producers) Nature of the events the organization produces

(dance—ballet/ethnic/modern; opera; theater—musical, drama, mime, media arts; other—specify).

Fees Paid to Performers
- Whether fees are paid to performers.
- The largest fee ever paid to a performing group or individual (nine categories, ranging from "less than $100" to "$10,000 or more" were listed).

Number of Performances/Programs
- Total number of performances offered in the most recent full year of operation (from "five or less" to "more than 150").
- Number of different productions or programs that figure represents.

Audience Figures
- Total attendance for all the performances presented in that year (from "1000 or less" to "more than 100,000").
- Size of area from which audience is drawn (from "three miles or less" to "an area ranging over several counties").

Ticket Prices
- Prices of the most expensive tickets sold at the facility (from "all performances free" to "more than $12.50").

Staff
- Whether paid staff is employed by the organization.
- Number of full and part time staff employed.

Budget
- Total organization budget for the most recently completed year of operation (from "$1000 or less" to "more than $250,000").
- Percentage of budget derived from earned income—from ticket and program sales and concessions; from private sector contributions; from the National Endowment for the Arts: from state arts councils; from other sources (specify).

Organization's Present Facility
- Name of facility where the group presents or produces most of its performances.
- Description of the facility. (Interviewers were instructed to keep probing until the interviewee mentioned one of eighteen possibilities, ranging from "traditional proscenium theater" to "hotel ballroom with permanent stage".)
- Age of the organization's current facility.
- Maximum number of seats in the company's primary performing facility (from "less than forty nine" to "over 2500").
- Opinion on the suitability of the number of seats for programming needs (too many, about right, too few).
- Ownership status of the facility (owned/rented/donated).
- Owner of the facility (school district, private, individual, etc.).
- Rental agreement, if applicable (by the performance, monthly, etc.), and rental cost.
- Whether rehearsals take place at the performance site.
- Rating of the facility from the point of view of audience comfort, sightlines, acoustics (from one to ten).
- Rating of the facility from the point of view of performers' support facilities, equipment, size.

Proposed new facility use
- Supposing that a new facility were available, the respondents were

asked whether they would be interested in performing there.
- If some degree of interest was shown, the number of days or evenings the organization would like to use the facility (from "one or two" to "more than forty").
- If classroom space were available in the new facility, would the group use it; for how many days or evenings?

Planning workshop participation
- Whether a representative of the organization would attend a workshop for a new cultural center.
- Whether the person invited should be the respondent or someone else in the organization.

From the results of the inventory, a list of probable users of the Hillsdale Performing Arts Center was compiled. Representatives of these groups were then interviewed in greater depth about their specific needs and the uses they envisioned for the facility. At the end of this thirteen week process, the consultants held a workshop for arts organizations and arts patrons to present a summary of their findings. With the help of a chart of projected annual usage prepared by the consultants (Figure 6-3), workshop participants reached a consensus on general requirements for spaces and facilities.

Figure 6-3   Hillsdale Theater Arts Program Feasibility Study, Projected performing arts facility demand and usage, 1986-87.

Small Theater 250-300 seats	Theater Performance Days	Rehearsal Hall
Probable Users		
Black Theatre Company	99	122
Friends of Shakespeare	12	—
Magic Theater Company	12	6·
The Moving Company	20	48
SUBTOTAL	143	176
Possible Users		
State Theater Company	72	54
Ala Carte Players	12	18
Bitteroot Stage Company	54	19
Hillsdale Little Theatre	38	69
SUBTOTAL	(176)	(160)
Realistic subtotal equals one half of estimate	88	80
Events Sponsored by the House		
Festival of Dance	6	6
Showcase Festivals	10	10
SUBTOTAL	16	16
Commercial Rentals	15	
TOTAL USAGE DAYS	**262 DAYS**	**272 DAYS**

Who Will Be In the Audience?

The second part of the arts program feasibility study involved a survey of the potential audience for events at Hillsdale Performing Arts Center.

Mailing lists of season subscribers and single-ticket buyers obtained from local cultural organizations and sorted by zip code helped to determine the size and location of potential audiences. Another list representing cultural interests *not* tied to specific local arts organizations was obtained from the offices of the public radio-TV station, which maintains a record of donors and subscribers to its monthly program listings. (The mailing list of a locally based magazine with a cultural focus or a printout of local subscribers to a national arts magazine would have served the same purpose.)

The consultants mailed questionnaires to 4,000 persons selected at random from the mailing lists of the four theater companies, the symphony, the art center, and the university theater. The questionnaire asked what determined their decision to attend a performance, listing such choices as proximity of the theater, the recommendations of friends, ease of parking, and the selection of repertoire. Respondents were also asked about their favorite leisure activities and the area of town where they pursued these activities. The concluding section of the questionnaire solicited opinions about a new downtown theater and whether its location would affect the respondent's attendance.

The 1,200 people who responded overwhelmingly mentioned the nature, quality, and reputation of the performing arts event as the chief factor in determining whether they would attend. The next most important factors were convenient parking, safe location, and the attractiveness of the theater. (Note that the cost of printing and mailing questionnaires, plus computer time for collating the answers must be figured into the feasibility budget for large-scale projects of this type.)

The consultants next held audience discussion meetings, one with people who received random mailings to arts list names, the other with the general public, informed via ads in the local media. Personal interviews with key community leaders outside of the arts community helped identify future sources of financial and political support, as well as potential sources of opposition.

Site and Building Feasibility

Reviewing Possible Locations

The consultants devoted a great deal of time to reviewing arts programming and space needs in order to develop a preliminary building program. Data was gathered from visits to existing theaters in the Hillsdale area. The consultants also reviewed the planning committee's aims in terms of the range of events to be showcased. Room types were enumerated and square footage assigned to the performance space. (Chapters 9 and 10 describe the considerations affecting the design of an arts facility.)

On the basis of the audience survey and anticipated programming, the consultant determined the number of seats required and the square footage of the lobby. Type and number of other audience services, such as the bar and restrooms, were also set out, as well as parking requirements for audience and staff.

The Consultants Develop Building Criteria

The consultants were now ready to generate the building program. Knowing exactly what activities were to be housed, they could analyze potential sites in terms of overall square footage needed.

At this point, the consultants also had to consider urban design issues. Although the location had to be chosen with a view toward enhancing downtown Hillsdale, the theater could not be singlehandedly responsible for urban redevelopment.

Testing of Sites Against Established Criteria

Consultants examined sites proposed by the committee, city leaders, and others knowledgeable about downtown Hillsdale. Of the twelve sites reviewed, nine were eliminated because they couldn't accommodate the building program, were not currently available, or were prohibitively expensive.

Each of the remaining three sites was studied in terms of land uses near the sites, surrounding businesses and neighborhoods, and future projects planned for the area by local government and private parties. Other factors influencing the choice of site were accessibility by foot, car, and mass transit; zoning and tax regulations affecting the area; and building requirements and codes for new and adapted structures.

The image that each site projected as a theater location also was a serious consideration. The special personality of a structure is based partly on the way it sits on the land and the angle at which a visitor approaches it. At the same time, the location had to permit large numbers of people to enter and leave conveniently and to accommodate the semi-trailers that transport scenery for a touring show.

Finally, each site was analyzed in terms of the costs of acquiring the land, building costs based on square footage needed, the comparative costs of maintaining and operating the theater at each site.

Financial Feasibility

Estimated Capital Costs

The financial feasibility study answered two questions: How much would the project cost, and where would the money come from to finance it? On the one hand, the consultants considered projected earned income based on audience projections, as well as likely sources of nonearned funding (see Figure 6-4).

Figure 6-4   Financial Feasibility Study, Hillsdale Performing Arts Center Income and expense projections
(For more detail, see Financial Worksheets, Appendix A)

Income (Earned)

Based on:

1. Number of events booked annually
2. Rentals collected from each event
3. Misc. rentals (offices, community room, receptions)
4. Concessions
5. Special events revenues

MINUS

Expenses

Based on:

1. Salaries and benefits
2. Administration and overhead
3. Utilities, maintenance, security, and insurance
4. Special events programming costs

EQUALS

Net operating position

$ to be supplemented
with contributed income

On the other hand, they estimated the price of acquiring the land, adapting the sites for building needs, demolition of an old structure on one of the sites, construction materials, equipment, architects' and engineers' fees, and all other costs for the building phase of the project. They then projected the capital in three different stages: (1.) a general estimate based on construction costs for the region; (2.) a more definitive outline budget based on programming needs; and (3.) a final estimate, made after the committee had chosen single plan from the three alternative site schemes.

Projecting an Operating Budget

The consultants also extended their financial feasibility analysis into the future, after the doors of the theater would be open to the public, and submitted an outline of cost-effective management structure. (See the Financial Feasibility charts in Appendix A.)

Suggested Funding Methods

Regarding the projected deficit and need for a subsidy, the consultants reminded the committee of the economic benefits that would accrue to the community as a result of locating the theater downtown. Hotel and restaurant income generated by the theater would be more than $1 million, they estimated. Money would be returned directly to the city in the form of sales, meal, and hotel taxes, as well as revenues from municipal parking lots used by theater patrons.

Synthesis and Implementation

Based on the data collected in each feasibility area, the consultants agreed that the project was well suited to downtown Hillsdale. They concluded that two theaters, seating 300 and 800 people, respectively, would best suit local needs.

The choice of site was more difficult. The consultants presented the pros and cons of each site, ranked their choices, and then turned the matter over to the committee. Before making its final decision, the committee discussed the choices with the city redevelopment agency and other local groups.

In the area of funding, the consultants suggested that equal amounts should come from public and private sources. They further advised that the city provide daily maintenance for the building, while the subsidy for arts programming would come from the endowment raised during the capital funding campaign, supplemented by state and federal grants.

The feasibility process for this project was a lengthy one. It took eighteen weeks for the first three phases of the study and another month and a half for the committee and its local advisors to choose a site. The consultants then responded with a financial plan tailored to that site and an outline for the design competition.

Feasibility studies are a way of measuring your dreams against the resources and interests of your community and of channeling your plans into a specific direction. Before you get wrapped up in details, you must know whether a new facility is appropriate for the arts programming you plan to present. And you must be prepared to find out that the project is unworkable.

The consultants you choose to conduct the studies should have skills in evaluating the need and demand for your arts programming, financial planning, and locating the best site for the project. As the fictitious case studies in this chapter make clear, the feasibility process involves close contact between the planning group and the consultant team. Your group will have to evaluate the information supplied by the consultants and draw your own conclusions based on groundwork you have already done.

Your group must be realistic about the extent of local need, however. Local government will require assurances that your project is economically viable and serves a broad segment of the community. Even a facility funded entirely with private donations needs sources of operating revenue. Be sure not to look only at one side of the issue. Evaluate the doom-and-gloom report as thoroughly as the glowing revenue projections.

Now that you have assembled the facts you are ready to make a decision. The next chapter presents various ways for you to evaluate the information you have gathered.

Your idea for a new facility has been discussed, explored and analyzed. Now, your committee must make a decision. Informed by feasibility studies and professional advice, your conclusion will follow from the answers to these key questions:

- Is there a proven need?
- Is the proposed site workable?
- Is the funding package financially sound?
- Is there sufficient support to see the project through?

7. Stop, Caution or Go?

After your consultants have prepared their feasibility reports, your committee must set aside time to reassess the entire project. If you do decide to proceed, you will need large sums of money and years of dedicated effort by many people. All those involved will be putting their reputations on the line. Now is the time to make sure that your plans are based on solid assumptions and a realistic appraisal of need.

SORTING IT ALL OUT

Do You Have a Proven Need?
Your first discussions should be about the overall concept of the new facility. Do your feasibility studies demonstrate sufficient need for the structure? How many nights and days will the facility be underused? Are the various uses you have planned for the facility compatible with each other? Is there sufficient local interest in such programs to provide a regular patronage?

Do the Numbers Work?
The second major area of concern is money. Has your financial feasibility study identified sources of funding to build the facility as planned? Where will money come from to support operations when the building opens? Have you projected programming and operating funds for at least five years after the facility is built?

Are You Able to See the Project Through?
Don't underestimate the manpower needed to turn your ideas into bricks and mortar. Your committee must support the project wholeheartedly. Some members might have to commit as much as two or three days a week for the next year and a half to planning and overseeing construction. This is the time to make sure your committee works well as a group and that the leadership is solid.

If all the pieces don't fit together reasonably well, stop and look for other alternatives to constructing a new facility, such as renovation or mixed use.

This decision takes time, but ultimately, you will do one of three things: (1.) stop the planning process at this point; (2.) rethink your plans or look for other options; (3.) go forward with the project. Your project may sit on the back burner for many months while you determine the best way to proceed.

STOPPING THE PROCESS FOR NOW: AN UNFEASIBLE IDEA

Your group may finally conclude that the idea is not feasible because of: (1.) insufficient audience demand; (2.) insufficient use by art groups; or (3.) economic difficulties. All three constraints are fairly common in "rapid growth" communities that currently have no home for the arts. The dedicated group that wants to build an arts facility often must put aside its plans in the face of greater community interest in building schools and recreation facilities and improving social services.

If your committee is faced with a "no-go" situation, you should now look for another way of solving your arts problem. It may be as simple as organizing bus tours to the nearest large performing hall. Or it may mean forming an alliance with another organization in order to gain a broader base of support. You may need to explore other ways of housing arts activities. If a high school is under construction, you may be able to hold events there. By keeping the arts in the public eye—even if you have to use a substandard facility for now—you will build community interest that may be valuable later.

RETHINKING THE PROJECT: THE PARTIALLY FEASIBLE IDEA

If the pieces of your project don't quite fit—and in most cases they won't yet fit perfectly—you need to adjust your plans until they are workable. This may mean gathering more information and perhaps commissioning additional studies. Or, the feasibility process may uncover problem areas that require specific actions rather than another study before the project will work.

The Cost Is Too High
If the cost of your project surpasses the funding goal suggested by your feasibility study, your group has several options: Instead of purchasing and renovating another building, you might renovate your present one. If you were planning to build a new facility, you might now commission a survey of buildings available for renovation. Collaborating with another group to

acquire a new building is still an alternative. Or, you might be able to "piggyback" onto other planned building projects—a convention center, a community services complex, a school, or a shopping center. Finally, you might come up with new strategies to tap into previously ignored sources of funding.

There Is Insufficient Need or Demand

If there are not enough patrons, artists, or performers to make a new arts facility feasible, you might consider building your audience through expanded offerings or more aggressive marketing techniques. By looking for other groups who would rent portions of your space, you may be able to increase the use of a new facility. (For example, classrooms or small meeting rooms might be rented out to business and community groups.) Your group may be able to add its own "extras," such as film and lecture series or popular touring shows, that would keep your doors open more often and justify the cost of a new facility.

The Site or Building Is Inappropriate

If you discover that the site or building you had in mind does not fit in with your other plans, consider reworking your plans, phasing the project over a longer period, or looking at other sites.

Political Barriers

If your plans test out in the above categories, but the city refuses to come through with public improvements or parking structures or the decision to float a bond, you need to do more politicking. This may involve making a pitch for the economic benefits of the arts to such groups as the Chamber of Commerce. Political roadblocks cannot be demolished with more feasibility studies. You can, however, choose carefully from the data you already have to make your point with local officials.

GOING FORWARD WITH THE PROJECT: A FEASIBLE IDEA

Generally, there are several rounds of rethinking, testing, and study before a group can actually go ahead with its plans. However, if you have prepared very detailed feasibility studies, and if your plans seem to fit in with the needs and resources of the community, you may be in the enviable position of moving ahead at this point. Whenever it comes, the decision to proceed will require a great deal of thought, collective action, and probably some reorganization of your committee.

Restate the Project Goals

The entire planning committee should now redefine the goals of the project for the final time. Everyone must understand and agree with the overriding concept, purpose, and scope of the facility. The same questions you have been considering since the planning stage will haunt you once more—but now you must be able to answer them fully. Who is the facility for? What will you be showing in the galleries? Who will be onstage? Do you envision a mixture of touring and resident groups? How many people will have to be accommodated in the auditorium, lobby area, gallery, parking stalls? Do these figures accurately reflect the attendance patterns in your community?

Your committee must now establish an overall project budget, including allocations for wages, supplies, overhead, and building design and construction, as well as the cost of land acquisition and document filing fees. A project schedule must also be worked out for the entire design and construction phase.

Acquire the Site

Your group cannot proceed to the design stage or launch the capital funding campaign until you control the land on which your facility will be built. You need to secure an option for at least one year, preferably longer. Whether you actually purchase the land now depends on how certain you are of your ability to raise funds. Generally—and particularly for large, expensive projects—it is best not to purchase the land until you are virtually positive that the project will proceed. On the other hand, legally securing your right to the land for a limited time through an option might prevent disaster. In one town, a group planning to renovate a historic building had negotiated tentatively with the owner while trying to raise matching funds for an Economic Development Administration grant. Meanwhile, the impatient owner received a firm offer from another party who promptly took title to the land and tore down the building. The arts group had to return the EDA money, and the facility project was stalled for more than three years.

Reorganizing Your Committee

When you finally reach the design and construction stage, it is time to take another look at your committee. Some people may have fallen by the wayside since you started many months ago. You may need to recruit others to fill in gaps in expertise, such as building development or large-scale fundraising, or to reinforce areas in which you will need more brainpower, elbow grease, or community contacts. At this point, you want representatives of every group that might use the facility on your committee.

Subcommittee Activities

The committee's work will now become more specialized. Subcommittees should be appointed to handle land acquisition, funding, public relations, arts programming and operations, and design and construction.

The executive committee, composed of representatives from each of the subcommittees, other project leaders, and your new facility manager, will coordinate the work of the subcommittees and make sure the right hand knows what the left is doing.

Planning the Capital Campaign

The task of the capital campaign committee is to raise money for construction, as well as for the operating endowment. Individual members should be responsible for various portions of the campaign—corporate donations, foundation grants, individual contributions, deferred giving, and bequests. The professional fundraiser your group hires will assist each of these efforts and coordinate the campaign. After the fundraiser and segments of the subcommittee have analyzed potential sources of funding in each of these areas, the capital campaign committee should hold a brainstorming session to make sure every possible source has been pinpointed and assigned a hypothetical donation. The subcommittee and funding strategist should also tailor an overall campaign plan to the design and construction timetable, so that money will be available to pay for salaries, materials, taxes, loan repayments, and emergencies.

Developing a Public Relations Campaign

Working closely with the capital campaign committee, the public relations committee is responsible for coordinating local support for the project. Directed by the public relations coordinator, who is hired or appointed by the planning committee, this subcommittee must keep the facility in the public eye throughout the design and building stage. While the PR consultant and graphic designer handle the press releases, posters, and advertisements, the subcommittee will organize telephone and door-to-door campaigns, get signatures on the petition for a bond campaign, attend meetings of the city council, and otherwise attempt to "sell" the project to the community.

Setting Up Programming and Operations Policy

People knowledgeable about the art field in question should be responsible for determining how the facility will operate when it opens. On an administrative level, this committee must establish the flow of authority from the facility manager or director through the various staff members, the board of directors, and auxiliary groups. An operating policy outlining the rights and responsibilities of user groups or the rules to be followed in acquiring or de-accessioning works of art must be drawn up. This committee will also work with the manager or director to write job descriptions and draw up an operating budget that will include arts programming, salaries, and building maintenance.

A program schedule for the first year or two must be developed while the facility is being built. Touring performers and major art exhibitions may require several years' advance scheduling in order to book them into your facility. The group may also need to do some research into available performers or exhibitions. If the facility will house a local, resident company, the committee should help plan repertory or concert series. When the arts group is a newcomer to the community, the committee may want to organize "trial balloon" programs at temporary locations around town in order to spark community interest and test local response to various kinds of programming.

Supervising the Building Process

The building committee is responsible for guiding the project through the design and construction process. This committee may begin by visiting arts facilities and researching building designs suited to the group's art form.

Other important initial tasks include selection of a design team (described in Chapter 5) and preparation of a preliminary building program. The actual design process that the building committee and design consultant team will follow is described in detail in the remaining chapters.

The Time Factor

There is no cut-and-dried answer to the question of how long it takes to build an arts facility. However, for a major public facility, the *minimum* time from initial exploration to ribbon cutting is likely to be five and a half to six years—if everything runs smoothly. Ten years is not uncommonly long. On the other hand, a small project or renovation may take as little as two years. Inevitably, the planning committee will underestimate the length of the process and begin setting up unrealistic deadlines.

Keep in mind, as Brian Arnott says in *A Facility Development Workbook,* that "the socio-political process which is parallel to the design process . . . could easily extend the time by 100 percent." An arts facility is only a small part of the ongoing activity within a town. Plans for schools, urban redevelopment, a sports arena, highways, or other projects will likely be under consideration at the same time. Community charities will be trying to raise funds for their programs. Local politicians will be vying for money for basic community needs and for their own pet projects. The support your project receives will depend on the availability of funding and city staff time.

From an architectural standpoint, an arts facility requires a much higher level of technical and interior "finish" than a house or office building. Rehabilitating an old building may take even longer than new construction if extensive preparation is needed.

Continue to Reevaluate Your Plans

Meanwhile, your group must reassess the project in ever greater detail. During the design phase, you will constantly balance design factors against probable funding sources. Community contact will be particularly important as you attempt to obtain approvals from the appropriate government departments and to market your concept to the public. Real estate issues will continue to be relevant as you select a final site and determine placement of the facility on the site.

Even when the doors finally open, your organization must continue to seek public support in the form of both audiences and operating funds.

No shortcuts allowed! It is tempting to telescope the process into fewer steps, but the constant reevaluations described in this book help you focus on what you really need in an arts facility and how to obtain it within the constraints of available resources.

With a clear mandate to go forward, your group can start to design the building. Working with a professional design team, your committee will review the design alternatives until you have a final blueprint ready for construction. To initiate the collaboration:

- Prepare a building program listing all the spaces that are necessary
- Incorporate the results of building feasibility studies and other research on design standards
- Hire the design team to translate your list into plans for the building

DEVELOP A
BUILDING PLAN

8. The Building Program

You have decided that your project is finally feasible, and your group has reorganized itself into a number of subcommittees. The focus at this point is on the building committee, which must work with outside experts to develop the actual plans for construction or renovation. The quality of the finished product will depend greatly on how well this committee does its job. As Brian Arnott says in *A Facility Design Workbook*:

> When the building committee neglects to guide, to direct, to supervise, to question, and to accept advice from its professional consultants, a less than satisfactory facility will result.

The building committee has an obligation to supply a sense of vision and to engineer a true collaboration between the outside consultants and the planning group. Its two chief tasks will be (1.) selecting the design team (the architect, acoustician, etc.) and coordinating its work; and (2.) preparing a preliminary building program that will explain to the design team your group's ideas of how the facility will function and the image you want the building to project.

Keep Your Professional Hats On

An effective building committee should represent a diverse range of social, political, and cultural viewpoints in the community. For some committee members, this will be a new experience, with a new vocabulary to learn. Initially they will be inexperienced in working with each other. Still, they must be encouraged from the beginning to voice their own opinions. Their professional acumen and experience can be invaluable to the design process.

Do Your Homework

The building committee must strive above all to understand the practical needs of the artists, staff, and audience who will use the facility. A public arts project requires the greatest amount of "self-education" on the part of the committee. The planners of a single user facility will already be well acquainted with the needs of the people involved. But whatever the scope of the project, there will almost certainly be budgetary pressures that force compromises or the reconsideration of essential parts of the facility. The committee must be informed enough about the operation of the building to guard against cuts that will reduce its functional quality.

SELECTING AND OVERSEEING THE DESIGN TEAM

Among the most important responsibilities of the building committee is selecting the architect and other members of the design team. Interview and selection methods should be carefully worked out in early committee meetings (see Chapter 5). Once the design experts are chosen, they and the committee must determine a workable design schedule. The time allotted for each phase of design will depend largely on the amount of money available at this stage. A time line should be built into the contract of each member of the design team.

Establish Procedures for Decision-Making and Mediation

Once the design team is ready to go to work, the building committee must establish a logical and workable chain of command. One member of the committee—preferably the facility manager—should serve as direct liaison with the architect. If disagreements arise between members of the design team, the committee needs a system for hearing both sides and determining what is best for the facility.

One common area of dispute in a performing arts facility is the relationship of acoustical standards to the architectural appearance of the building. While the acoustician represents the interests of musicians, actors, and audience, the architect is more concerned with visual aspects of the building. In a visual arts facility, differences may arise over the place of natural light in the gallery area. It is the committee's job to mediate such disputes, always keeping in mind the ultimate aim of the facility.

Good communications among committee members and between the committee and the design team are vital to the success of the project. Remember that a facility planned from many separate perspectives will seem disconnected in its finished form.

THE BUILDING PROGRAM

The path that leads from your feasibility studies to a finished building is mapped out in a document called the "building program." Seeing this program through to completion is the building committee's second great responsibility.

The building program lists each space in the facility in terms of use, dimensions, and functional relationship to the rest of the building. It specifies who will use each space and for what purposes. Drawing up a building program requires seeing the relationship between the activities you plan for the facility and the physical spaces you need to house them. You must decide which spaces are absolutely essential and which might be dispensable in the face of budgetary constraints. You must also anticipate which spaces you must have when your building opens to the public and which areas might be added later.

The building program is particularly important because it allows you to evaluate the facility before actual design begins. Because the program is created so early in the process, it will of course be open to change. You will be able to isolate pieces of information from your feasibility studies and channel them directly into the final "recipe" for the building. As you continue to work out the details, you will retest your initial goals for the building, always taking care that the apportionment of spaces reflects the scope of your arts programming.

Your Preliminary Building Program

The planning group should first try to assemble a preliminary building program, with a narrative description of its goals, desired image, and planned functions for the building. In addition, you should itemize site requirements, the physical and environmental qualities you are seeking, and specialized equipment and furnishings.

The *final building program*, developed by your design experts, will probably incorporate substantial changes. But don't think of your own efforts as wasted. The exercise of developing an actual building program— "preliminary" as it is—will make you a better client, more aware of your needs and better able to respond to the questions and recommendations of your designers. Second, you will have organized the information the experts need from you into a manageable form. This information will allow them to focus on the refinement of the program according to proven architectural standards.

Defining the Purpose and Function of the Facility

Who and what will the facility house? The question must sound very familiar by now. But this is the last time you will be asking it—because it is about to be translated into a design for a costly and time-consuming construction project.

You must explain to your design team the details of the arts programming you envision. This is the crucial information that will determine exactly what spaces are necessary within the building. Your committee must be sure of the overall square footage that will accommodate the types of exhibitions you are planning, the size of the stage you will need, and the number of seats that makes the most sense economically. Specific site requirements—do you want a sculpture garden? how many cars need to be accommodated in the parking lot?—must also be nailed down.

Review the design standard chapter (Chapter 9, 10 or 11) for your particular art form for an understanding of the main design features you need. For more detailed research, consult other references (see Further Reading for suggestions). Finally, visit other arts facilities. Armed with knowledge from your research and your feasibility studies, you will now be able to get the most out of such tours.

Defining the Image of Your Facility

A building's public "face" is the first hint a potential patron receives about the nature of the art inside. The location, scale, and style of a building and its environment make an impression on the visitor even before he or she decides to enter.

- The building can appear welcoming to people unacquainted with the art inside and still be inviting to people already familiar with your group's work.
- The building can look as though it belongs with surrounding structures—by means of repeating or contrasting scale, forms, textures, and colors—or it can stand apart from them as a monument. (It is possible for a building to "respond" to the architectural style of its neighbors without being a carbon copy.)
- Many older structures present a pleasant, if formal, image. But some traditional architecture may appear overly grandiose and forbidding to today's visitor.

If you are renovating a building, it will already have an image in the eyes of the community, although you may be able to alter it somewhat. In new construction, you have a much freer rein, although the site will determine certain aspects of the building's image.

Whatever style or image you choose, it should make people feel comfortable, whether they have come to view an exhibition or to take a pottery class. The facade of an arts facility is surprisingly like a storefront. As Brian Arnott says in *A Facility Design Workbook,* "Both socially and economically, the public areas of an arts facility are its marketplace." Keep in mind that the building must advertise its special presence both to vehicular traffic and to pedestrians. Passersby should understand immediately where to enter and how to locate each part of the museum or art center. No one should feel conspicuous or confused; the initial visit should be a welcoming—not a daunting—experience.

As you work with your architect to establish the building's image remember that you represent the community-at-large. The architect will design the face of the building based on what you want it to say to the public and whether there is any special symbolic quality you want projected. If there will be an outside design review by historic or neighborhood groups or the planning commission, be sure to include the qualities these groups will be looking for in the building exterior.

As a rule, architects do not want to see drawings of what you think the building should look like. If you find it difficult to describe the image you want, collect photographs of other buildings that reflect some of your own artistic goals. You might be interested in the entryway of one building and the silhouette of another. Be prepared to explain precisely what it is about this door or that wall that you like. But don't expect your architect to copy these details; he or she will use them to better understand you as a client.

An alternative approach is to think of other arts facilities and try to state your overall impression of each one. Does the architecture give you a clear picture of the artistic purpose of the organization? How? Does it clash with what you know is the purpose? Answering such questions might help you verbalize what you want as an image for your building.

Organizing the Material: Your Building Program Workbook

Figures 8-1 through 8-4 suggest forms for compiling your preliminary building program. When complete, these forms can be assembled into a workbook that will serve as your mandate to the designers. The workbook should summarize all the information you gathered in the planning and feasibility stages and incorporate any revisions you have made.

General information about the facility, your group, and its plans should include:

1. History of your institution and plans for the future
2. Nature of your current arts programming and changes you foresee
3. Image of the facility
4. Reasons why you have decided to build/renovate now

A description of your site requirements might include, among other considerations peculiar to your project:

1. Parking and pedestrian access
2. Outdoor functional areas (e.g., courtyards)
3. Service entry location (e.g., loading dock)
4. Future expansion needs as you now envision them

If you are planning an addition to your present facility or are renovating a building, you will have to provide:

1. General description of the existing building
2. Functions and sizes of each room or area
3. Floor plans, if available

Finally, include any other information relevant to the project:

1. Budget data
2. Feasibility studies
3. Other consultant reports you might have commissioned

The bulk of your preliminary building program will consist of descriptions of the various spaces needed to house your arts programming. These should include:

1. What exactly will be happening in this space?
2. What is the proposed size of the space? How many people must it accommodate? (State square footage if you can make a reasonable estimate.)
3. What aesthetic qualities should the space have?
4. What spaces must be adjacent to each other? Which should be located near each other?
5. Special needs:
   - Equipment
   - Environmental standards (acoustical/heating and air condition/relative humidity, etc.)
   - Storage space
   - Number of doors required, where they lead, and how big they need to be
   - Security requirements

Be sure to include all areas where art is presented and produced, audience support areas, and staff areas, including offices and any other spaces required by your plans. Remember: you are not designing the facility at this stage, just describing as fully as possible what you envision when you picture each space.

Make a sheet for each of the spaces, then write a description of each one (how big? what kind of equipment is needed?), and explain the function it serves. Indicate how each space functions in relation to the building as a whole. (How should you position the workshop area in relation to the stage? Where is the box office located? How does the administrative office relate to the exhibition space?)

The arts generalist or the consultant for your particular art form can help you visualize these spatial relationships.

One of the best ways to tackle this process is mentally to walk through the building. In a performing arts facility, imagine what must be done in order to present a touring show. How will the scenery be unloaded? What route will the performers take from their dressing rooms to the stage? How will the technicians maintain contact during the performance? Where will props for the next scene be stored? Does the person manning the lighting console have enough room if the ballet corps is waiting in the wings? How will the stage be adapted for the orchestra concert tomorrow?

Consider visitor needs. Are facilities adequate for patrons to get a drink and visit the restrooms during intermission? Will everyone in the house have a full view of the stage? Are people likely to trip walking up to their seats in the balcony?

Don't forget management requirements. Can normal office routine continue during the matinee without interfering with the performance?

In a visual arts facility, consider how a traveling exhibit will arrive at the facility, how it will be checked in and assembled for display. Then imagine visitors entering the building. What kind of impression do you want them to have on reaching the front door? How should they be greeted in the lobby? How will they know what is on view, and where they will be apt to go first? What route will they take to view the art? Where should classrooms—if any—be located?

The Final Building Program Emerges

The design team will review your preliminary building program, along with your feasibility studies. After several meetings with the committee, during which the designers may pose detailed questions, the team will prepare its recommendations for the final building program. The designers may suggest that you combine the uses of several areas, eliminate certain rooms, or add other spaces that will help you to accomplish your goals. When all the information is presented to you, you will review it and decide whether the building program and projected costs will work within the context of your needs and resources. (For example, you may not have foreseen the need for a meeting room initially, but you now realize that it could be an important part of the building.) When conflicts arise with your original plans, you must either reevaluate the decisions of the feasibility study or alter the standards you have set to fit the construction budget.

Once your committee has approved the final building program and the preliminary cost estimate that accompanies it, the project proceeds into the schematic design phase covered in Chapter 12.

Figure 8-1   Building Program Worksheets

General Information about the Organization

History of the Organization and Future Plans

Statement of Artistic Intent (current arts programming and changes foreseen)

Figure 8-2   Building Program Worksheets

General Information about the Facility

Reasons for Building or Renovating

Image of the Facility/Purpose of the Facility

Figure 8-3   Building Program Worksheets

Spaces Inside the Facility (complete one per room)

Room Type: _____

Degree of Necessity: IMMEDIATE:_____ LATER:_____

Number of Occupants: _____   Total Area (sq. ft.) _____

Purpose and Activity Description (What will be happening in the space?)

Relationships to Other Rooms or Functions
MANDATORY   DESIRABLE

Special Needs for the Space (equipment, storage, numbers of doors, ceiling height, security, daylight, surfaces, environmental systems, furnishings)

Figure 8-4 Building Program Worksheets

Spaces Outside the Facility

Site Requirements:

Space Type _____ Total Area/Capacity _____

Purpose and Activity Description (What will be happening in the space?)

Relationships to Other Spaces (interior rooms, exterior functions or facilities)
MANDATORY   DESIRABLE

Special Needs for the Space (equipment, furnishings)

DEVELOP A
BUILDING PLAN

9. Design Standards: Performing Arts

This chapter presents an overview of all the parts that make up a facility for the performing arts. If you can grasp the basic standards that pertain to the performing arts, you will be better able to evaluate the way your architect handles crucial working areas of the facility. Of course, you will not be able to create a design for your facility directly from the list of parts in this chapter. Rather, you will be able to assemble a "shopping list" of crucial spaces—a preliminary building program which can be worked up by your architect into a final building program.

Even if your project is very small—a converted storefront or church, for example—or even if you are planning a renovation instead of new construction, this section will help, because certain issues are inescapable. Areas of the building that are absolutely necessary, no matter what the size of your project, are plainly indicated as such in this chapter.

After you know what a performing arts facility is supposed to contain, your visits to other facilities will also be more meaningful. You will know what to look for in terms of spaces, dimensions, and technical equipment. Look at the technical books listed in Further Reading for more details on various parts of the performing arts facility. Other pertinent information for groups involved in a renovation or mixed use project can be found in Chapter 11.

BASIC COMPONENTS OF THE FACILITY

There are three basic parts of a performing arts facility: performance space, performance support areas, and audience and administrative support areas.

The **performance space**, the heart of the facility, is made up of the stage and seating for the audience. In any performing arts facility, the design of the stage and the size of the house are the primary considerations. Only after these key decisions are made can the rest of the facility be planned. The factors that determine stage design are the nature of the programming and the desired relationship between performer and audience. The audience seating area depends on the size of the audience you can expect and the intended use of the facility, which will affect visual principles and acoustical formulas. These in turn determine the shape of the hall, the arrangement of seats, and floor and stage elevation.

Performance support spaces, commonly known as the backstage area, include dressing rooms for the performers, production preparation areas (where sets and properties are constructed), technical facilities (lighting positions, sound system installations, mechanisms for raising the curtain and adjusting the stage), and storage areas.

Audience support spaces, created for the comfort and convenience of theater patrons, include the lobby, box office, refreshment area, restrooms, and coat check. *Administrative offices* are also included in this section.

Performance Spaces

The first step in creating a performing arts facility is to be absolutely clear about how the stage will be used—by what type of group, and for what kinds of performances. As you will see, stage requirements differ significantly for music, dance, and theater. Other critical decisions include the size and shape of the theater and the desired relationship between audience and performers.

STAGE TYPES

There are three standard types of stage: the proscenium; the thrust (sometimes called three-quarter round); and the arena (theater-in-the-round). The so-called "black box" or experimental theater—a nonproscenium, flexible space—is a popular fourth type of contemporary stage. Proscenium, the type most adaptable to a variety of staging demands, is the only practical choice for touring shows. For intimate drama, arena theater can work very well; every member of the audience feels close to the stage.

Proscenium Stage
On the most common type of stage form, the proscenium, the action appears to take place in a room with the fourth wall removed to let the audience see what is happening. The frontal relationship between performer and audience is well suited to most traditional plays, ballets, musical comedies, and operas. Because it offers flexibility for a variety of performances, it can be considered

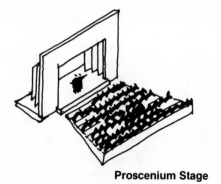

Proscenium Stage

End Stage

the workhorse of the theater. The proscenium stage is generally equipped with a flyloft, wings, and backstage facilities. Although it allows for more sophisticated machinery than do other forms—thus permitting rapid and dramatic changes in scenery—it usually requires more technicians to run it.

It is possible to design a proscenium that converts to a thrust stage and also accommodates a shell for music performances. One variation of the proscenium is the "end stage," which features access from the audience at one end. Although it has a flyloft and wings, it lacks the proscenium arch and the working areas needed for scenery.

Thrust Stage

The thrust stage creates an increased sense of intimacy because the audience surrounds the action on three sides. The actors can enter from all sides. The thrust stage can accommodate only productions developed for multidirectional acting, making it a poor choice for touring company use or for art forms other than theater. However, the thrust stage requires minimal scenery, stage support space, and equipment, and therefore can be less expensive to build and operate.

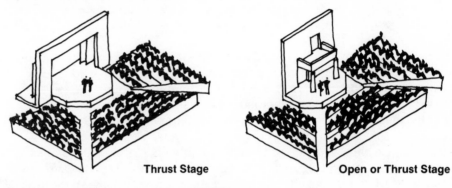

Thrust Stage   **Open or Thrust Stage**

Arena or Theater-in-the-Round

In arena theater, the audience completely surrounds the stage, requiring the acting to be multidirectional. It is the most intimate stage design and is best suited to a small theater and square-shaped house. An arena theater is unsuitable for traditional stagings of standard repertory because actors must enter from behind the audience or from under the stage, and no provisions can be made for scenic backdrops. Because choreography tends to be frontal, an arena theater is also a poor choice for presenting dance.

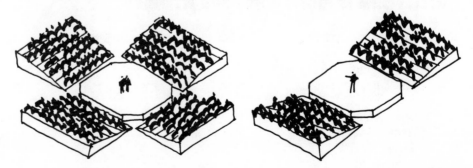

Theater-in-the-Round or Arena   **Center Stage or Two-Sided Arena**

Black Box

A flexible theater space that allows for a variety of stage and audience seating arrangements, the black box is often used for experimental productions. Well-adapted for remodeled spaces, such as warehouses, black box theaters are also frequently included as a secondary part of a performing arts complex. Because a black box usually seats only 50 to 200 people, it cannot economically serve as a town's sole performance space.

Multiuse Stage

Although stage design is hotly debated among theater consultants, scenic designers, and directors, most experts agree that the proscenium is the basic "bread and butter" design. The so-called "multiuse" stage, which can be converted from one type to another, is no longer highly touted. Even when properly designed, convertible stages tend to be:

- More expensive to build
- More expensive to operate because of the labor required to prepare for each performance
- Daunting to the average technician because of the special expertise involved in running the equipment

The reality of a multiuse stage is that it serves one use best; no one type of stage serves all performing arts forms at an optimum level. If you must build a theater for many types of performances, design your stage for the kind of program you will be showing most often. Other uses to which you put the theater must be adapted to the chief purpose of the hall.

There might be some in your group who would like to adapt the performance area for banquets or rodeos or other non-art functions. Be sure to keep your art needs uppermost, or you'll end up with a second-rate facility. Most performing arts, for example, need a raked (slanted) house so the audience can see what is happening on stage. Flat floors do not work for performances — even if they would best accommodate the annual banquet. Also be realistic when you plan the size of the house. A theater built to accommodate thousands for a wrestling match cannot effectively be closed off for an intimate chamber concert. Acoustics also can pose a serious problem in multiuse situations.

WHICH FORM IS RIGHT FOR YOUR NEEDS?

After examining the options for stage design, your group needs to determine:

1. The planned use of the facility:
   Musical comedy
   Symphony
   Solo recital
   Rock
   Jazz
   Theater
   Experimental theater

Ballet
Modern dance
2. The relationship you want between audience and performer:
Proscenium
Thrust
Arena
Flexible (black box)

If your house is primarily for music, acoustical considerations will be paramount, determining the shape, volume, and surface treatments within the hall. A house built mainly for dance requires special attention to sightlines, so the audience can see the dancers' feet.

PARTS OF THE STAGE AND KEY DESIGN REQUIREMENTS

To work out the plan that suits your needs, your group needs to be somewhat familiar with theatrical vocabulary and the working parts of the stage. The following is a simplified guide to the performer's side of the curtain.

The stage consists of a series of spaces embedded within each other. The **performance area**, which the audience sees, is the heart of the facility and varies in size according to the program being presented. The **stage enclosure** defines a volume contiguous to the stage space, communicating with the house. The entire stage volume behind the proscenium arch from the stage floor upward is known as the **stagehouse**. Wrapping around the performance area is the **scene space**, which houses *flats, props, portable wagons,* and other elements of the scenery.

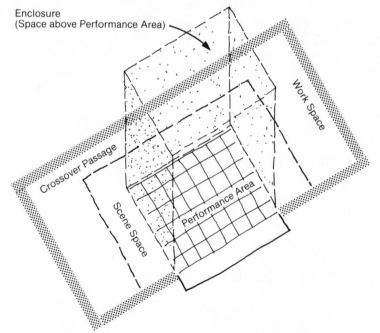

Enclosure
(Space above Performance Area)

Work Space

Crossover Passage

Scene Space

Performance Area

Basic Organization of the Stage

The back walls of the stagehouse must be unobtrusive and free of all obstructions. Never put windows in these walls. Masking the back wall and the area at the rear of the stage is the **cyclorama**. Be sure that between the cyclorama and the back wall there is sufficient **crossover space** for performers, plus working space for technicians and their equipment. This entire stage support area should be roughly equal to the square footage of the performance area.

The height of the **proscenium arch**, which frames the performance area in a proscenium theater, should be designed with regard to sightlines from the audience. You will likely want a high arch, with the ability to "mask down"—to frame the top of the stage with a short horizontal curtain or flat, called a "teaser." The depth of the performance and working space from the proscenium opening to the rear wall of the stage, should be one and one-half times the proscenium width. A depth of 40 or 50 feet is not excessive for most uses.

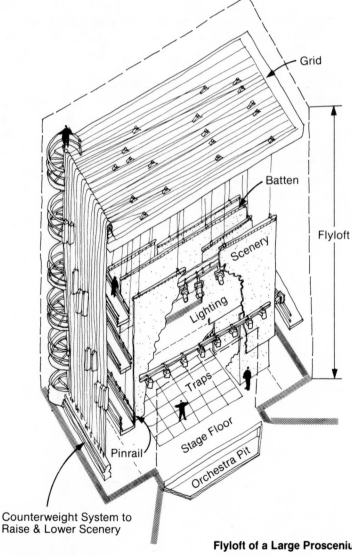

Flyloft of a Large Proscenium Stage

Wing space is the area on either side of the proscenium opening, out of sight of the audience. A rule of thumb is that the total width of right and left wing spaces should equal the width of the proscenium opening.

The **stage floor** should be flat for the comfort of performers and ease of scenery handling. Dancers require a "sprung" or resilient, wood floor covered with a sheet of portable vinyl flooring. But because resiliency is a desirable quality regardless of intended use, wood is the best material for all stage floors. Soft pine is a good choice because it easily accommodates the screws and nails used to attach scenery to the stage. Tongue-and-groove hardwood will make an expensive but top-quality floor. A less expensive option is to use a permanent subfloor covered with a hardboard surface that can be replaced when it begins to wear out. Never build the stage on a concrete base, because the floor should be "trapped" (as in "trap door") to accommodate stage equipment and technicians. You will want at least eight feet of workable space under the stage.

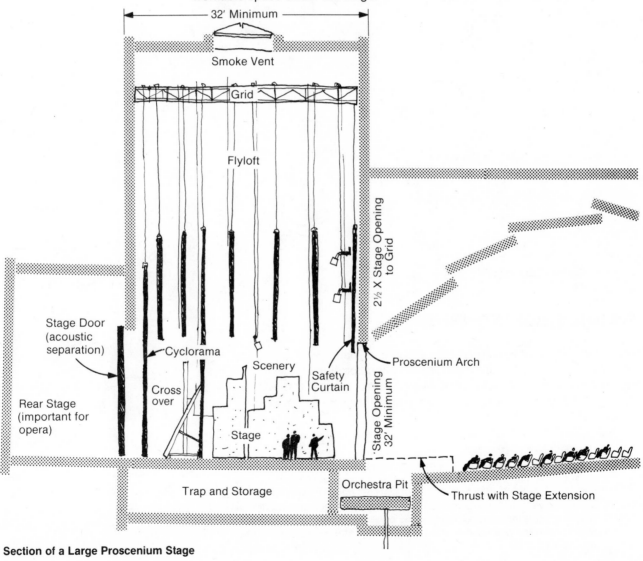

Section of a Large Proscenium Stage

Adequate space overhead is also essential. The area directly above the stage where scenery, curtains and lighting instruments are hung is called the **flyloft**. The height of the loft should be at least two and a half times the height of the proscenium arch so that full-size drops can be stored out of sight of the audience. The flyloft is frequently cut out of a performing facility for budgetary or zoning reasons, but the result is a severe limitation on programming and an inability to present large touring shows.

The **orchestra pit** in front of the stage should be large enough to accommodate the largest orchestra you expect to present and deep enough to allow the conductor and musicians to remain out of sight of the audience. Design the pit so that it can be covered over as an extension of the stage when not in use.

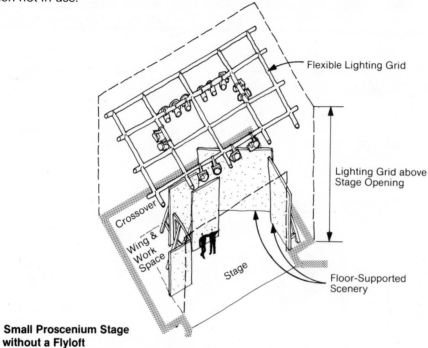

**Small Proscenium Stage
without a Flyloft**

SPECIFIC STAGE REQUIREMENTS

Below are specific stage requirements for drama, dance, opera, musical comedy and light opera, orchestral music, choral productions, and instrumental and vocal recitals and small chamber groups. (Source: *Design Guide: Music and Drama Centers* prepared by Hardy Holzman Pfeiffer Associates.)

"LEGITIMATE" DRAMA
In the so-called "legitimate" theater—which presents plays, as opposed to vaudeville, pantomime, film, or operetta—the actor is paramount, and scenery is generally built to human scale. Actors routinely enter from left and right sides and move across the performing area. Because drama involves a continuously evolving series of events, the director must be able to control changes in context, pace, center of attention, and atmospheric tone.

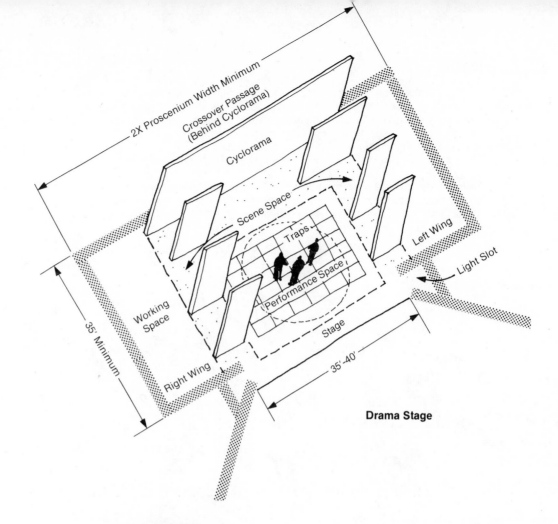

2X Proscenium Width Minimum

Crossover Passage
(Behind Cyclorama)

Cyclorama

Scene Space

Traps

Left Wing

Light Slot

Working
Space

Performance Space

35' Minimum

Stage

Right Wing

35'-40'

Drama Stage

Performance Space

- Acting area is approximately 35 feet wide by 20 feet deep (40 by 25 feet is the usual maximum).
- Floor is level, normally 30 to 36 inches above the front row of the house.
- Traps are recommended in key acting areas.

Enclosure

- A stagehouse and flyloft are strongly recommended.
- Proscenium opening of 35 to 40 feet is standard, though it can be larger.

Scene/Working Space

- Wrap-around scene space is required for flats, drops, wagons.
- Allow ample horizontal working space for the largest set piece, plus actors' passage, waiting areas for actors, technicians' work space, counterweights and pinrail (to which rope used to hang scenery from the flies is attached), curtain space, and stage lighting board.
- Use inside clearances and keep the plan shape compact and rectangular.
- Overhead working space must allow room for the longest piece that will be hung from the flies as well as for borders and grid space. (The grid is the open framework of beams over the entire stage from which scenery and lights are suspended.) There must also be space for a technician to pass above the grid.
- Understage should have at least eight feet of clear working space.

DANCE

Large dance movements may occupy an area as high as fifteen feet above the floor. Dancers must be able to enter from various points along the sides of the stage. In most dance numbers, scenery is minimal, but stage lighting is complex. Although recorded music often is used, a dance facility should be able to accommodate a live orchestra. All music must be heard clearly onstage.

A dance concert usually consists of a series of separate events with rest periods during which the stage is reset. Changes that can be made swiftly will require a pause; more complicated changes take place during intermission. Versatile and sophisticated technical equipment is essential, particularly in the case of lighting controls.

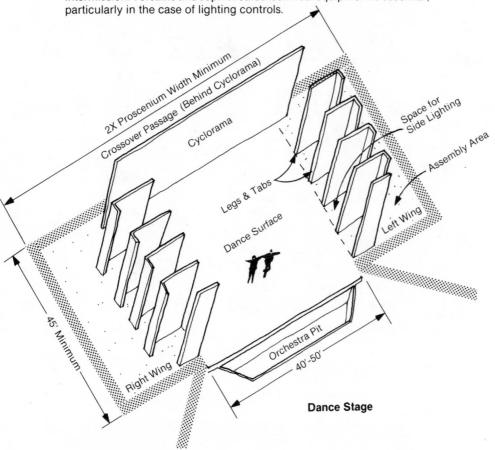

Dance Stage

Performance space

- Acting area is typically 45 to 50 feet wide by 40 feet deep, although a 40 foot width will accommodate modern dance and small companies.
- Because resiliency is essential, the floor cannot be built on concrete. There should be no point on the entire floor where a dancer's foot could come into contact with a nonyielding surface. The floor may be built up on crisscrossed sleepers with neoprene cushions between; sponge mats are not springy enough and can cause injuries. The surface must be smooth and nonslip, free of splinters, holes, and protrusions (no nails or staples allowed). Often, a removable linoleum, vinyl, or hardboard surface is attached to the floor with gaffers' tape. Touring dance companies will specify flooring requirements on their contracts and will refuse to perform on a dangerous floor. Many tour with their own floor covering.

Enclosure

- In large halls a high proscenium is necessary for a clear view of the performing area. An intimate hall may require a nonproscenium arrangement.
- Stagehouse requirements depend on the amount of scenery used.
- At least 25 feet of unobstructed overhead space is needed to allow for lighting instruments and complicated dance maneuvers.

Scene/Working Space

- Wing space on either side of the performance space should be adequate enough for dancers to prepare their entrances and to exit safely.
- Dance performances frequently require a cyclorama or other backdrop.
- An orchestra pit with room for 20 to 50 musicians is very desirable.
- There should be an adequate sound system for dance companies that work with taped music.
- Onstage and backstage areas used by dancers should be warm—between 75 and 80 degrees—with no drafts.
- Unimpeded crossover space is a must. It should be at least six feet wide—sufficient for costumed dancers to pass each other without disturbing the cyclorama or drapery. The floor construction and covering in both the crossover space and the passageway from the stage to the dressing rooms should be comparable to that of the stage.

OPERA

As a mixture of song, music, and spectacle, **grand opera** involves a great deal of background movement, multiple points of entry, lavish costumes and settings, and elaborate stagecraft, special effects, and scene changes. Usually, there is a large cast of singers and musicians supporting lead soloists. **Operatic recital** emphasizes music and song over action and scenery and may involve only two or more small groups onstage. Minimal scenic devices and dance activity are required. The middle ground between vocal recital and grand opera is occupied by **musical drama**, which uses song, speech, music, dance, and scenic elements on a scale comparable to operatic recital.

Performance Space

- Grand opera requires a stage 50 to 70 feet wide by 55 feet deep to accommodate a large chorus which constantly reassembles itself in new relationships to the soloists. Traps, multilevel constructions, stage elevators and lifts are used extensively.

Enclosure

- A stagehouse and flyloft are strongly recommended.
- The proscenium opening is larger than for other performing art forms because of the size of most opera productions.

Scene/Working Space

- Opera stages are technically very sophisticated; scenery tends to be vast and expensive because of its dramatic importance.
- Grand opera requires substantial scene space and offstage working areas on all sides, including a large, fully equipped flyloft and scene elevators below stage. The flyloft must furnish generous, flexible lighting points behind the proscenium and above the stage. Side-lighting towers in the wings also are helpful.
- A large orchestra pit—accommodating 80 musicians—is essential for grand opera. Although the orchestra should be out of the audience's direct line of sight, eye contact between singers, musicians, and the conductor must be maintained. Singers and musicians must be able to hear each other clearly. The pit should be acoustically designed to make sound reverberate at a low intensity so as not to overpower voices.

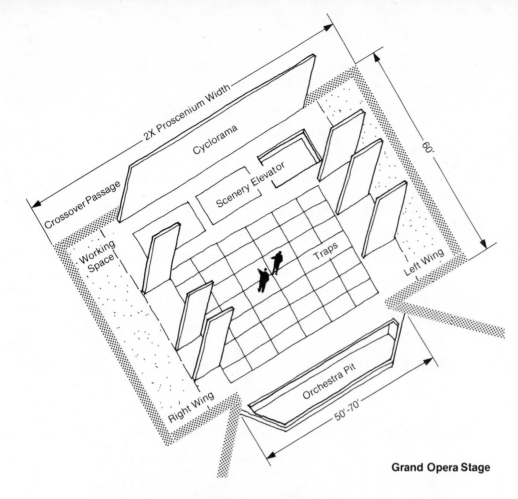

Grand Opera Stage

MUSICAL COMEDY AND LIGHT OPERA

Similar to drama in storyline continuity, these musical forms also rely heavily on stagecraft and technical support. Speech, song, and dance alternate and musical transitions require expert control. With up to 50 people onstage at once and quantities of scenery to manage, extensive preparations and an excellent communications system are needed to coordinate the activity.

Performance Space

- Although attention is focused downstage, background chorus activity and cross-talk between widely separated members of the cast require a wide, deep acting area that can be masked down as desired. The opening should be 50 to 70 feet wide.
- The floor should meet the resiliency standards of dance but must allow pieces of scenery to be attached to it.
- Traps and cyclorama are desirable.

Enclosure

- A 30 to 35 foot high proscenium arch is recommended, along with a flyloft stagehouse.
- Wing space is as important as flyloft space.

Scene/Working Space

- Wrap-around space must accept a large variety of elaborate scenery. There must be structural support for stand-up sets with recesses and overhangs, as well as for portions of the set that are "flown," or hung from the flies.

- Sets mounted on wagons are also useful but require substantial additional working space.
- Symmetrical working space will simplify maneuvering during scene changes.
- Live music is essential; allow orchestra pit room for 15 to 30 musicians.

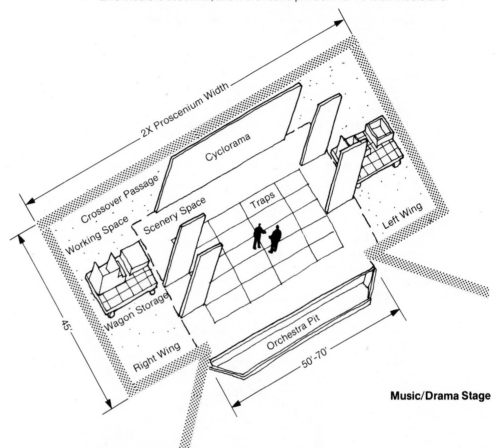

Music/Drama Stage

ORCHESTRAL MUSIC

The characteristic sound, intensity, and physical arrangement of an orchestra vary with its size and composition. Although a hall is usually designed for the "most likely" user and style of music, try to provide for variations as well. Music concerts consist of a series of uninterrupted performance periods of varying length. In the intervals, instruments may be changed, reorganized, and retuned while the audience takes a break.

Performance Space
- Orchestra setups are kept as compact as practicable, so that players can hear and see each other and share sheet music.
- The stage area averages 18 to 25 square feet per musician; proscenium widths range from 55 to 80 feet.
- There must be flexibility for changes in setup needed to achieve balance among the sections.
- A flat floor with portable riser platforms is best.
- The stage should be designed for the largest expected group. Smaller ensembles can be accommodated on a large stage by adjusting the enclosure and arrangement of musicians.
- Stage floor construction should dampen resonant vibration.

- Stage dimensions for different groups work out as follows:

Band or ensemble, 30 to 50 musicians	800- 900 square feet
Medium-size orchestra, 50 to 80 musicians	1200-1500 square feet
Medium-size orchestra plus chorus of 50 to 100 voices	1800-2300 square feet
Symphony orchestra, 80 to 125 musicians	2000-2400 square feet
Symphony plus large chorus of 100 to 200 voices	2800-3500 square feet

Enclosure
- There are two ways to direct sound toward the audience:
    1. With a removable shell erected in the stagehouse.
    2. By means of a permanent construction with structural qualities similar to those of the house.

Scene/Working Space
- Stagehouse functions are minimal; most support activity takes place backstage or from control areas in the house.
- There should be space adjoining the performance area for performers to assemble and for "standby" storage of pianos, extra chairs, and music stands.

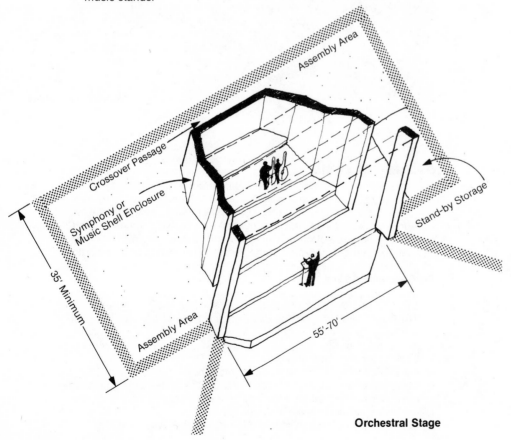

Orchestral Stage

- There may also be separate rooms for broadcast recording equipment and lighting switch gear.
- Freight elevators should be carefully planned to make loading most efficient.

CHORAL MUSIC

Because choral music has some of the characteristics of dramatic speech, intelligibility is crucial. Choral requirements fall somewhere between those of a large recital hall and a medium-size orchestral facility, depending on the number of voices involved.

Performance Space
- Singers are usually closely grouped so they can hear and see each other.
- Instruments and music stands are not required.
- Singers may be seated for long or intermittent performances, or they may stand throughout the concert.
- There should be five to nine square feet of stage area per singer.
- Additional room should be allowed for a piano or other instrumental accompaniment.
- Portable risers adjustable in eight inch increments are preferable to fixed risers.
- The performance area is normally twice as wide as it is deep.

Enclosure
- Requirements are similar to those for recital and orchestral halls. In larger halls, a shaped enclosure or shell will enhance the sound of choral music.
- The enclosure should blend, balance, and contain the sound energy.

Scene/Working Space
- Offstage assembly space must be larger than in other music facilities, and there should be entries from both sides of the performance area.
- An orchestra pit is desirable, particularly for large scale events; the alternative is a very large open stage arrangement.
- Piano, risers, and chairs should be stored in an area adjoining the stage.

RECITALS AND SMALL CHAMBER GROUPS

Instrumental and vocal recital rooms are the most intimate music spaces. The presentation format is similar to that for orchestral concerts, but musicians are fewer in number and share a much more personal relationship with the listener. Acoustics must provide greater definition among instruments.

Performance Space
- The platform area depends on the size of groups expected; allow about 18 to 25 square feet per musician. Portable risers may be used for larger groups and for choral performances.

Enclosure
- Surfaces surrounding the performance space may be treated with adjustable panels that reflect sound, absorb it, or both in order to adjust hearing onstage. A high degree of diffusion is desirable.
- The ceiling or suspended reflectors over the stage should be no higher than 20 feet; walls should not be parallel.

Scene/Working Space
- No scenery is involved, unless the hall has secondary uses.
- Piano, risers, and chairs are stored in areas adjoining the stage.
- There should be a lounge for musicians.
- Dimmers are necessary for house and stage lights.

AUDIENCE SEATING AREA

The house—the area where the audience sits—is the second major part of the performance space. The goal is to allow everyone who bought a ticket to see and hear clearly, and thereby participate as fully as possible in the production. The house also conveys the organization's artistic intentions and sets the mood and tone for performances.

How Many Seats?

Seating is determined by balancing ticket demand with the amount of money you can make from ticket sales, the cost of the touring groups you plan to bring in, mortgage rates, and operating expenses. The magic formula you choose may make or break the facility. As Joe Golden points out in *Olympus on Main Street*:

> Every seat more, or every seat less, has an impact on something: costs, revenues, sight lines, acoustics, safety, maintenance.

Economically a house should be as large as possible, consistent with the size of the potential audience. Aesthetically it should be no larger than is absolutely necessary for maximum impact of the performance on an audience. Often the two considerations are in conflict. Sometimes, for example, the size of a house could be increased substantially on the basis of market potential. But if it gets too big, the aesthetic experience may be so diminished that the market potential drops, too. Invariably, house size becomes a compromise among the various aesthetic, acoustical, marketing, and economic considerations.

Figure 9-1 will give you an idea of the types of activities that can be supported by different size halls. This list is intended only as a guide to matching the scale of performance to the number of seats. Financial considerations will require additional calculations.

Seating Arrangements

For a quick preliminary estimate of house size, multiply eight square feet times the total number of seats. This figure includes an allowance for aisle space. Within this area, seats are arranged to provide the greatest number of full views of the stage. There are two standard seating arrangements: American (or conventional); and continental.

American or conventional seating (Figure 9-2) provides for more intersecting aisle space than does the continental model. The rule of thumb in conventional seating is that the center seat be no more than six seats from each aisle.

The advantage is easy access to all seats and the need for fewer house exits. Fewer ushers are needed to supervise entering patrons. The disadvantage is that the aisles take up valuable space that might have been used for higher-priced tickets close to the stage.

Continental seating, in which long rows of seats extend nearly the full width of the auditorium (Figure 9-3), ensures that none of the best viewing positions are lost to aisle space. With wider space between the rows than in conventional seating, the audience enjoys increased leg room. On the other hand, people seated toward the center of each row may have to cross in front of as many as 30 people to get to their seats. Allowable maximum length under most current building codes is about 60 seats, depending on distance to an exit and aisle width. More exit doors are required than in conventional seating. If patrons are seated during the performance, special efforts must be made to minimize inconvenience to the rest of the audience.

Figure 9-1 A guide to prototypical relationships between number of seats and types of activities
(Source: Brian Arnott, A Facility Design Workbook.)

150-300 seats	Community theater productions Local music recitals Some touring music recitals Touring solo artists Modern dance performances (small companies) Film Lectures Meetings
450-850 seats	Community play production Many touring play productions Music recitals and concerts (small companies) Very modestly staged concert opera Modern dance performances (small companies) Film Lecture Meetings
900-1300 seats	Community musical play productions Most touring play and musical play production Most community orchestra concerts Touring music recitals Modern dance performances (except large touring companies) Some modestly staged opera performances Film Lecture Meetings Small conferences
1500-1900 seats (or more)	Community musical play productions Touring play and musical play productions Orchestra concerts and other music performances Grand opera performances Modern dance performances (large touring companies) Local and touring ballet performances Variety acts (popular music, country & western) Light and "soft" rock Film Conferences; small conventions Meetings

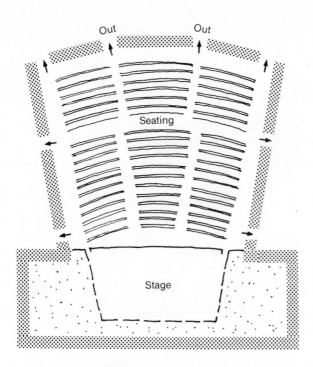

Figure 9-2 American Seating Plan

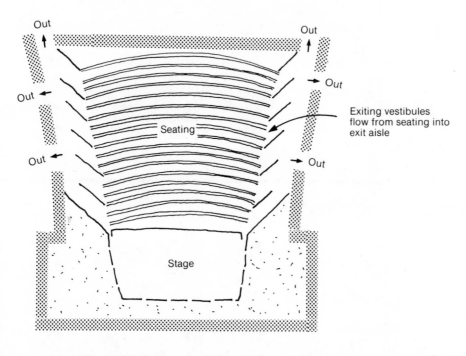

Exiting vestibules
flow from seating into
exit aisle

Figure 9-3 Continental Seating Plan

The Individual Seat

Since good seats are not necessarily expensive, seat types should be chosen primarily for audience comfort. Some criteria for auditorium seats:

- Seats should not be too narrow; 21 inches "elbow to elbow" is standard.
- A good seat back and padding on the seat, back, and armrests ensure maximum comfort.
- The seat material should permit easy maintenance.
- Seat covering colors should not be distracting.
- Allow for leg room; recommended minimum distance from the back of one seat to the next is 30 inches.
- If your budget is very tight, consider seats other than those advertised in theater supply catalogues. Church pews, stackable chairs, or cushions on seating platforms may work for a black box type facility. Or seats might be salvaged from a derelict movie theater. (Cleaned and fumigated, they won't reveal their undistinguished past.)

VISUAL PRINCIPLES THAT INFLUENCE THE DESIGN OF THE HOUSE

An optimum view of the stage throughout the house depends on three factors:

- Slope of the house floor
- Staggering of seats
- Elevation of the stage

The Slope (Rake) of the House Floor

If the floor is flat, patrons have a hard time seeing over the people in front of them. For this reason, most theater floors slope gently upward toward the back of the house. The floor may be ramped (a continuous slope) or stepped. For safety reasons, a ramped floor is limited to a maximum slope of 10 percent; steeper slopes must be stepped. Be sure to provide for wheelchair-bound patrons and standing room positions when figuring the slope of the house.

Staggered Seats

The positioning of seats in the rows depends on the degree of the rake. **One-row** vision, in which seats in each row line up directly with those in front, requires a very steep rake to allow for proper viewing angles. **Two-row vision** involves staggered seating and permits an unobstructed view between the two seats in front of the patron. Because this arrangement does not involve a steep rake, it is highly recommended.

Elevation of the Stage

The stage should always be below eye level of patrons sitting in the first row. Ideal height is between two feet, six inches and three feet, six inches from the floor at the first row of seats. The viewing angle of the audience varies with art form. In dance, for example, patrons must be able to see the dancers' feet. Make sure the stage floor is level with all support spaces backstage to expedite movement of scenery and equipment.

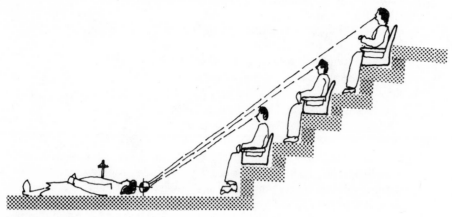

Flat Floor Stage

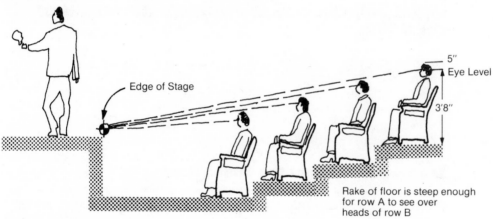

5"
Eye Level

3'8"

Edge of Stage

Rake of floor is steep enough
for row A to see over
heads of row B

One-Row Vision

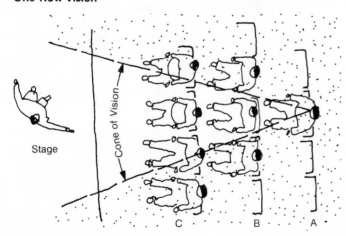

Cone of Vision

Stage

C   B   A

Plan of One-Row Vision

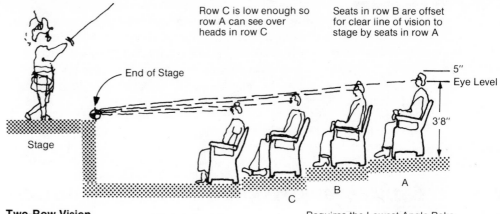

Row C is low enough so row A can see over heads in row C

Seats in row B are offset for clear line of vision to stage by seats in row A

End of Stage

5"
Eye Level

3'8"

Stage

C

B

A

Two-Row Vision

Requires the Lowest Angle Rake

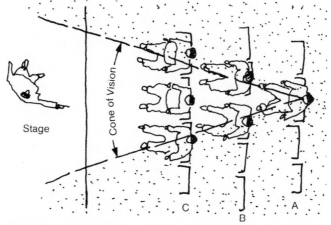

Stage

Cone of Vision

C

B

A

Plan of Two-Row Vision

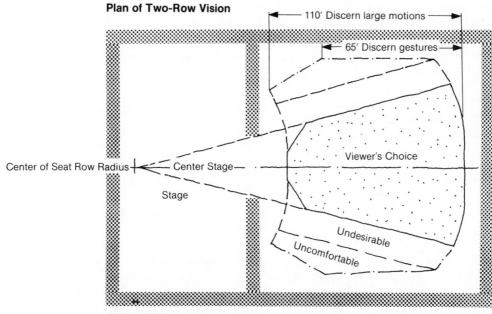

110' Discern large motions

65' Discern gestures

Center of Seat Row Radius

Center Stage

Viewer's Choice

Stage

Undesirable

Uncomfortable

Horizontal Sightlines

The Balcony

Building a balcony provides more seats within a given distance of the stage. The more intimate the drama, the more a balcony is useful in bringing the audience closer to the stage. Balconies should be raked to a level consistent with safety, ease of access, and the best viewing angle. Even the holders of the lowest-priced tickets are entitled to see more of the performers than the tops of their heads.

Be sure to consider the placement of balcony railings, which are required by safety codes, so that they do not block the view of balcony patrons.

ACOUSTICAL PRINCIPLES THAT INFLUENCE THE DESIGN OF THE HOUSE

Acoustics are the qualities of the hall that affect the transmission and reception of sound. (Sound reinforcement systems and equipment used for electronic enhancement of sound are discussed on pages 125-126.)

The quality of the sound that reaches the audience from the stage is a combination of direct sound and that reflected from all surfaces of the hall. The object is to balance these two sound qualities by eliminating as many sources of distortion as possible and distributing sound evenly throughout.

You must also take into account the sound quality your performers require. Although sound is very hard for a nonacoustician to describe, performers may know of other halls with desirable qualities that could serve as models.

Acoustical quality can be affected by:

- Shape of the theater (each has a unique sound quality)
- Width, depth, and height of the house
- The presence of a balcony and balcony size
- The number of seats and the size of the audience for a given performance
- Size, shape, and location of the reflective material within the acoustical system
- Seat materials and composition of walls, ceilings, and carpeting (all can affect sound reverberation time)
- Placement of technical equipment, such as catwalks

Acoustical design, probably the most controversial aspect of performing arts facility construction, is the responsibility of an acoustician—not the architect. An acoustical engineer who understands the artistic requirements of the art forms you are presenting will probably be your best choice for the job. You might consider contracting with an acoustician to come in for one day at the beginning of the project to help you to assess your needs.

To find the right acoustician, get a list of buildings outfitted by each potential consultant and look at those comparable in size to the one you are planning. Or, find houses whose acoustical qualities you like and ask who designed them. The best groundwork for choosing an acoustical expert is to find out what has been done correctly and incorrectly in the past.

Noise and Vibration Control

For maximum expression of their art, both musicians and actors must have as little competition from unwanted sound as possible. The acoustician, architect, and mechanical engineer must work together closely to ensure that the facility is designed for absolute quiet and complete lack of vibration. The following are pertinent considerations for noise control. (Source: *A Facility Design Workbook,* prepared by Brian Arnott.)

- Location of mechanical equipment rooms
- Sound buffer zones between noisy and quiet areas
- Proper design of heating and air conditioning
- Incorporation of appropriate detailing to ensure against noise entering quiet areas from outside the building

Performance Support

The type and extent of "backstage" support depends—once again—on the groups that will use the facility. A "booking" theater that presents mostly touring attractions may not need the extensive support areas of a theater with a resident repertory company that requires room to build sets and store costumes from year to year (see Figure 9-4). But never underestimate the need for adequate backup and preparation space—performances cannot happen without them.

Figure 9-4   Varying amounts of support space needed by a production house and a booking house

Production House (resident company)	Booking House (touring Companies)
Maximum number of administrative offices	Fewer administrative offices
Scene shop/storage/equipment/paint shop Costume shops/storage/equipment Property shop/storage	No production shops; minimum number maintenance shops and basic storage space
Full range of lighting instruments	Basic lighting equipment
Rehearsal space	Rehearsal space not absolutely necessary
Stage configuration to suit specialized needs of resident company	Traditional (proscenium) stage
Dressing rooms for company	Maximum number of dressing rooms

There are three categories of performance support:
1. Facilities for the performers
2. Production preparation and storage facilities
3. Technical facilities and equipment

FACILITIES FOR THE PERFORMERS

The type and number of such facilities will depend on expected cast sizes and special needs of different performing arts groups. Will you need to make special provisions for stars? Will you be dealing with large instrumental groups or choruses?

Professional performers often spend as many as eleven or twelve consecutive hours in the theater. They need light, fresh air, and comfortable, constant temperatures in order to function within a demanding work schedule.

Dressing Rooms, Toilets and Showers

Facilities for performers must be completely separate from the public portions of the theater. All dressing rooms should be as close as possible to the stage, preferably on stage level, and have direct access to the wardrobe department. Sixteen square feet per person is the minimum workable space in the dressing area. Generally, there are two separate large rooms for male and female performers, as well as several smaller "star" dressing rooms.

A larger facility might include star dressing rooms, shared changing facilities for other performers, a musicians' room, and separate rooms for a conductor and soloist. Remember that flexibility is essential to meet the varying demands of different types of productions. A community theater cannot, of course, provide for the largest possible cast that will ever perform there. The occasional large scale production will require temporary dressing room arrangements.

Each dressing room should have a wash basin with hot and cold water, and toilets and showers should be convenient to all rooms. There should be at least one toilet and shower for every six performers and one basin for every four persons. Every performer needs a dressing table and chair with incandescent light similar to stage lighting. Each station should have individual light switches and electrical outlets. Other requirements include a locked drawer and cupboard for each performer's personal possessions, hanging room for day clothes and costumes (about 24 inches of rack space per person), shelves for hats and wigs, and shoe racks. Every dressing room should also have a full-length mirror. Consult Actors' Equity standards for more detailed dressing room requirements.

Changing Rooms

Many performers do not require substantial makeup preparation or costume changes. Orchestra members and choral groups, for example, can be accommodated in changing rooms. In smaller theaters, rehearsal space, a classroom, or an actors' lounge might double as a changing room. Allow 25 square feet per person in the changing room, and provide a hanging cupboard, wash basin, and mirrors. If possible, include a cubicle with mirror on each side of the stage for minor changes and adjustments during performances.

Lounges

In a theater, as in any work environment, rest areas are required. Be sure to provide an **artists' lounge** where performers can relax, mingle, wait for calls, and have coffee. It should be furnished comfortably and preferably have windows. A canteen or vending machines also are welcome. The lounge need not be near the stage, but if it is, the area must be acoustically isolated so noise does not carry into the performance area.

The **green room** in a large theater serves as a more formal lounge, where performers may meet guests and the press. Kitchen facilities should be provided. In smaller theaters, the artists' lounge can double as a green room.

Rehearsal Space

Performers need to rehearse in an area approximately 50 by 50 feet, or as close as possible to the size, height and character of the stage. Sound baffles should eliminate noise from the street, public areas, and workrooms. The room should have a floor similar to the stage floor, proper ventilation, and a small storage area. Access to daylight can make the room a more pleasant place to work.

For dancers, a rehearsal room must be equipped with mirrors, a sprung wood floor, barres, and a piano. Ceiling height should be at least 13 feet. For musicals and drama, the rehearsal room must be as large as the acting area of the stage with additional space at the back and sides for the cast to assemble. A piano is essential. Music rehearsal rooms should have sound qualities as similar as possible to those of the actual stage. An orchestra, choir, or chorus will need a concert platform similar to the one they will use during performances.

A rehearsal room also can house classes, meetings, and receptions, but you should determine ahead of time what these other uses will be and plan the storage space, lighting, and floor surfaces accordingly.

Chorus Room

Pressure can be taken off the hectic backstage area by providing a "chorus room," an acoustically separate space near the stage that can double as a warmup space for musicians. The room may also be used for small rehearsals, public gatherings, or as a lounge.

PRODUCTION PREPARATION AND STORAGE FACILITIES

A theater booking touring companies must have backstage and wing space adequate for cleaning and assembling prebuilt scenery and props. Space must also be provided for temporary storage of flats and props. Recommended minimum standards require one wing to be wider than the proscenium opening to accommodate scenery.

A theater designed for a resident company, on the other hand, is much like a cottage industry engaged in light manufacturing. Space allotted to production preparation will always be greater than in a house built strictly for touring needs. Activities such as welding, woodwork, and scenery and wardrobe construction need to be located near one another but must not encroach on each other's territory. Although it is not absolutely necessary for production facilities to be housed in the theater—in cities, they are often located in low rent, manufacturing districts—having everything under one roof is desirable, where possible. Separate facilities make production coordination, company administration, and maintaining company morale more difficult.

Loading Dock and Receiving Area

The best model for a loading dock is right in your neighborhood—at the local supermarket. A performing arts facility presenting road shows needs sufficient space for large semi-trailers to maneuver into proper position for unloading, and truck parking space is essential. The American Ballet Theater travels with thirty 40 foot tractor trailers, while a smaller dance company like Ballet West travels with five trucks. The more efficient your loading facility, the more valuable time (and money) you will save.

Allot approximately 50 to 100 feet of space adjacent to the loading dock so that the truck can back straight up to the receiving area. Provide a level area in front of the loading dock at least as long as the largest trailer you expect to accommodate (probably 40 to 45 feet).

Dock height should be anywhere from 44 to 55 inches; the top of the trailer will rise 13 to 15 feet above the dock itself. Average truck stall width is 12 feet.

A critical design issue that is often overlooked is the placement and size of the loading door. This is the kind of "small" error that can significantly drive up labor costs and limit the kind of shows your facility will be able to present. Check with touring companies you plan to book about the standard size of the flats they use, and remember that each one will have to pass through the loading door! The loading entrance should be in a direct line to the stage so that bulky pieces of scenery will not have to be maneuvered around corners.

Be sure the floor of the receiving area and loading dock are at stage level. Otherwise, you will need a large freight elevator serving all floors of the facility. Separate the noisy loading area from the stage by at least two sets of doors.

To be sure you have planned properly for this vital area, visualize the truck pulling up and the scenery being unloaded. Will the doors be tall and wide enough? Is the area protected against wind and rain? How difficult is it to move a large, odd-shape item onto the stage? Surprising as it may sound, many performing arts facilities are built with loading docks so poorly designed that trucks have to be unloaded in the parking lot.

General Storage

Because sets, large props, and stage equipment must be stored when not in use, it is virtually impossible to have too much storage space. Though most desirable close to the stage, storage areas may be located throughout the building. Doorways to stage-area storage must be large enough to accommodate large flats; shelves and bins can help organize smaller items. Be sure that all spaces are well lit.

Instrument Storage

Pianos and other musical instruments owned by the facility require a separate, secure storage area with controlled temperature and humidity. Make sure the doors are wide enough to permit easy entry of a concert grand piano.

Scene and Paint Shop

Scenery is constructed and repaired in the scene shop; the paint shop may share this space or be located in a separate area. Ideally, the combined size of these spaces is equal to the stage area plus the wings and stage apron. Ceiling and doors must be high enough to accommodate sets and the scenery wagon used to carry them. The scene shop should be convenient to both the loading area and the stage. Be sure to insulate the shop to protect the rest of the facility from fumes, dust, noise, and vibration.

Set construction space should be equipped with workbenches, a janitor's tools, sink, and space to store finished flats, as well as pieces that are drying. Backdrops are painted either on vertical paint frames or flat on the floor, which requires a very large floor area.

Properties Shop and Storage

A workroom for the preparation of props should be adjacent to a prop storage area. Props can be stored on shelves as they are built until needed for a performance. A small performance prop room near the stage will hold all props needed throughout each performance.

Wardrobe Shop and Storage

Design, fabrication, and maintenance of all costumes is handled in the costume construction area. Among the required furnishings are cutting tables, sewing machines, ironing boards, dress forms, materials and supply storage, hanging space for finished garments, a curtained fitting area, and full-length mirrors. Even, incandescent light is essential, and daylight is also desirable.

Dyeing, laundry, and drycleaning operations require heavy-duty industrial machines, a double sink, counter space, and a dyeing tub.

The costume storage area should have ample space for hanging long costumes and room for cabinets, drawers, and shelves. The area must be clean, well-lit, and dry.

Costume storage may be divided into short term and long term; the short term area should be easily accessible to the wardrobe shop and dressing rooms. For long term storage, proper ventilation is necessary.

Electrical Shop and Storage

The base of operations for theater electricians, the electrical shop is a dust-free area where equipment repairs can be made. Color gels for special lighting effects are also prepared here. Storage areas house electrical accessories for the entire theater, plus slide and film projectors, lenses, and lighting equipment.

TECHNICAL FACILITIES AND EQUIPMENT

The facilities needed for lighting and sound and control of scenery depend on the size and skills of the production crews and on the level of technical sophistication desired by the organization. Quality before quantity is the watchword for selecting technical equipment. Second rate equipment is liable to break down more often. The best equipment needs little maintenance and provides a good foundation for future expansion.

On a limited budget, it is best to develop a high quality, portable electrical system. Make sure you have all the outlets you require, and start by purchasing a small number of the best available light fixtures, adding a few more lights each year.

Lighting Systems

In the theater there are three different lighting systems: house lights, work lights, and stage lights.

House lights must be bright enough to allow audience members to find their seats and read the program comfortably. Incandescent light should be on a dimmer control circuit separate from the stage lighting. Put the aisle and exit lights on another, nondimming circuit.

Work lights illuminate the house and stage for rehearsals, maintenance, and show preparation. They should provide maximum visibility without a great deal of electricity and can be controlled by switches separate from the stage lighting board. Consider placing house work lights and stage work lights on separate circuits, because they will not always be used simultaneously.

Stage lighting should be chosen and positioned by a lighting consultant and your artistic director. Design the stagehouse with a walkspace above the grid for maintenance of the light fixtures positioned on overhead rigging. All fixtures must be adjustable and movable. The lighting system should in no way interfere with sightlines or acoustics in the hall.

Auditorium lighting positions for a proscenium stage consist of *ceiling slots* and *wall slots*. The location of the slots is determined by stage size, but there are usually one or two of each, 15 and 30 feet from the proscenium. Access to these positions by way of catwalks (lighting bridges) and ladders is important.

The stage lights are controlled from the *lighting control room,* located at the rear of the house, possibly in a glassed-in, soundproof room. The lighting operator working here needs an unrestricted and undistorted view of the entire performance area.

Follow-spot positions at the rear or sides of the hall house the spotlights that follow cast members around the stage. Scenic projectors are also operated from this area.

Before selecting *lighting components,* check with a lighting consultant and investigate the contract requirements of touring companies, if you plan to present them. Be absolutely certain that the facility's electrical capacity can accommodate future growth, as well as the road show with super power amplifiers, motorized devices, and special lighting equipment.

Each performing art form has a different set of lighting requirements:

- For **dance productions**, primary light comes from the sides of the stage, usually from spotlight trees that sidelight the performers from a low angle. Cable connections must be designed into the stage area, and wings must be deep enough to accommodate these lighting fixtures.
- For **music concerts**, light is beamed from directly above the stage. Light must be bright enough for the musicians to read their music without producing glare. Outlets for music stand lights should also be provided.
- **Dramatic productions** require great flexibility in lighting positions so that the moods of different plays can be captured through lighting plots. Usually, lighting is directed from a more frontal position, and the actor's face is illuminated from both sides.

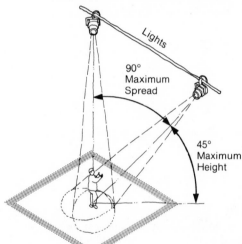

Optimum Angles for Lighting the Actor's Face

Sound Systems

In addition to the acoustically designed configuration and surfacing of the hall, many auditoriums now include sound "enhancers" that simplify and reinforce the sound quality and create theatrical sound effects when needed.

Electro-acoustical enhancement adjusts the reverberation time of a performing space—particularly important when the facility is to be used for art forms with radically different acoustical needs. Music, for example, requires a long reverberation time to make it sound full and smooth. But reverberation can ruin the intelligibility of speech during lectures and plays. If a hall is "tuned" for orchestral music, audio equipment can help alter the sound field for a theatrical presentation. Likewise, a hall designed for theater can be adapted to some extent for music concerts via electro-acoustics.

Sound reinforcement amplifies and selectively balances direct sound. A properly designed system yields a nearly natural sound quality; a poor system can destroy the nuances of a performance.

In the arrangement most commonly used by touring companies, speakers are placed on either side of the proscenium. Placement of permanently installed speakers will depend on the room configuration and the intended use of the hall. Your acoustical consultant will position them to produce a natural sound throughout the hall and to avoid time lag between the words mouthed by performers and the sound heard by the audience.

The sound reinforcement system should be controlled from a *sound control booth* at the rear of the auditorium, so the operator can hear the sound the way the audience hears it. This booth can be located near the lighting control booth but should be acoustically separated from it. Location and wiring connections will be specified by the sound system designer.

A theatrical sound effects system, separate from the reinforcement system, is used to create special directional sound, such as a train going around the stage, a doorbell, gunshots, or thunder. This system should be flexible, with loudspeakers that can be placed in a variety of locations. Music for plays and dance is usually handled through an adaptation of the sound effects system, though in some cases, reinforcement speaker clusters may be added.

A minimum sound package for a theater includes:

Tape decks
Speakers
Amplifiers
Mixers
Microphones
Phonograph
Control booth sound operators

The Communications System

In addition to production equipment, a theater needs a behind-the-scenes communication system to allow artists and technicians to talk with each other, for directions from the stage manager to the technical staff for stage door security, and for warnings to the performers.

Additional communications systems include:

- A public address system to make general announcements to the audience or backstage groups.
- Monitors to permit latecomers gathered in the lobby to hear the performance on stage.

Other Technical Positions

The stage manager's command post is backstage, where he or she can oversee the crew during performances. Large productions will require a stage crew room with toilets and lockers where the crew can relax between duties. Room must also be provided in the wings for the person who raises and lowers the curtain.

Audience and Administrative Support

The third major component of a performing arts facility consists of the public areas (lobby, box office, coat check, and refreshment stand) that directly serve the needs of the audience and the offices for administrative staff.

PUBLIC AREAS

The building's exterior details —the facade, landscaping, driveway, and entry —are the patron's first introduction to the artistic experience awaiting inside. Depending on the way it is conceived, the facility may give people the impression of grandeur, community openness, off-beat artiness, or commercial slickness. It is important to settle on just one image rather than trying to be all things to all audiences.

Everything should be clearly identifiable; a patron must not be left to guess where the entrance is. The drop-off point where car passengers disembark should be protected from the elements with a weather shelter or canopy. A tasteful banner or other sign can inform the passerby of events currently taking place.

Access for the Handicapped—and Others

The Rehabilitation Act of 1973, Section 504, states that:

> No otherwise qualified handicapped individual in the United States shall, solely by reason of his handicap, be excluded from the participation in, be denied the benefits of, or be subjected to discrimination under any program or activity receiving federal financial assistance.

Translated into architectural terms, this means that buildings must be constructed so that handicapped persons can maneuver wheelchairs into and throughout the facility, including the lobby, auditorium, and restrooms.

Any arts facility, however, should be designed for "human access" so that all kinds of people—visitors with baby strollers, the elderly, children, the infirm—can move through the building with ease.

Lobby

Visitors should pass through a vestibule isolating the lobby from cold air and outside noise. The ticket taker can be positioned right at the door or in the outer lobby area. The lobby is a place for socializing, relaxing with friends before the performance begins, enjoying refreshments during intermission, and picking up literature on coming events. By making the lobby a pleasant place, you can help put patrons in a receptive mood for the performance to come.

Lobby size is based on building code requirements. Allot approximately five to eight square feet per seat, plus 20 percent of that figure for circulation. An additional 20 percent of square footage should accommodate toilets, coat storage, and the first-aid room. Clear signs are needed to guide people to restrooms, telephones, the refreshment bar, souvenir shop, and other public areas.

Transitions

In addition to a vestibule between the outer doors and lobby, double doors with noiseproof crash bars should be installed between the theater and lobby. Doors must close silently, with no creaking or clicking.

AUDIENCE SERVICES

Restrooms

A two and a half or three-hour performance usually has at least one—and often two—intermissions of 10 to 15 minutes. Restrooms, water fountains, and phones should be sufficiently numerous to avoid very long lines during these brief intervals. Try to provide enough stalls in the toilets so that lines do not extend outside the restroom doors. *Design Guide for Music and Drama Centers* recommends 260 square feet in the restroom for a 300 seat house, 350 square feet for 650 seats, and 500 square feet for 1400 seats.

The Box Office

The box office, of course, must be easily found. If it is accessible without having to pass through the entire lobby, the interior of the theater can be closed to the public during nonperformance hours, thus reducing security, maintenance, and energy costs. Check with the facility manager for ticket sale procedures that will be in effect; estimated sales volume will determine the location and size of the box office. Keep the ticket window away from areas of main traffic flow, the street entrance, stairs, and ramps.

Make sure the box office is large enough to accommodate the number of personnel required, ticket racks, telephones, safes, and the automated equipment used for verifying and registering charge orders. (See Chapter 13 and Further Reading for more information on managing a box office.)

Coat Check

Fifty square feet per 100 patrons is the recommended size. A long counter situated away from main traffic paths will accommodate more attendants and speed the coat-claiming process at the end of the performance. A self-service coatroom is another option that reduces congestion somewhat.

Food and Beverage Service

Whether it is a snack bar, a liquor bar, or a full restaurant, food and beverage service may be a big moneymaker for your facility. This is especially true if your group is permitted to have a liquor license. Locate the refreshment bar adjacent to or within the lobby, again avoiding the main flow of traffic. Consider how heavy crates of liquor will be delivered to the bar area; stairs should be avoided if possible. Storage space is always required, no matter how modest the service, and the area should be lockable.

If you are thinking of installing island bars, be aware that they require more staff to serve customers than do bars set against the wall. It is also hard to find room for bottles, glasses, and rubbish away from the view of patrons.

If you are planning sit-down meal service, consider whether it will be compatible with the major use of the facility. Are there already numerous restaurants in the area, or will you attract patrons unable to dine elsewhere? Will the restaurant be economically viable? What prices will your audience pay for an evening's meal? A restaurant consultant can give you down-to-earth advice about the type of service appropriate for your needs.

Restaurant service may be periodic or continual. **Periodic service** means one seating a day, possibly a dinner theater arrangement, with meals prepared elsewhere. **Continuous service** requires a larger kitchen in which to prepare meals. For either type of restaurant you should provide ten to twelve and a half square feet per seat. Consider, too, how you will deal most efficiently with garbage disposal.

ADMINISTRATIVE SPACES

Staff Offices

A production house for a resident company will need offices for a full staff, including an executive director; resident director and designer; development, publicity and marketing managers; operations personnel; a financial department; and secretarial staff. A house that books touring companies, on the other hand, will employ fewer people. In designing your administrative spaces think ahead to possible future expansion; like storage, office space often tends to be in short supply.

Because long hours are the rule in the arts, offices should be properly illuminated, sufficiently roomy, and graced with an exterior view if possible. Cramped, uncomfortable office space will only result in staff unhappiness and lower productivity.

For the sake of flexibility, some arts managers swear by the open-plan office, in which partitions divide one large space. However, each work area must be acoustically isolated in order to minimize distractions.

Whatever plan you choose—and you should consult your staff on their preferences—try to locate the offices in a central position near the public entrance. Make sure the offices—particularly those with noisy machines—are acoustically isolated from the theater. In at least one new facility, the duplicating machine cannot be operated during a performance because of inadequate sound baffling.

Mailroom, Duplication and Supplies

Either one room or separate areas can be designated for sorting mail, sending mail out, copying, and storing supplies and dead files. Remember that the space must accommodate addressing machines (or a word processor or computer) and postage and duplicating machines.

Conference Room

Most facilities will require a room seating about 20 people to accommodate meetings of the staff, the board of directors, and executive committees. In a small facility, the conference room can house a basic reference library.

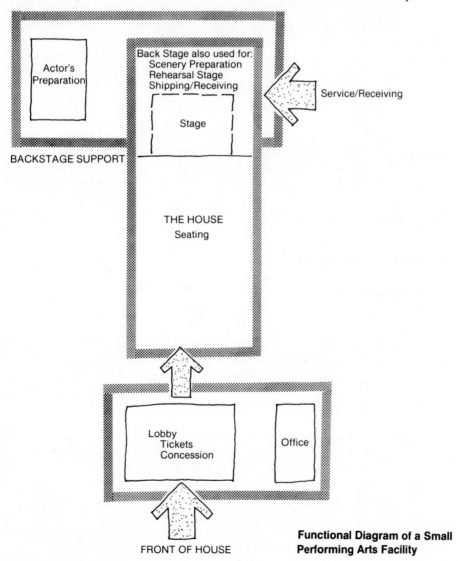

Functional Diagram of a Small
Performing Arts Facility

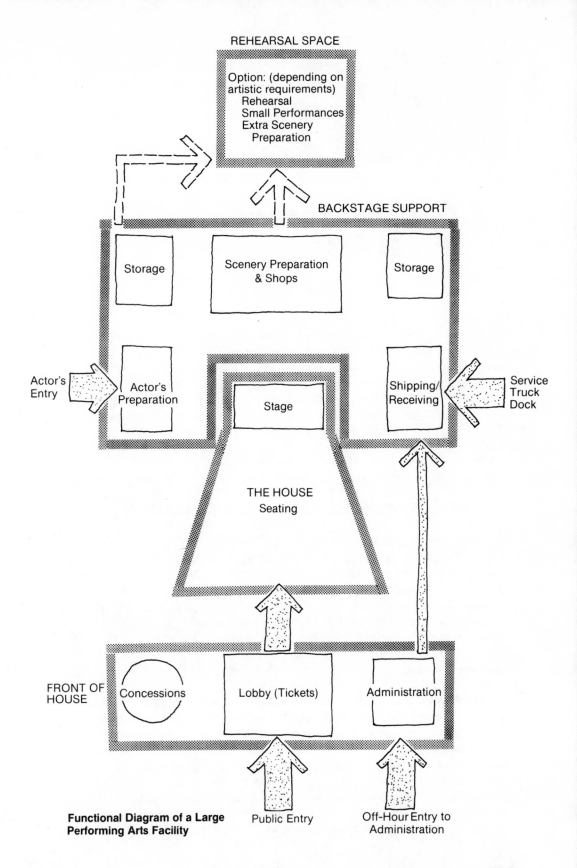

REHEARSAL SPACE

Option: (depending on artistic requirements)
Rehearsal
Small Performances
Extra Scenery
Preparation

BACKSTAGE SUPPORT

Storage

Scenery Preparation & Shops

Storage

Actor's Entry

Actor's Preparation

Stage

Shipping/ Receiving

Service Truck Dock

THE HOUSE
Seating

FRONT OF HOUSE

Concessions

Lobby (Tickets)

Administration

Functional Diagram of a Large Performing Arts Facility

Public Entry

Off-Hour Entry to Administration

DEVELOP A
BUILDING PLAN

10. Design Standards: Visual Arts

U nlike performing arts facilities, which must be constructed according to certain technical standards, the few fixed rules that govern a museum or arts center deal mainly with atmospheric control and security. Therefore, you must know exactly what kind of art you want to show and what relationship you wish to establish between the art and the visitors before you can begin to plan the number, size and positions of the galleries. This chapter describes in general terms the various parts of a visual arts facility. For detailed help in planning the specific features your group wants, consult the reference books listed in Further Reading.

THE PRIMARY FUNCTIONS: ART AND EDUCATION

Whatever the focus of their programs, all visual arts facilities have two primary functions: exhibiting art, and educating the public about it. There are, however, many different approaches to these two functions. Exhibition can involve the display of a permanent collection, a series of changing exhibitions, or a combination of the two. Education can involve anything from docent tours of the exhibits to formal lectures, studio art classes, and special programs that include music, dance, and film or video. The approach chosen and the amount of space devoted to each function will vary depending on the type of facility.

Prototypes: Museum, Gallery and Community Art Center

There are three basic types of visual arts facilities: the museum, the gallery, and the community art center. A **museum** typically has a permanent collection and is committed to the exhibition and conservation of significant works of art. The decision to assume responsibility for a permanent collection will considerably influence the design of a facility and subsequent operating costs. Flexible gallery space also is needed for changing exhibitions. A museum education department offers lectures and classes, sometimes including studio art courses, for both children and adults.

A **gallery** features traveling or gallery-originated art exhibits on a regular basis and has no permanent collection. It is usually committed to the presentation of a particular kind of art. Often, the facility consists of one exhibition space with staff offices.

A **community art center** serves as a meeting place where educational and artistic functions provide a focus for community activities. It usually has at least one gallery space for changing shows but does not house a permanent collection. The center offers studio classes in painting, ceramics, photography, and other art and craft media and may also present performing arts events, lectures, and special programs.

The type of arts facility you choose will depend on the interests of the community, the availability of art exhibits in other local facilities, and your group's philosophy. But whatever type you build, you need to plan for certain basics:

- Public support spaces, the areas encountered by the visitor on the way to the galleries and other major parts of the building
- Exhibition space, the public galleries themselves
- Technical support areas, including storage, workshops for conservation and the preparation of exhibits, and shipping and receiving
- Administrative support areas, such as offices and conference rooms
- Educational spaces, including the lecture hall or auditorium, studio art classrooms and the library

Finally, this chapter will deal with two other important areas in the design of a visual arts facility:

- Temperature and humidity control
- Security systems

PUBLIC SUPPORT SPACES

Integrating the Social and the Aesthetic

In recent decades, there has been a trend away from the "temple of culture" where galleries were the dominant public spaces. Newer visual arts facilities are airy, spacious places that attract people not only to view the art but also to meet friends and relax in the refreshment area, bask with a book in a pleasant garden, or even do their Christmas shopping in well-stocked gift shops. The classic Beaux Arts building, with gallery "arms" extending outward from a central rotunda falls somewhere between these extremes.

The purpose of the new designs is to increase earned revenues by attracting more visitors. Most museum-goers have infrequent contact with art, walking through the doors perhaps only once a year. A smaller number go frequently and account for a disproportionately large number of visits. To capture the uncommitted crowd, arts facilities have tried to shed the image of a cloistered browsing place by opening up the galleries and making the visitor feel "at home" in a pleasant atmosphere. Shops and cafes are additional attractions to people unlikely to venture in only to see the exhibits.

The result is that a modern facility has a bustling, social atmosphere. While some people are standing still to look at an individual object, others are moving through, scanning the gallery to see what is in it, or leaving in search of more art, the restrooms, or a breath of fresh air. And with increased numbers of visitors and a liberalization of the old hush-hush atmosphere, museums today tend to be noisier places.

It is especially important, therefore, that the "social" spaces of the facility—predominantly the lobby, restaurant, and gift shop—don't intrude on areas devoted to contemplation of the art. This division of functions holds true whether the facility is a large museum or a small community art center.

First Impressions

The location, scale, and style of the facility make an impression on visitors even before they decide to enter the building. Many older, formal structures are distinctive in design but may appear overly grandiose and forbidding to today's visitor.

If you are remodeling the facility where you have spent many years, keep in mind that the old facade is probably out of character with the art currently exhibited inside. When remodeling a structure not previously associated with art, you have to deal with the former image of the building. A jail, for example, may need some creative restructuring in order to provide a suitable home for art.

The Entry and Lobby

Public spaces should provide a transition between the hustle and bustle of the outside world and the special precincts where art is displayed. The lobby should be sufficiently large to permit visitors to get their bearings, check the room map, familiarize themselves with services offered by the facility, and gather membership and class information. A clear orientation system in the lobby can help reinforce a visitor's initial favorable impression of the facility.

Some points to keep in mind in planning the lobby:

■ Prominent, easy-to-understand **signs** should tell visitors what kind of art is on view—and where—and what activities are currently taking place. The reception area is also the place for attractive announcements of future exhibits, class schedules, and social events sponsored by the art organization. On the other hand, orientation displays should not overwhelm the exhibition function of the facility.

- An **assembly area** may be necessary to accommodate bus groups. A coatroom with low hooks is a thoughtful addition in any facility that expects frequent visits from school children. In a larger facility, a separate entrance for groups and a parking lot for buses may be most practical.
- Adult visitors also need a pleasant **rest area** where they can sit and rest or wait for friends.
- **Lighting in the foyer** should allow the visitor's eyes to adjust from bright daylight to the low levels of light required for conservation of art objects.
- The **reception area**, where visitors may pay an admission fee or buy tickets to a special exhibit, should have room for queues to form. For practical as well as security reasons, the reception desk should face both incoming and outgoing traffic.

Access for the Handicapped—and Others

Wheelchair access to public buildings is mandated by law (see page 127). However, any arts facility should be designed for easy access by all kinds of people. Don't forget that some of your biggest supporters may be frail, elderly people. Heavy doors can be a problem even for the able-bodied. Ask yourselves whether everyone can easily open the front door and use railings and other physical features of the building. A special "handicapped access" should be marked with clearly visible signs. If you are working with an architect known for creating imposing structures, insist on consideration of visitors' needs in the entrance design. A ramp entrance, for example, is easy for everyone to manage.

Food Services

If you are planning to operate or sublease a restaurant or snack bar, get down-to-earth advice from a restaurant consultant about the type of service most appropriate for your facility and about the need for a restaurant in the neighborhood. The restaurant should be situated so as to prevent cooking odors and noise from drifting into the galleries. When allotting space, allow ten to twelve and a half square feet per restaurant seat, in addition to the kitchen area. A kitchen where meals will be prepared must be larger than one designed to handle only meals catered elsewhere. And don't forget that food services require their own storage spaces and provisions for deliveries.

Bookstore/Gift Shop

Because the sales area is essentially a retail store, planning advice from a local merchant or marketing professional can be helpful. Locate the store in the lobby or other entry point but separate it from the gallery area to keep noise and crowding from interfering with the viewing of art. If the store is not located near the entrance, be sure to advertise its existence in the lobby. Within the store, provide adequate storage space and plenty of display space to attract interested buyers. The cash register should be positioned so that one person can survey the entire sales area.

Other Basic Needs

Of course, you must provide drinking fountains, toilets, and a public telephone for your visitors' needs. Local building codes will mandate the number and size of the restrooms.

EXHIBITION SPACES

The first step in designing exhibition spaces is to have a clear idea of what you will be showing. How many exhibits are planned per year, and how often will they change? What kinds of traveling exhibitions do you hope to schedule? If you have a permanent collection, how many pieces will remain on view? Will you be showing some very large-scale art? Mostly small pieces? Three-dimensional objects to be displayed in cases or on pedestals? Fragile prints and drawings?

With firm program plans in hand, you can determine the degree of flexibility you need, the layout of your galleries, and the size and environmental qualities of the spaces. There are few fixed rules, so the guidelines in this section are necessarily general. For more details on gallery and exhibition design, see the books listed in Further Reading, particularly *Communicating with the Museum Visitor,* published by the Royal Ontario Museum.

The guidelines here reflect the belief that exhibitions of paintings, prints, drawings, photography, and sculpture will continue to be the "bread and butter" of any visual arts facility's annual programming. Providing for such newer developments as video and performance art is not that difficult, even for the small or medium-sized museum or art center. The key is flexibility: Can you turn gallery space into a performance art site for an evening with a minimum of fuss? Do you have sufficient, conveniently located outlets to accommodate video monitors? If you plan to emphasize nontraditional art forms, be sure to talk with artists who work in these media about their specific needs.

Orient the Visitor

Unlike the performing arts, in which the audience stays in one place to watch the action on stage, the visual arts require movement and choice on the part of the spectator. Your galleries and other public spaces must be designed to help the viewer organize the experience of looking at and considering a sequence of objects.

The entry and lobby areas should direct visitors to the galleries, where they should be able to survey what there is to see, select a starting point, and move to it as directly as possible. From that point, you want the arrangement of spaces to yield a continuously unfolding experience, allowing the visitor's attention to be drawn easily from object to object, gallery to gallery.

Some factors to keep in mind when designing your exhibition spaces:

- Viewers should be able to move through the exhibit without being forced to walk past objects they have already seen.
- There must be adequate space for visitors to move at different speeds. Some will move continuously, while others will stop to examine particular objects in greater detail.
- A viewer tends to turn to the right upon entering a gallery. Circulation patterns should be designed with this in mind.
- The ability to survey the gallery area in one sweep will help viewers understand what is on display and decide what they want to see.

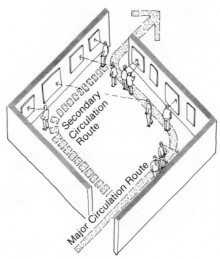

Right Hand Preference Circulation Patterns

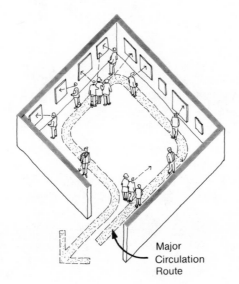

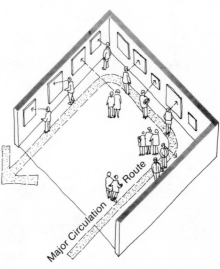

Provide a Pleasant, Varied Environment

A crowded, warm, or noisy environment can make the most ardent art lover irritable. Be sure the facility has sufficiently roomy corridors and aisles as well as other "transitional" areas such as courtyards or skylit spaces. Viewers need places to sit down and rest, reflect on the art, take a break from the visual richness of the galleries, or simply get their bearings. Frequently, these spaces are illuminated by daylight, in contrast to the gallery areas, which are lit primarily with electric light. Seats at appropriate distances from large, important works of art give visitors a chance to pause and examine the art without standing for long periods of time.

These amenities also vary the "pace" of the visit—an important element in the design of a visual arts facility. When viewers become tired, satiated with the sheer quantity of the art, or discomfitted by noise, their gallery experience ceases to be rewarding. Visual diversity helps keep the viewer interested. A low level of ambient lighting in the gallery area can be contrasted with dramatic highlighting. Variations in ceiling heights and different wall colors throughout a sequence of galleries help ward off visitor fatigue. Of course, none of these features should ever upstage the art.

It is essential to control noise and vibration in the exhibit space; air conditioning and other equipment should be selected and located accordingly. The mechanical engineers on your project should be aware of the need to mask distracting sounds.

Critical Dimensions for a Visual Arts Facility

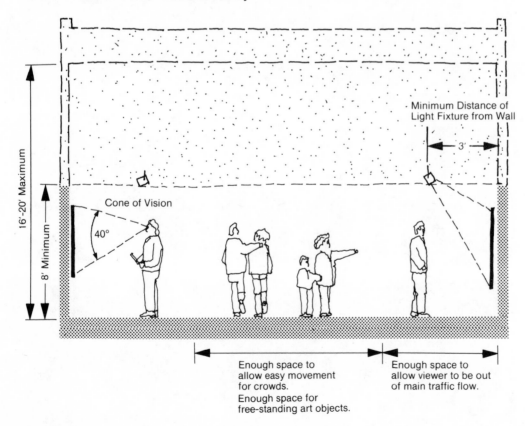

16'-20' Maximum

8' Minimum

Minimum Distance of Light Fixture from Wall

3'

Cone of Vision

40°

Enough space to allow easy movement for crowds.
Enough space for free-standing art objects.

Enough space to allow viewer to be out of main traffic flow.

The Physical Elements

The color, texture, and materials you choose for walls, ceilings, and floors will establish the aesthetic mood of your galleries.

Walls

Walls and ceilings are backdrops for the art, and must never compete with it.

Because walls also serve as a support system for the art, they should be as flexible as possible to accommodate a variety of shows. Surface material must be able to withstand the constant rehanging of works. Position outlets and thermostats carefully so that valuable wall space is not wasted.

Walls are also spatial devices which, with the help of floor or ceiling tracks, can be arranged in different patterns and sequences. Many galleries construct temporary wall systems for each exhibit, cueing the paint color to the mood and tonality of the art.

Ceilings

Ceilings should be neutral in color and texture so they do not draw the viewer's attention away from the art.

Ceiling height is an important consideration. If ceilings are too low, heat from the lights may damage the art, and viewers may find light hitting them squarely in the eye. You also want ceilings high enough that the largest piece of art will pass comfortably through every door on its path from the receiving area to the gallery. A rule of thumb is that ceilings should be no lower than eight feet and no higher than twenty feet. A fourteen- to sixteen-foot height is a good choice for most galleries. You might want to include a ceiling that can be lowered to create a more intimate exhibition area for certain shows.

Ceilings also must be carefully designed to house the lighting, heating, and cooling systems without exposing the art to sunlight or dry air from vents and without detracting from the aesthetic quality of the gallery space.

Floors

An often overlooked surface in the gallery area is the floor, which like the walls and ceilings, is also a background for the art. Beware of decorative patterns that call attention to themselves. Floors must be strong enough to handle the heaviest work of art the gallery will exhibit, and the floor material must resist wear and be easy to maintain.

Lighting

Lighting plays a key role in establishing mood and ambiance in art galleries, just as it does in the theater.

The Daylight Debate

There is much discussion among art facility designers about daylight versus electric light in the galleries. All the experts agree that direct sunlight on works of art must be avoided. Drawings, prints, and photographs in particular can be irreparably damaged by exposure to infrared rays. Those who favor skylights or windows in the gallery argue that dangerous rays can be screened out while visitors enjoy a light-filled, airy environment.

If you do decide to allow daylight into the gallery space, keep in mind that:

- The light rays must be filtered or the illumination confined to reflected light.
- The orientation of the sun changes during the day and according to the season. Establish the angle of the sun's rays within the gallery in order to arrange arts objects for maximum protection.
- The intensity of light reaching the gallery will vary with atmospheric conditions and time of day, so artificial illumination will still be needed to maintain a constant light level.
- The introduction of natural light will affect the temperature and relative humidity in the room. It is important that works of art be kept at a fixed humidity level to prevent warping, peeling, drying, and other deterioration.
- Certain types of traveling exhibits may only be loaned to facilities with gallery space that has no access to natural light. (See the yearly catalogues put out by SITES and The Art Museum Association of America.)

In nongallery areas, on the other hand, natural light is always welcome. Thoughtfully integrated into the lobby and other public spaces, it can be a relaxing link with the natural world.

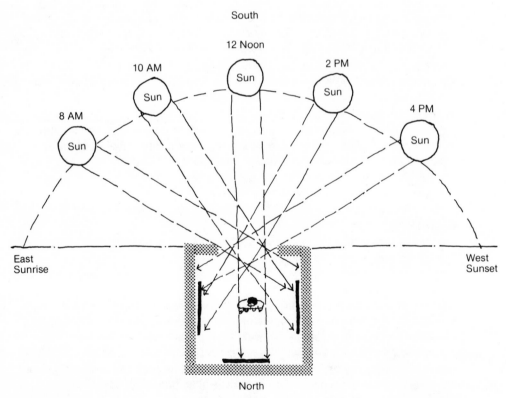

Natural Light in the Gallery

Position of the sun changes during the day.

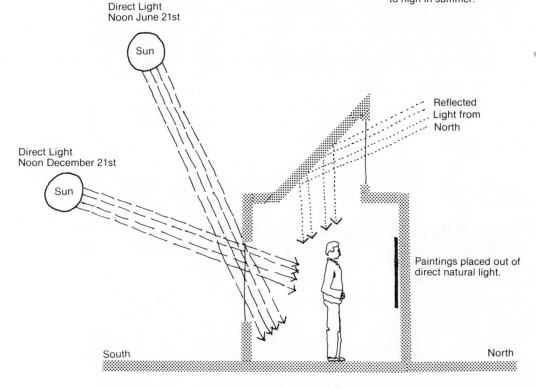

As seasons change, the height of the sun in the sky changes from low in winter to high in summer.

Direct Light
Noon June 21st

Sun

Reflected Light from North

Direct Light
Noon December 21st

Sun

Paintings placed out of direct natural light.

South

North

Natural Light in the Gallery

Electric Lighting

Flexibility is most important for gallery lighting. Of the professional systems available, track lighting is the most flexible and inexpensive. A grid section suspended from the ceiling may easily be augmented as your needs change.

Don't shortchange yourself on lighting supplies. Even if you buy only one fixture a year, get the best one possible. Be sure you have enough electrical outlets to support all your lighting needs and that the electrical system can handle the load.

Fluorescent tube lighting does not provide a sufficient spectrum of color for a gallery and should not be used to light art. However, if the budget permits, you may want to install an additional, cool-toned lighting system, to be used only during installation of exhibits. Ultraviolet light should never be permitted to come in contact with works of art.

For performances that take place in the gallery, you may need extra portable lights to provide adequate illumination. If you use the permanent fixtures, you will want to be able to keep certain lights focused on the event while others are turned off. Dimmers would be useful for these occasions, but they are hard to adapt to the low-voltage systems preferred in galleries. On a high-voltage system, the dimmer control poses no problem, but the light gives the environment an orange cast.

The following are some basic rules for the installation of a lighting system:

- Lights should be at least 36 inches from the wall.
- Art objects should not be warmed by the light. Low-voltage lights (5.5 to 12 volts) may be worth the higher cost because they provide lower heat levels and increased energy efficiency.
- Buy the same style canisters for the entire gallery area to avoid a slapdash appearance.
- Arrange the lights to avoid reflections on the surface of art works and shadows cast by painting frames. Viewers should not encounter glare or see their reflection in any protective glass.

Because lighting is such a complicated subject, a consultant's services can be invaluable. The Art Museum Association of America offers a consultation service—and splits the cost with the requesting institution.

Special Requirements for Outdoor Sculpture

An outdoor "sculpture garden" or courtyard can provide visitors with a restful break from touring the galleries. Make sure the landscaping, placement of benches, and layout of pathways enhances visitors' appreciation of the art in addition to creating a pleasant environment. The sequence of sculptures a visitor encounters, the way in which they are scaled in proportion to each other and to the plants, variations in level and distance between each piece, and the use of texture and color all affect the viewer's experience outdoors.

Of course, sculpture to be placed outdoors must be made of materials that won't disintegrate in snow, rain, sun or wind—unless the artist intends the work to weather. For security reasons, all objects must be bolted down on concrete slabs and properly lit at night. The area should have no blind spots, unless it is an interior court. Keep in mind that objects not protected within the walls of the facility may be more difficult to insure.

TECHNICAL SUPPORT AREAS

Virtually no museum has enough storage or work space because of a widespread reluctance to put money into places the public never sees. Ideally, a visual arts institution should devote 50 percent of its floor area to technical and administrative support space. Organization of this back-up space should be a major priority of the building committee.

Support space includes both "clean" and "dirty" preparation areas, work areas for the registrar and graphic designer, a shipping and receiving department, administrative offices, and—most important—storage.

Exhibition Support

Shipping and Receiving

Each time the facility plays host to a traveling exhibit, the crated art will enter and leave through the shipping and receiving area. Every step in the receiving process—vehicle access, controlled entry, and unloading and uncrating—should be carefully plotted out during the design stage.

For maximum security, trucks should be able to back straight up to the loading dock, where art works will be transferred by a hydraulic or mechanical lift directly to the receiving area. The dock should be 44 to 55 inches high—approximately even with the truck bed. Average truck stall width is twelve feet. Trucks will also need approximately 50 to 100 feet of space in the street or parking lot in order to back into the dock area.

The shipping area must be sufficiently large to accommodate several incoming and outgoing exhibitions at the same time. Frequently, the crated-up old show is still sitting in the receiving area when the new one arrives. Remember that the largest object you will ever exhibit must be able to fit through the doors—and pass through each support or exhibition area in the building. A large, heavy-duty freight elevator serving all floors of the building is standard equipment.

Works of art are unpacked, inspected, and repacked for shipment in the crating area. Storage for empty crates, a crate construction space, and a secure, temporary holding room for materials in transit are essential here. A secure area must also be provided for the registrar to examine and catalogue each incoming item. If the budget permits, install a darkroom for developing photographs of incoming works of art.

The Workshop: Exhibit Preparation

Every facility, no matter how small, needs an area for carpentry work. At least three people must be able to work together in the space, with room left over for storage. A preparator should be able to saw a 4 by 8 foot sheet of plywood, have space to move on either side of the table, and have room to stack each piece as it is cut.

The shop should be isolated from art storage areas but must have direct access to the loading dock. A sink and drains are standard equipment in the "dirty" area. The "clean" areas, where matting and framing are done, should have limited access to insure careful handling of the art awaiting preparation for display. Good lighting and proper ventilation for solvents are essential.

Conservation

Any facility with a permanent art collection has a legal and ethical responsibility to conserve it. Most museums share regional conservation facilities rather than install their own labs. Early in the planning process, make arrangements to use the facilities of the closest regional center, but be sure the labs are appropriate to the size, value, and type of art in your collection. Dust-free, humidity-controlled, secure space large enough for a work table should be provided.

Storage

Each major area of the museum needs its own storage area. Ideally, the vault should have two rooms: a larger one for objects remaining in storage a long time and a smaller, short-term holding room. The latter, invaluable for submissions to juried exhibitions, is especially important in a community art center. Access to the short-term area should not require entry into the long-term storage room. The storage area may also be divided according to special climate needs and object size. In any case, the entire vault should have padded shelves, slots, and cubby holes to guard against chipping and breaking.

Don't accept leftover space for this very important function, and make sure to safeguard whatever location you choose. If the storage area will be in the basement, protect it from potential flood damage, leaking overhead pipes, and damp walls. On the top floor of the building, guard against roof leaks, wide variations in temperature and humidity, and security risks. A top-floor storage location also requires careful plotting of the route to the loading dock.

Special archival storage areas should be equipped with temperature and humidity controls and a large table. No ultraviolet or natural light should penetrate this area; both are detrimental to the preservation of art objects.

ADMINISTRATIVE SUPPORT SPACE

Administrative offices should not be afterthoughts worked into the remaining alcoves and spaces after the galleries have been designed. In the interest of staff morale and productivity, offices should be designed with adequate light, air, and space.

In a small museum, plan space for a staff of five to eight people, including the director, one or two curators (who may also constitute the education department), a business manager or administrator, a secretary/receptionist, a registrar, a preparator, and guards. A larger museum will have more curatorial staff, more guards and preparators, a bookkeeper , public relations director, membership chairperson, fundraiser or development director, and education department. The staff of a small arts center may consist of an executive director, a part time assistant, and teachers of studio art, while a small gallery may have only one full time staff person.

Administrative offices should be located between the workshop areas and the galleries and have easy access to both. But avoid a fishbowl atmosphere. Do not attempt to have the secretary double as a guard by providing him or her with a window looking out onto the gallery area.

An open space office arrangement offers the advantages of lower construction costs, the need for less square footage, and increased flexibility. On the other hand, staff members engaged in detailed work may need the privacy and quiet of separate offices. If you do choose an open space plan, take care to provide adequate sound baffles. Carpeting is insufficient for noise control, and low acoustical panels make for poor working conditions.

In addition to office space, administrative support areas include:

- A conference room to accommodate 20 people for staff, board, and volunteer meetings. This room, essential even for a small facility, can also be used by the education department and for viewing artists' slides. There should be a built-in projection screen, built-in storage, and a means of darkening the room during the day.

- A kitchenette with a sink, refrigerator and counter that can be used to service catered receptions. In a small facility, the space may double as a staff lounge.
- An office supply room for stocking everything from pencils to cartons of paper and publications. There should be space for a copier, copy collation, and package wrapping.
- Storage area for audio-visual equipment and a designated location for film and video presentations.
- A guard's office where the central alarm system controls are located.

EDUCATIONAL SPACES

Educational programs typically offered by a visual arts facility include lectures, film and videotape showings, live performances, and studio classes in painting, sculpture, ceramics, textiles, jewelry, photography, or glass-blowing. Gallery tours led by volunteer docents are also within the domain of the education department. Each activity requires a properly equipped space and specialized equipment that ranges from audio-visual devices for the lecture hall to looms, kilns, and darkroom paraphernalia for studio art classrooms.

The Lecture Hall

Lectures, films, and music and dance programs require a proper hall. (If you plan to present performing arts events, consult Chapter 9 for specific information on the design of stage spaces.) An auditorium may also be a source of additional revenue for your organization. If meeting halls are scarce in your community, local groups may be happy to pay for using yours.

The size of hall you need depends on the type of events you will be scheduling. A small classroom can accommodate 35 people for a class on art appreciation. A small lecture hall seating 100 people may be suitable for a guest lecture. A medium-sized auditorium (200 to 300 seats) or a larger hall (500 to 600 seats) may be necessary for a larger community or an organization planning to schedule many popular events. You may be able to use the gallery floor for certain performances, provided that security is adequate and that the audience, seated in folding chairs on the floor, can see the action clearly.

For security reasons, the public should be able to enter the auditorium directly for after-hours performances or lectures without walking through the gallery area.

The Library
In a larger institution, you may want to include a library or resource center. The scale and furnishing of the room will depend on the extent of the library's holdings and whether you plan to open it to the public.

Studio Art Classrooms
The requirements for a studio art classroom will vary depending on the activity planned for it. This section offers only basic design guidelines; for more detailed information, consult *Design Guide: Arts and Crafts Centers*. Whatever classroom activity you plan, be sure to keep noise and dust away from the art galleries, as well as the technical support areas.

Spaces for Drawing, Painting, and Printmaking
Drawing and painting classes of forty to fifty students with two instructors will require about 1200 square feet of studio space. Draughtsmen and painters favor northern light; electric lighting in the room should duplicate daylight as closely as possible. Make sure floor surfaces are washable. If the area will also be used for printmaking, floors should be acid-resistant (treated concrete is a good choice). Equipment needed for the studio includes drawing tables, easels, work tables with cutting surfaces, stools and chairs, work sinks, paper cutters, a slide projector and screen, and slotted storage for canvases. Printmakers will need printing presses, drying racks for prints, and separate storage for toxic chemicals used in etching and silkscreen processes.

Sculpture and Three Dimensional Design
Sculpture studios for clay modeling and wood and stone carving will occupy a work area of 1000 square feet, plus 200 square feet of storage, for classes of twenty students and two instructors. Workbenches and stools used in any arts and crafts area are adequate for most sculpture projects, but students will require floor and table sculpture stands and specialized hand tools used for carving.

Pottery and Ceramics
A ceramics classroom for twenty students and one supervisor should be about 1200 square feet. Standard equipment includes potters wheels, work tables with metal tops, wedging boards, sinks, and glaze spray booths. Where possible, separate the dusty process of working with clay from other arts and crafts activities. A dust removal system is desirable in the clay preparation area. Room surfaces should be nonporous and easily cleaned; floors should be sloped and equipped with drains. Provide storage near the service entrance for large, heavy sacks of clay and clay-mixing equipment, and set aside a separate area for the drying of fragile pottery before it is fired.

The kiln room (200 square feet on the average) must be separate from the general work area because of the heat. Many art centers choose electric kilns, which generate a relatively low amount of heat and can be used for bisque and low-fire ware. But advanced ceramics programs require gas kilns, which operate at higher temperatures.

Glass-Blowing

A covered outdoor space or a well-ventilated foundry-type room is the best setup for glass-blowing, which generates a great amount of heat and cannot be combined with any other studio activity except ceramics. A work area of 500 square feet should be adequate for ten students and a teacher. If the classroom is indoors, furnaces should be near an exterior wall, and mechanical exhaust systems must be provided. Concrete floors and masonry walls are advisable. The major equipment needed includes the melting or pot furnace, annealing (firing) oven, and special benches with arms for rolling the blowpipes. In addition, provide a heavy-duty work counter with an asbestos top and storage shelves or cabinets for materials, tools, and the cooling pieces of glass.

Photography

Photography requires three distinct areas: a classroom; a photo lab for film processing; and a finishing area where prints are dried, trimmed, and mounted. To accommodate 25 people, the classroom should be approximately 500 square feet. As a multiuse area, it should be equipped with a chalkboard, a mobile rear projector, film and slide projectors, and stacking chairs.

In the photo lab, you can build either a single, large darkroom or smaller rooms with space for two to four students. Both types require light-trapping entrances. Equipment needs include enlargers, contact printers, developing sinks, film-drying cabinets, print washers, a safelight, timers, metal-lined cabinets, papercutters, and a refrigerator for film. Stainless steel sinks with hot and cold water are a must.

According to *Design Guide: Arts and Crafts Centers,* the following space allocations are appropriate for a photography department set up to serve classes of twenty-five students:

Film-loading cubicles	65 square feet
Black-and-white film processing labs	600 square feet
Color film processing labs	200 square feet
Storage area	100 square feet

The print finishing area, which does not require special lighting, can be combined with other crafts activities. Required equipment includes dry-mounting presses, a sink, print-drying cabinets, print dryers, a copy camera, a papercutter, work tables, and counters.

TEMPERATURE AND HUMIDITY CONTROL

Atmospheric control, virtually invisible to the average visitor, is never the less a crucial aspect of a visual arts facility. In *Museums in Motion,* Edward P. Alexander acknowledged the status of devices that monitor the air surrounding art objects: "Though it may be difficult to raise money for such a purpose, in the long run air conditioning is more important for the museum than the acquisition of art."

Maintaining a constant humidity of 50 percent is ideal. Below 50 percent, paper and leather become brittle, canvas goes slack, and textiles dry out. Above 50 percent, mold and mildew grow on glue, leather, and paper; wood swells, canvas tightens, and metals oxidize at a faster rate. Major traveling shows cannot be acquired unless you meet this 50 percent standard. Even if you aren't able to achieve ideal levels, you must at least maintain constant humidity and temperature levels—24 hours a day, 365 days a year.

Smaller facilities that cannot afford elaborate mechanical devices will find a hygrometer adequate for measuring relative humidity. Humidifiers and dehumidifiers can maintain proper moisture levels.

To minimize costs you may zone the atmospheric system, providing galleries and art storage areas with special temperature and humidity controls, while lobbies and other support areas are outfitted with ordinary ventilating systems.

Air conditioning and heating/ventilating systems should be properly filtered to prevent dust and pollution from entering the facility. Locate ducts so that art objects are not directly in the path of hot or cold air flow. In colder regions, the building should also be well insulated. Double-pane glazing will guard against temperature fluctuations and cut energy costs. For a listing of more detailed information on temperature and humidity control, see Further Reading.

SECURITY

The building should be designed for maximum security round-the-clock. Most thefts occur during visiting hours. Rule number one is that *there should be only one way of entering and exiting the museum* (even though additional emergency exits will probably be required by code). Both staff and visitors should use this door; if you want a special staff exit, you will need additional security.

Take care to protect the art when visitors are in the building. Paintings should be securely attached to the wall and small sculptures encased in tamper-proof cases. A pot on a pedestal should be fastened with museum wax so that an accidental bump won't knock it off.

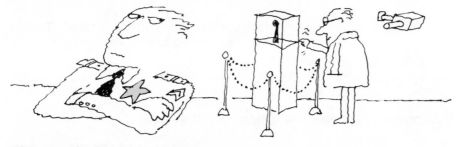

Electronic Security Systems
Electronic systems are used in both peripheral and interior areas. Peripheral security precautions include the attachment of magnetic devices to all doors,

windows, and skylights. It is wise to install these on interior shop doors as well, so that an intruder's passage through the building can be marked by a series of tripped alarms. For interior security, a sonic system is best, even in small museums. This type of alarm, triggered by movements disturbing the air currents within designated areas, is required for insurance purposes and by most traveling exhibition programs. Remember that the system must be adjusted each time you move your temporary walls.

The alarm system, which should be on a separate electrical circuit with a battery back-up, can be set up either to scare the thief or to catch him. Panic alarm bars—equipped with alarms loud enough to scare mischievous children and alert museum personnel—should be installed on the emergency doors. A silent alarm that sounds a signal at the police station is best for apprehending a burglar.

Closed circuit video cameras are useful for the loading dock or other areas that don't require constant monitoring, but they should not replace guards in the galleries. It is difficult to make sure that monitors are watched continuously, as professional thieves are well aware. However, it may be worthwhile to install an inexpensive dummy camera that is not even hooked up as a deterrent to impulsive theft.

Guards

No matter how effective your alarm system may be, it can't replace a trained guard. Identifiable by a uniform and staff badge, he or she should walk around the galleries rather than remain seated behind a desk. Try to avoid taking the guard off the floor for such duties as watching an incoming art shipment. In a facility planned with security in mind, the preparator's or registrar's office might be situated near the shipping and receiving area, thus permitting supervision of art deliveries without a guard. Also consider the impact of room design on gallery surveillance. Avoid odd-shaped rooms with nooks and crannies, and plan connecting exits and entrances carefully.

Because your precise security needs will vary according to the type of art you plan to exhibit, you should check with your insurance broker for additional requirements. If you will be hosting traveling exhibitions, familiarize yourself with the security standards imposed by the major exhibit sources. The requirements for SITES exhibits, shown in Figure 10-1, are representative for any traveling exhibit of museum quality.

Figure 10-1   Smithsonian Institution Traveling Exhibition Service Security Requirements ("SITES")

HIGH SECURITY
High security is required for exhibitions containing highly valuable articles that are sensitive to light, humidity, and temperature. These include paper, wood, and textiles, gold, silver, other precious metals, jewels, and archaeological treasures.

The following conditions must be met by organizations desiring high security exhibitions:

Space
- Museum or limited access gallery. An open mall, hallway, or lounge area is not acceptable.

Protection

- Trained professional guards in sufficient number to adequately protect objects. Guards need not be armed.
- Night guards and/or electronic system.
- Provisions to prevent the public from touching wall-hung objects by means of an appropriate hanging system, the use of stanchions, platforms, and/or guard supervision.
- Locked glass cases for small objects. Plexiglas cases are not acceptable for high security exhibitions unless prior approval of their design is obtained from SITES.
- Handling of objects by curator or registrar, or equivalent museum professional.

Environmental Controls

- Temperature and light control are required for all exhibits in this category. Humidity control is required for certain exhibitions.
- Fire system, and other fire protection devices according to local ordinances.

MODERATE SECURITY

Moderate security is required for most SITES exhibitions which contain original art works, prints and graphics, original specimens, artifacts, or original photographs.

The following conditions must be met by organizations desiring to exhibit moderate security exhibitions:

Space

- Limited access, gallery-type area. An open mall, hallway, or lounge area is not acceptable.

Protection

- Professional guards or other trained persons whose sole duty is the supervision of the exhibition.
- Locked glass cases or secure Plexiglas cases for small objects. Plexiglas must be screwed to wall or base cabinet, not just rested on top of the unit.
- Exhibit area must be locked and secure during closing hours. Alarm and/or guards during night hours are preferred but not required.
- If the registrar or curator will not be handling the objects, a preparator, exhibits technician, or other person trained in handling museum objects must take charge.

Environmental Controls

- Temperature and light control are required. Humidity control is desired.
- Fire protection according to local ordinance.

LIMITED SECURITY

Limited security is the minimum security required for certain exhibitions. These exhibitions include panel exhibitions containing no original material or artifacts, and some photography and children's art shows which are considered less of a security risk.

The following conditions must be met by organizations desiring to exhibit limited security exhibitions.

Space

- Shows may be exhibited in a gallery or lounge area, preferably not in a hallway. No SITES exhibition is to be displayed outdoors or in tents or temporary buildings.

Protection

- Supervision by guard, volunteer, student, or receptionist. Someone must be in the room with the exhibition at all times and may be performing other duties as well as watching the exhibition. No SITES exhibition is to be left unguarded at any time while open to the public. Even panel and photo exhibits can be the object of theft and vandalism.
- Exhibit area must be locked and secure during closing hours.

Environmental Controls

- Direct sunlight should be diffused or eliminated to prevent fading of panels and photographs.
- Fire protection according to local ordinance.

FIRE PROTECTION

Fire protection must be designed for the safety of both art objects and visitors. The amount of fire protection you have will affect your insurance rating and the types of traveling exhibitions your facility can attract.

Types of fire protection include:

- Fire-retardant materials within the exhibition area
- Heat and smoke detector systems, typically connected to the ductwork of the airhandling systems
- Fire alarms that ring within the facility or at a local firehouse
- Hand fire extinguishers
- Carbon dioxide systems
- Zoning the building so that the smoke is not picked up in the ventilation systems and carried to other parts of the building

Sprinklers are not included in this list, because the water would have devastating effects on fragile works of art. Even in a workshop area, you would risk damaging a painting waiting to be crated. If you are renovating a facility, ask an insurance agent to walk through with you and tell you what you need to do to increase the rating and lower your premium. Advice from a fireman will also be useful.

Functional Diagram of a Small Visual Arts Facility

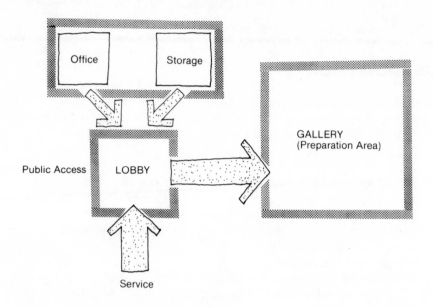

Office

Storage

Public Access

LOBBY

GALLERY
(Preparation Area)

Service

Functional Diagram of a Large Visual Arts Facility

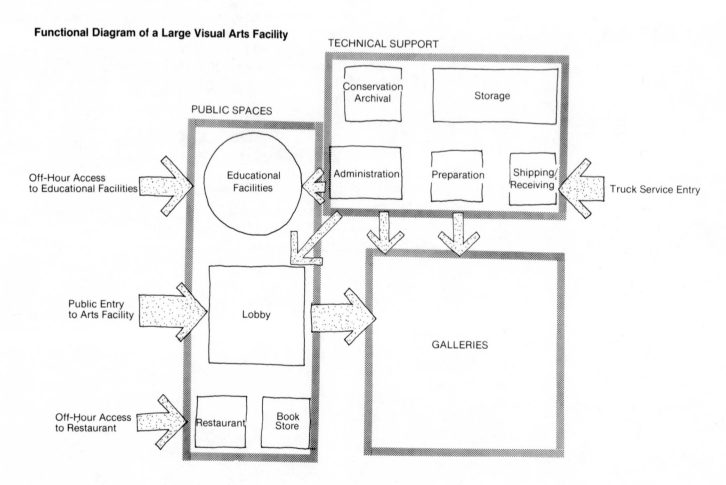

TECHNICAL SUPPORT

PUBLIC SPACES

Conservation
Archival

Storage

Off-Hour Access
to Educational Facilities

Educational
Facilities

Administration

Preparation

Shipping/
Receiving

Truck Service Entry

Public Entry
to Arts Facility

Lobby

GALLERIES

Off-Hour Access
to Restaurant

Restaurant

Book
Store

152 DEVELOP A BUILDING PLAN

DEVELOP A
BUILDING PLAN

11. Special Cases: Mixed Use, Renovating, & Remodeling

I f you are renovating an old building, or if your arts space will be only a portion of a larger building project, you will follow the same basic working methods described in this book for a new, single-use facility. You will face the same kinds of real estate, design, and funding issues, and you must still undertake feasibility studies to determine your needs and resources. But you will also need to consider the specifics outlined in this chapter.

The section "Mixed Use Projects" presents special design considerations for a facility that will be part of an office building, hotel and entertainment complex, shopping center, school, or other nonarts development.

"Renovating Old Buildings" discusses ways of evaluating the worthiness of old buildings and the special issues involved in remodeling certain types of buildings for arts use.

"Remodeling Your Facility" explains how to make small design changes in your present building.

MIXED USE PROJECTS

The integration of the arts into nonarts facilities is an increasingly popular strategy that allows greater public exposure to the arts while providing needed capital and ongoing support for the facility. If your group is planning to be a part of a mixed use complex, consider the following.

Make Your Needs Known
Approach the developer or school board as early as possible with a clear concept of your facility and list of space requirements.

Will You Be Visible?
The arts facility should be clearly identifiable in the mixed use building. The structure must have well-designed, well-placed signs to indicate the kinds of

activities that go on within its doors.

In a shopping center, smaller shops largely depend on crowds attracted to the department stores, yet they must also have strong identities as specialty stores. In a similar way, an arts facility should do its share to attract people to the mall. Though it depends on patrons who come for other purposes, the arts group must establish an identity as specific as that of a jewelry store or bookstore.

Assess Your Location

Your facility must be located in a part of the complex that is easily accessible to both patrons and service people. In a school, for example, the audience should not have to traverse the length of the building to reach the theater. Security also mandates a separate entrance for the arts facility. In a shopping center, beware of being marooned on an upper floor or other location that attracts few passersby.

Visual art in an office building must be displayed so people can see it properly. A gallery with properly designed wall surfaces may be located just outside major circulation areas but in clear view of people entering the lobby.

Obtain Design Control

You needn't necessarily use the same architect who will design the entire shopping center or school. Your own architect can work with the general architect to produce a usable space that is properly integrated with the rest of the complex.

A Multiuse Facility

Many problems arise when a standard school cafeteria or gymnasium is turned into a part time theater. However, if the room can be planned from the outset with the performing arts in mind, you can avoid the irritations that come with second rate status. There are three key points to keep in mind when designing a theater for a space with another use:

1. **Sightlines.** Avoid placing the seats on a flat floor, which does not permit people in the back rows to see the stage properly. Foldout bleachers attached to the walls or a collapsible floor may solve the problem.
2. **Acoustics.** Cafeterias tend to be large, open spaces with highly reflective walls and dead spaces that produce echoes. You may be able to install acoustical panels that hang from the ceiling, adding to the room's decor by day and helping focus the sound quality of a performance at night. A vestibule or baffle system will keep your performance space acoustically insulated from the cafeteria kitchen.
3. **Stage Size.** Lack of wing space and adequate stage depth can be a serious drawback. If a properly appointed proscenium stage is out of the question, consider using a portable thrust stage.

Some other considerations to keep in mind in a multiuse facility. Be sure your facility has proper lighting; fluorescent lights, often found in cafeterias, are unsuitable for theater. Performers will need access to rest rooms. A band or chorus room may be used as a dressing room; an adjacent classroom can house the lighting controls. The theater must be on the ground floor to facilitate scenery delivery. (See Chapter 9 for a full discussion of the individual features that make a theater work.)

RENOVATING OLD BUILDINGS

When creating your own facility, you start with a clean slate. But with preexisting buildings, you always have to consider their potential for adapting to your uses. You need to study the structure's soundness and exterior appearance, its means of public access, its interior space configuration, existing environmental controls and security systems, and the cost of enlarging or refitting the building to your standards.

To find out if the building is structurally sound, have it inspected by a building engineer. If it has not previously been used as a public building, will costly alterations be necessary to bring it into compliance with local codes? The size of the building should satisfy the space requirements outlined in your feasibility study, and the layout should be compatible with the functions you have planned. If you are working with a historic structure, find out whether the changes you have in mind might interfere with its architectural character.

Just as in choosing a site for a new facility, you must check out whether an existing building is accessible by car, foot, and public transportation and determine if there is sufficient parking space nearby. If not, how difficult would it be to provide a parking area? Consider the public perception of the neighborhood. Do people frequent the area only by day? Or do loiterers make it undesirable even during the daytime? You may want to think twice if you will need a massive public relations campaign to convince people that your facility is located in a safe and pleasant area. On the other hand, you may feel that by renovating the building you will contribute to the revitalization of the neighborhood. Are other groups like yours moving in nearby?

If the present location is a drawback, you may be able to move the structure to another site. The feasibility of this will, of course, depend on the size of the building, its structural stability, and the route the movers would have to take. If relocating is a serious option, get an estimate of costs from a professional mover.

Evaluating the Old Building

Renovation involves updating the structural, electrical, plumbing, and occupancy requirements to present day codes. Certain areas will also require the costly step of bringing the building up to earthquake standards. Remember that maintenance of an old building may be more expensive over the years than upkeep for a modern one. Old adobe structures, for example, require continual work to keep the unsealed adobe from dissolving. An older building designed for other uses—a water tank or a jail, perhaps—may have a negative image that will have to be overcome before your facility will appeal to potential patrons.

Examine the present condition of the building carefully and determine exactly what needs to be altered to accommodate your program.

What to Look For on the Exterior

Settling

Is the building plumb both vertically and horizontally? It should stand at right angles to the ground, and structural members should also form right angles. You can determine whether the building is settling by checking the fit of windows and doors.

Exterior Walls

In masonry, check for major cracks; in wood, look for dry rot and termites. If the building has ornate trim, check whether any parts are missing or about to fall off.

Roof

In a flat-roofed building, walk around on the roof and check for leaks or bubbling of the roof material. Examine a sloped roof to see whether it is bowed from years of holding winter snow. Notice the condition of all roof materials, skylights, and drains.

Exterior Drainage

Check whether water collects on the site or flows away from the building.

What to Look for Inside

Floors

Look for slanting, sagging, or warping in wooden floors and unevenness and cracking in concrete floors. If possible, peer under the floor to see how it is constructed. Many pre-1920 buildings have no foundations, and settling can be a problem unless major alterations are made.

Also check the live load of the floor. In a commercial building, information about the weight the floor will bear should be posted on the wall. If it is not, ask the owner for the previous Certificate of Occupancy issued by the city or county.

Stairs and Corridors

Take a good look at stairs and corridors. What is their condition? Are they made of wood or steel? Are they open or enclosed? Are they wide enough to accommodate your equipment, scenery, or exhibits and to comply with fire codes? Three feet eight inches is a general code requirement for the "means of egress" (see Appendix B, Building Codes).

Elevators

If there are elevators, ask to see them in operation and try operating them yourself. Notice the load capacity, usually posted inside the elevator. Will the size accommodate scenery and materials? Are the elevators conveniently located in relation to possible storage, performance or exhibition spaces, and main circulation areas?

Walls and Ceilings

Note the materials used in wall and ceiling construction and check for signs of dampness and leakage. If you spot leaks try to determine whether they originated in the roof or exterior masonry or are localized around plumbing, windows, or vents.

Check if there is insulation in the walls. If not, consider how you would go about installing some.

Columns and Load-Bearing Walls

If possible, discover which walls and columns are essential for structural support, because these cannot be removed without substituting costly support beams.

Is the spacing of interior structures suitable for your use? Will columns disturb sightlines? Will you have to cut through major load-bearing walls to create circulation areas between galleries?

Windows and Sashes

Check for misalignment, rotten frames, or broken window panes that must be replaced. Open and close all windows. Consider whether the windows are appropriately located for your use. You might have to wall them up if you plan to turn the place into a theater.

Basement

Look for a "ring" around the walls that could indicate flooding. Check possible dampness in the walls, and see if the boiler leaks.

Note the basement construction. Many old buildings in the West have earthen cellars.

Plumbing

Test the plumbing by turning on all the faucets and flushing all the toilets. Is the floor rotting around the toilets? Is the plumbing in the basement leaking? Examine walls for leakage stains, and inspect the hot water tank for water capacity and overall condition.

Electrical Power

Make note of the type (AC or DC) and amount of current and voltage supplied to the space in which you are interested. Usually, each floor will have a fuse box or circuit breaker panel with the amperage marked on it. If not, look in the basement near the main service box for the building. Four-wire, three-phase, 200 amp, 120 volt AC service is the minimum requirement to light a small theater; anything less will severely limit your stage lighting capability.

Consider additional power required for the rest of the facility. The local power company will give you a free assessment of your needs.

Try to determine the condition of wiring in the building while you are looking at the fuse box in the basement or attic. Rewiring an old building may be very costly.

Heating, Air Conditioning, and Ventilation Systems

If possible, ask that each of the systems be turned on so that you can check their efficiency and noise level. If the building is still occupied, ask current tenants about comfort throughout the year.

Make a note of the types of heating and air conditioning systems, and analyze them in terms of your needs. An old steam radiator, for example, might produce too much moisture for a gallery space. A local heating contractor can help you decide whether you will be able to upgrade the old system adequately.

Fire Prevention and Emergency Systems

Check the type, location, and condition of the fire prevention system, and ask when it was last inspected. If there are fire extinguishers, look at the date on the tags—it will be a good indication of the last time the space was inspected.

Structural System

Have a structural engineer or local architect assist you in assessing the building structure and how its component materials will affect renovation. For example, a large barn may look as though it would make a perfect theater, but building codes do not permit theaters in wooden buildings because of fire risk. In certain sections of the country where buildings have to meet new earthquake standards, old concrete structures can be difficult to bring up to code.

Special Building Types

The buildings most frequently renovated for use by arts groups are movie theaters (for the performing arts) and storefronts (for visual arts or small performing arts groups). Warehouses and banks are also popular choices of arts organizations. Before you select one of these buildings, be certain it can be made to suit your art form within the constraints of your budget.

Old Movie Theaters

If you are thinking of taking over a former movie theater or vaudeville house, remember that there is a considerable gap between the charm of an old building and the technical updating it will need to accommodate modern performances. Most movie or vaudeville stages constructed prior to 1930 are 50 to 80 feet wide but only 20 to 30 feet deep. A Broadway show, a major orchestra, or a ballet company require a minimum of 35 feet. Movie houses not built for vaudeville lack crossing space backstage, and sightlines to the rear of the stage are unusually poor. The stagehouse will also be too small for modern needs; in the old days no provision was made for temporary storage of scenery or for a large troupe of dancers to assemble before going onstage. Even the orchestra pit will probably be inadequate. Only 20 to 30 musicians were needed in the old-time movie house, while contemporary productions often require 40 musicians, and as many as 60 to 80 for opera.

Backstage support space will be equally disappointing. Most old movie theaters had 10 to 20 dressing rooms, each accommodating two to four people, located at least one level above the stage. Facilities most in demand now are "star" accommodations (often with private bathrooms) at stage level and large chorus rooms with space for 20 to 40 people. You also won't find a green room in an old movie house.

For a resident company, you will need to add construction shops and storage facilities, neither of which were included in the old houses. Likewise, the loading area will need to be upgraded to accommodate scenery, costumes, and instruments, which in the old days entered through the same stage door the performers used. Company administrators, too, will probably be chagrined at the office space, which was not designed for separate departments of public relations, accounting, bookings, personnel, and so forth.

The audience will also fare poorly in an unmodified old movie house, where seats are smaller and closer together than in modern theaters. Although you can reduce the number of seats to make the orchestra section roomier, you can't change the arrangement in the stepped balconies or loges.

Because vaudeville shows had no intermissions, lobby space tends to be cramped. You will also need to enlarge the box office, which was designed for two persons dispensing tickets to one performance rather than for a whole staff handling advance sales and mail, phone, and charge orders.

Whether you will be able to enlarge the stage depends on the availability of space behind the theater. Often, movie houses are surrounded by buildings on three sides, or an alleyway to the rear may have to be retained as access to a retail or commercial property. If there is room, expanding the stage and backstage area will be absolutely necessary for your operations. Your committee will have to decide whether the cost of properly outfitting the facility justifies acquisition of the building.

Storefronts

Older ground floor commercial spaces were generally built with lofty ceilings and without structural columns—two selling points for an arts facility. Direct access from the sidewalk will help attract patrons. Basement storage, a common feature of a storefront, will also be useful to your group. For the performing arts, large display windows may need to be walled up to prevent light leaks.

Warehouses

Warehouses contain large open spaces and are usually built to bear heavy loads. However, changing the structural system or cutting doorways in concrete walls can be very expensive. The warehouse may also lack sufficient plumbing, electrical, and heating systems. In a concrete building, the wiring and pipes may be exposed, and proper insulation may be lacking.

Some warehouses have very low ceilings unsuited to the performing or visual arts. A two story warehouse will not have the proper number or size of exits mandated for a theater by the building code. Old brick warehouses may not rest on adequate foundations. Check the condition of the foundation before committing yourself to an expensive new base for the facility.

Churches

Because they were originally designed for public assembly, churches often require little work to turn them into performing arts spaces. You will have to install a proper stage and lighting, but social areas and Sunday school classrooms may be suitable, with some remodeling, for support spaces. A former church may also be used as a visual arts facility because the high-ceilinged, unobstructed central area makes ideal exhibition space. A cramped lobby area is the one serious drawback to a church.

REMODELING YOUR PRESENT FACILITY

Sooner or later every arts group will have to do a certain amount of remodeling—even if it amounts only to a coat of paint, the rearrangement of offices, or the installation of a new stage floor. Other common reasons to remodel are the need to install better equipment or to remedy maintenance problems. However, if you are considering major structural changes or a new addition to the building, you should look at the steps involved in new construction or renovation. Adding new galleries or a backstage area will affect the entire functional quality of the building and must be considered in terms of a major facility renovation.

If you are happily situated in your neighborhood and on your lot, or if you have discovered that moving to another, larger facility would be too expensive, remodeling may be the right solution to your building problem. But undertake the project only if the building is structurally sound. If you are renting the facility, consider whether the project is worth the investment of time and money should you be forced to leave at a later date. On the other hand, the landlord may assist you in the project because it will increase the value of his or her property.

Planning the Remodeling Project

You probably have a fairly good idea of what you want and where you want it, but you may have overlooked possibilities that offer greater economy or a more efficient arrangement. First, with the help of an architect if necessary, draw a careful plan to scale of your present room layout. You or your landlord may already have a set of plans, or you might consult the architect who designed the building.

After you have the plans, look at several alternatives before you proceed, keeping in mind the following points:

- Interior walls that carry none of the load of the roof or floor above can be easily removed.
- Load-bearing walls may also be removed, but the process is more

160 DEVELOP A BUILDING PLAN

complicated and very expensive.

- Doors may be made into windows and windows expanded into doors. You can also close up existing openings altogether—or create brand new ones.
- You can move light fixtures and outlets fairly easily; heating ducts and radiators are more difficult to rearrange. If you can possibly avoid it, do not cut into any wall containing plumbing lines.
- If new plumbing fixtures are being added, locate them near existing lines to save money.

Refer to Chapter 9 and 10 for the building program standards for your art form. Then, using the above suggestions, generate a series of plans, color samples, and costs before determining which rearrangement will be most satisfactory. Be sure to ask opinions of the staff members who will be using the room. And don't forget aesthetic considerations. The remodeled area should reflect the high artistic standards you have set for yourselves.

Document your plans with the help of an architect or contractor. You should have a set of drawings in case you need a building permit to proceed with the remodeling project.

Building Permits

If you are making electrical or wiring changes or altering the structure of your building, you must have a set of plans in order to obtain a permit from the local building department. Your fire insurance might be voided if you install a new electrical outlet and wiring without a permit. If you put in new waste lines for a toilet or basin without a permit, you might later be ordered to take them out and redo the work if it does not conform to code. If you are adding a room or other basic structure, materials and workmanship must meet basic safety requirements. (See Appendix C, Building Codes, for more information.)

A building permit signifies that work conforms to local building codes and ordinances and that you are competent to handle the work. If a contractor does the job, he takes out a permit. The work will be inspected by the building department to see that it has been done correctly and safely.

The Building Process

Doing some of the work yourselves will save money, but the extent of your efforts obviously depends on the skills of your group and the kind of remodeling you are undertaking. Don't attempt all the work in a major remodeling job. In many communities the building code requires that wiring and plumbing be done by licensed professionals. In determining what part of the work your group can do, consider:

1. **Your interests.** If your group can find time for only one task, choose the job people seem more enthusiastic about doing and pay someone else to perform the rest.
2. **Your skills.** If someone in your group can do cabinetry or has experience in laying floors, that's great. But if no one knows anything about plumbing, call a plumber rather than wasting time and money learning on the job.

3. **Dangers involved.** Certain tasks, like reroofing a steeply inclined roof or rewiring the building, should be contracted out to an expert. Why risk increasing your liability insurance or injuring a stalwart member of your committee?
4. **Time available.** Tasks have a way of taking twice as long as you expect. If you are unfamiliar with the type of work involved on a major alteration, or can only spare time on weekends, you may be well-advised to hire an expert.

One way to proceed is to farm out larger portions of the project—such as foundation work, wall demolition, and rough wall construction—to a contractor. Members of your group can carry on from that point, completing construction, painting, laying and finishing the floor, and possibly installing some of the fixtures.

Whether the contractor does everything or your group finishes the project, you should have an architect or other advisor outline specifications for the remodeling work. For example, if you are planning to change single pane windows to double pane insulated windows, you'll want an expert's advice on keeping water from seeping in and on the type of hardware that should be used.

Scheduling

Regardless of who actually does the work, you must develop a construction schedule. The pace should allow plenty of time for each part to be completed and for floors to be refinished before visitors are allowed in the space. The schedule must establish a logical order for each activity—you want the electrician to rewire the space before you refinish the floor—and each work party should have sufficient time and space to do its job well. A crew can't come in to paint the walls if another group is still stripping the floor.

How to Keep Going While the Dust Is Rising

The rest of the arts facility, as well as visitors, must be protected from noise, dust and debris produced by the remodeling process. Obviously, off season is prime remodeling time. Seal doorways into other rooms with plastic to keep out wafting dust, and cover the floors with paper. Be sure to clean thoroughly between tasks.

DEVELOP A
BUILDING PLAN

12. Design & Construction

The design phase of your project involves translating all the planning work you have done into detailed drawings that will be used to describe and construct the building.

Whatever the size of your project, you will be working with an architect at this stage, and it will be his or her task to perform the actual design work. So this chapter won't tell you how to design your own building. Instead, it explains the major steps your architect and other designers will take in translating your words and ideas into design documents. By learning the basic steps involved in design and the type of work done by the construction specialists, you will be a better client.

At this stage, the committee's main job will be to evaluate and approve the designs your experts prepare. The architect should explain to the entire building committee how to read architects' drawings and understand three dimensional models, which are all you will have to judge whether the designs meet the standards you have in mind. If you can only look uncomprehendingly at the building plans, you are forfeiting an extremely important opportunity to make your opinions known.

The design process involves three major steps:

1. **Schematic design**, results in a set of schematic drawings that lay out:
   - relationships of the spaces within the building.
   - the external relationship between the building and the site it occupies.
2. In **design development**, the schematic plan is refined into specifics—dimensions of rooms, types of equipment, interior wall finishes, and structural systems.
3. A set of **construction documents** is prepared. These are working drawings and specifications that will guide the construction team.

This chapter treats each step of the design process in turn, also touching on design competitions. The latter part of the chapter deals with major aspects of the construction process.

SITE ANALYSIS AND PLANNING

Before your designers can begin they need more detailed information about the site your committee has chosen. The architect or landscape architect will analyze foundation conditions (the soil, water table, and drainage), topography (the slope of the land helps to determine placement of the building), and climate and microclimate (variations in temperature, rainfall, snowfall, angle of sunlight, and wind unique to the site). This information will determine the orientation of the structure to maximize human comfort and minimize energy costs. The shape of the land, plant cover, and location of other structures on the property all have a considerable influence on the quality of light available to the building and the level of noise inside it.

A site analysis will also yield data about the visual layout of the site and the influence of traffic, utilities, massing of the building, ambient noise level, neighborhood land uses, and local zoning ordinances. Many of these areas will already have been investigated in the feasibility study, but the architect is now concerned with how they will determine the placement and architectural features of the facility.

Site planning involves arranging the building, parking lots, peripheral roads, service areas, outdoor seating areas, and all other aspects of the building design in order to make best use of the land in question. Lack of forethought might make future expansion impossible or difficult.

Once the data are in, the designers will prepare a graphic and written analysis outlining the principal constraints of the site, as well as its positive features. The actual site plan and architectural design of the building will then be developed from this analysis.

SCHEMATIC DESIGN: EXAMINING DESIGN OPTIONS

The first step in the evolution of a three dimensional building plan should be a schematic design, in which the descriptions and lists you have drawn up as the building program begin to be transformed into spaces bounded by walls.

Schematic design may take from one to six months to complete. The architect, working from the final building program, will create a series of drawings (sometimes called "bubble diagrams") that roughly indicate the organization of activities within the building and on the site. The drawings will show interrelationships between spaces and the relative proportions of different parts of the building. The next step is to refine the drawings into a series of alternative designs for the facility.

Are Alternatives Necessary?
Alternative designs will be presented at two stages. The first involves the big

picture—the options for organizing the elements of the building and the site. Once a decision has been reached on these, the architect will look at alternatives for individual components of the project. For example, there might be several design schemes for the entryway and lobby.

The number of design possibilities will vary according to the scale of the project. If you are remodeling an existing wing, there may not be many alternatives, but in a large project with few constraints, there will be a greater range of design solutions. Architects always look at different ways of tackling each design problem. This process should be of interest to you as a client, and you should take an active part in arriving at each solution.

Don't narrow your options until you have explored the whole range of possibilities your architect offers you. Consider each design from different vantage points—the quality of the overall structure, the interrelationships of the parts, and the details of those parts. Make up a list of criteria to help you evaluate each alternative, always keeping in mind the overriding purpose of the facility.

The process of generating alternative solutions will help you determine whether a new building or a renovated one would best suit your requirements. If you are considering only one building for future renovation or one site for new construction, you should know the full range of possibilities, from the most inexpensive to the costliest. The design you choose will probably be somewhere between these extremes. Considering alternatives is particularly important in a renovation project, where you must find the best way of meeting your program needs within the confines of the existing building.

Each design alternative may have political and economic ramifications which you will have to weigh against the need for certain building features. A flyloft, for example, may violate local zoning codes, but if you feel this feature is central to the success of your theater, you might be able to work out a variance with the city planning department. In other cases, retaining the design features you require may mean finding new sources of revenue. Even in a small remodeling project, the time you take to evaluate alternatives will reassure your group that you are indeed choosing the best way to go about it.

Choosing the Right Scheme

After exploring various options, you must finally make the decision to adopt one—or none—of the designs. The design alternative phase is the last point at which you can decide against going through with the project—before so much money and energy have been committed that you could not turn back without engendering community ill will.

If you are going ahead, you are now about to choose a plan that you will present to potential donors, government officials, and the community at large. Make sure again that you have dealt adequately with the major issues. Will you be projecting the community image you had in mind? Do the proportions of the building look harmonious? Are all the necessary spaces designed into the building? Who will use each space, and what technical activities will occur there? Have you made allowances for housing all the technical equipment needed for your art form? How functional are the spaces in the building? Will your committee be able to raise enough money for both construction and operating costs?

Beware of Shortcuts

On the surface, this process sounds unnecessarily long and tedious. In fact, some arts groups try to shortcut the schematic design phase, thinking it more economical to move quickly into the final design rather than spend time and money fussing over the merits of alternative schemes. But it is essential not to lock yourselves into one approach too soon. Problems and questions should come up now, while it is still possible to work out solutions that will incorporate your program needs into a well-designed building. Why settle for less than you need and want?

Products of the Schematic Design Phase

When you make your final decision to proceed with one of the alternatives— or a hybrid of several alternatives—your group will have in hand:

- Sketches of the project
- Plans, elevations, and sections (views of the building as if it were cut through the middle, exposing interior relationships)
- Small scale working models that give a sense of the mass, proportion, and relationship of parts within the facility

Based on these visual aids and the work you have been doing with your designers, your committee will be able to understand the working relationships within the building, as well as the orientation of the building to its site and the design of major outdoor spaces. Before proceeding to the next phase, the architect will want your written approval of the schematic plan.

Should You Hold a Design Competition?

If you are thinking of holding a design competition, the logical time to do so is after the final building program has been prepared and before the schematic design phase. A design competition does not replace the schematic design phase. Rather, it is a way of selecting the design team and exploring various design approaches. Each of the competing teams will come up with a different way of organizing the building and site. From these submissions, a jury will select the most appropriate design for the situation, taking into consideration the architects' ability to conceptualize solutions and the team's technical competence. The building committee then hires the winning team to work through the design of the facility. Remember that the finished building may, in fact, look completely different from the winning scheme. Design competitions are intended as a means of selecting the general approach, not a way of producing an instant final design (see Appendix B, Design Competitions).

DESIGN DEVELOPMENT: HEART OF THE ARCHITECTURAL PROCESS

Before you can actually build the facility, your architect must further refine the design. At the end of this refining process, your group will know the exact dimensions of the rooms, the type of equipment to be supplied, the structural system, building finishes, and all the other design specifics.

Design development will involve your entire design team—all architects assigned to the project; all other design specialists, such as theater consultant, museum consultant, and acoustician; engineers; specification writers; and the cost estimator.

From now on, the project will be a balancing act between conceding to the pressures of time and money and taking as much care as possible with the design and construction. There will be many demands on the project from now until the ribbon cutting ceremony. The building will have to be approved by various government departments. The fundraising campaign will be at its most energetic level. Meanwhile, construction costs will be escalating, and the deadline you have set for the opening will loom nearer.

However, by taking the time to examine the details of the building plan, you can make sure everything you want is included in the drawings—and that no extraneous details have found their way into the design. In this way, you eliminate redundant costs and the necessity of making major adjustments once the facility has opened its doors.

Your Last Chance to Make Changes

This phase represents your last chance to make significant changes in the design of the facility. You must be certain that potential users, major funders, board members, and all other concerned parties have seen, understood, and approved the design drawings before you proceed any further. Are your prime consultants and specialists satisfied with the building? Do they feel any crucial aspect of the facility has been sacrificed or misconstrued? Is your committee satisfied that public areas of the building fulfill community needs?

All too often, the building committee becomes so protective of the design that it is afraid to show the plans to potential critics. This is a mistake. The more people who scrutinize the design, the more likely you will be to end up with a facility that best meets your needs. It is the building committee's responsibility to ensure that the design drawings are checked and approved before authorizing the preparation of construction documents —the "working drawings" from which the facility will be built.

Products of the Design Development Phase

At the conclusion of the design development phase, your design team will provide you with:

- A site plan showing the location of buildings, paved surfaces, planted areas, grading (the degree of slope of the land), utility lines, and other pertinent information
- Building plans, interior and exterior elevations and sections that describe the size and character of the entire project
- Structural, mechanical, and electrical plans

- An outline of specifications
- Cost estimates

Testing the Design

About halfway through the design development process—and again at the end—you will be responsible for reviewing the design to check on room locations, dimensions, and spatial relationships.

- Mentally test the design by running your intended programming through the building one more time. Imagine the staging of the most elaborate production your group will present. Will the entire chorus fit backstage? Can you get the set through the scene shop doors? Are the backstage restrooms and dressing rooms on the same level as the stage? Or consider the most extensive exhibit you expect to house in the gallery. Is the exhibition space tall enough? Will the lighting ruin fragile works on paper? Will security be sufficient for the type of exhibits you hope to obtain?
- Make sure separate parts of the building program function independently and in relation to each other.
- Be sure you have taken into consideration the work of the technical consultants. Have each specialist review the entire design to make certain that the dimensions and layout of the building coordinate with the specialized artistic requirements.

Securing Outside Approvals

At the end of the design development process, all individuals or departments with the power to veto aspects of your project should review the decisions of your committee. Again, it is infinitely easier and less costly to make changes in the drawings than during the actual construction process. Ask an insurance broker to review the drawings and suggest options that will lower premium rates for the finished building. An energy consultant might be able to recommend energy-saving design details. Lending institutions will need to check over the plans to make sure the project meets their standards for investment. You will also need to consult with your local planning and building permit departments.

Cost Estimates

By the end of the design development phase, a precise cost estimate based on detailed plans, elevations, sections, and outline specifications will be established. The actual cost of the building should be within ten percent of this final figure. If the cost exceeds the budget for the project, the committee has two choices: raise more funds or reevaluate the program. If a decision is made to trim the program, the building committee will likely attempt to cut back on support space or specialized, expensive equipment. However, you must make sure that a more modest facility continues to meet the needs of the arts organization.

Keeping your project from running over budget will be a big concern. Remember, though, that there is a great difference between an economical building and an inexpensive one. When you are tempted to work with cheaper materials, consider long term maintenance. The end result may not represent a savings. Determine which items must be of high quality and which may be less durable or less visually distinctive. Again, a good cost estimator can help your group develop an accurate accounting of costs and make design adjustments that save money without sacrificing functional quality.

PREPARATION OF CONSTRUCTION DOCUMENTS AND CONSTRUCTION OF THE BUILDING

The final step before construction can begin is translating design decisions into construction documents—the drawings and specifications that will be put out for bid by contractors. These documents must be carefully checked before the bidding process by all the design consultants and any other individuals responsible for review of the project.

What Are Construction Documents?

Sometimes called "working drawings," construction documents show clearly and concisely all information needed by the contractor for making a bid and building the facility. In fact, these drawings constitute part of the contract between the contractor and the owner of the building. Specialists working for the architect will provide drawings of the electrical, mechanical, and plumbing installations, in addition to the architectural and structural diagrams.

While it is very late in the design process to make changes in the plans, you should still review the drawings with your architect. Feel free to ask about particular details, like the position of the loading dock or the placement of heating vents. A good way for you as a lay person to understand a complicated set of drawings is to have the architect "walk" you through the building, pointing out how it functions for your needs.

Construction Specifications

Construction documents also contain the specifications for types of materials, equipment, construction systems, standards, and degree of workmanship to be used in the building. You should clearly understand these specifications, particularly for equipment that will directly affect your performances or exhibition design, such as the type of track lighting or stage floor material to be installed.

Do not be afraid to ask questions. As the sponsors and users of the building, you must be sure it meets your expectations on a detailed level as well as in general concept.

Products of the Construction Documents Phase

The successful outcome of all your hard work depends on the construction documents. Included in this very extensive set of drawings are:

- A site plan with building and utility locations
- A landscape and grading plan
- Building floor plans, roof plans, interior and exterior elevations, sections, and details
- Structural plans
- Mechanical plans for plumbing, heating, ventilating, and air conditioning
- Electrical plans for lighting and the power supply

Obtaining a Building Permit

Building permits are issued by the city or county building department after review of the working drawings to make sure they comply with zoning and building codes. The building codes, which vary from one locality to another, are compilations of health and safety regulations passed over the years. (See Appendix C, Building Codes.) Although fire safety is the major consideration, the codes also deal with structural soundness, plumbing requirements, and maximum allowable building heights. Code issues are important in renovation projects and in all public construction, especially theaters. A fire, a collapsing skywalk, or similar disaster in a public facility would put the city at fault, either for inadequate enforcement of the law or for having an insufficiently detailed code on the books.

Because of the possibility that changes might have to be made to bring the building plans up to code, your architect should obtain all necessary approvals before the project is sent out to bid. Inspectors usually visit the building site during construction and will certainly show up when the facility is completed to issue a **certificate of occupancy** (also known as a certificate of inspection or certificate of completion). This document indicates that application was made for the building permit, that the drawings were up to code, and that the building was in fact constructed within code restrictions.

Remember that the process of obtaining a building permit may take a considerable period of time. City council approvals may even be required on large public projects.

Zoning

The local building department will decide, based on a review of the plans, whether your facility can be built within existing zoning laws.

The Cast of Characters

During the construction process, you will be dealing with a number of different professionals: The **prime**, or **general contractor** (the G.C.) is responsible for coordinating all the on-site activities, including the work of all subcontractors. The G.C. may be replaced by a **construction manager** whose chief tasks are to keep project costs in line and coordinate the work of the subcontractors. Managers must be supervised to ensure that proposed money-saving changes will not severely affect programming. For example, pouring a concrete stage is cheaper than building a wooden stage with a proper trap and equipment, but this adaptation would seriously limit the range of performances that could be presented. It might also involve costly additions later, such as building a special floor for dancers.

Each **subcontractor** is responsible to the G.C. for performing a specific task. The electrical contractor, for example, works on-site only at certain times during construction to install and test the electrical system.

The **suppliers** or **product manufacturers** will be delivering items ordered and, in some cases, installing them in the building.

The **field supervisor**, sometimes called the **super**, is the main project coordinator under the G.C. and should be present during all conversations you may have with a subcontractor. The super is the chief spokesman with whom you and the clerk of the works will be dealing.

The **clerk of the works**, along with the architect, is responsible for seeing that the contract documents are being followed. Any changes need to be discussed by the clerk, the architect, and the super. It may be necessary for you to have your own field supervisor on hand to check the progress of the G.C., particularly for a large civic project requiring coordination between the city and the contractor.

When you don't have a clerk, the **architect** is responsible for seeing that contract documents are followed, coordinating shop drawings, authorizing payments for your approval, and representing your interests on the site. The architect should make certain that shop drawings submitted by suppliers or subcontractors conform to the design scheme so that all components are correctly built and installed.

The **inspector** is the city representative who visits the site to approve the plumbing and electrical systems and who "certifies" the building on completion.

Selecting the Building Contractor

One of the most important steps in creating a building is the selection of a contractor. There are two hiring options: you can select a general contractor who will take full responsibility for seeing that the building is constructed on time and within the bid or negotiated price; or you can hire a construction manager to act as your representative on the project for a negotiated fee. The construction manager generally replaces the contractor on large or complex projects, giving the client more control over subcontractors. Although the construction manager oversees the work, the owner of the building assumes all risks inherent in the construction process.

A general contractor can be chosen by competitive bidding or through direct selection. Under **competitive bidding** the construction documents are sent to interested contractors, who submit bids or prices they would charge to construct the building. The bidding process may be open to all interested, qualified parties or only to selected contractors. All public projects require competitive bidding, and the contract is awarded to the "lowest responsible bidder".

In the **direct selection**, or negotiation system, the architect and building committee choose the contractor who seems most qualified to handle the project. They then negotiate a construction contract that sets forth either a *stipulated sum*—the price for the contractor's services—or a *cost of work plus fee* agreement—in which the contractor is reimbursed for his expenses and also receives a fixed fee for his services.

Check Out the Contractor's Qualifications

Qualifications are especially important for the sophisticated kind of construction that an arts facility represents. Be sure to investigate a contractor's general reputation, financial integrity, demonstrated quality of performance, and adherence to scheduling demands, as well as the scope of prior projects. On public jobs, because of the "lowest bidder" rule, it is crucial to establish acceptable standards for integrity and performance. Bidding must be limited to contractors who meet your standards.

Construction Procedures

Success during the construction phase depends on a close working relationship between you, the client, and the architect and general contractor or construction manager. Have your architect outline the steps in the construction schedule, as two issues will be particularly important from your point of view: authorizing payment and the formal completion of the project.

Authorizing Payment

When you sign the construction contract with the contractor, his fee will be broken down into three segments: payment to begin construction, progress payments through the middle of the project, and the final payment at completion. Keep close watch over the items you have specified to make sure they have been correctly chosen and installed when the contractor requests payment. If he has bungled the job, make sure the situation is rectified before authorizing payment.

If you find that the contractor was at fault, your architect can issue a **field order** outlining the steps the contractor will take to remedy the situation without changing the contract fee. If you, the architect, or the clerk of the works made the error, the architect can issue a **change order** describing the correction and adjusting the contract fee to cover the cost of the change.

Your architect or clerk of the works should review all completed work and upon "substantial completion" of the job submit a certificate of payment to you authorizing the contractor's fee.

Final payment, due when the architect issues the final certificate for payment, covers the remaining five to ten percent of the contract fee. As you near the completion date, the atmosphere on the job site can become very hectic, because you will want to get into the space as soon as possible, and the contractor will be anxious to vacate. Time is money for both of you.

Tied to the completion date in the contract is a **bonus and penalty clause** providing for a bonus if the contractor finishes the project satisfactorily ahead of time, and charging him a penalty if the work is not finished by the deadline. Therefore, despite the last-minute bustle, you should be able to resolve loose ends and get the building completed according to your specifications.

Giving Your Formal Approval

In a final inspection of the building, the architect compiles a **punch list** of items that are incomplete or incorrectly finished or installed. By all means do not skip this step! Once you occupy the building, it will be difficult to get errors rectified. To be on the safe side, don't schedule events too soon after the planned opening date of the facility. Be sure the proper equipment warranties have been filed with the manufacturers. Have the contractor submit an affidavit stating that all debts and claims against him for labor and materials he has subcontracted or purchased have been paid, and that all liens against the contractor have been released.

Is It Possible to Speed Up the Construction Process?

You may hear of a construction method, known as fast-tracking, which allows the building process to start early, before all the details of the plan are fully worked out. Quick decisions are required on such basics as walls, floor plans, and room arrangements. To some people, fast-tracking means saving big dollars on construction costs and sprinting through the building process to meet an early opening date. Others who have had experience with this method are more likely to talk of poorly constructed buildings full of compromises and unresolved technical problems.

Remember that arts facilities are very specialized buildings that require extensive special equipment, layout, and last minute tuning. While fast-tracking may save construction budget money, it may cost you more in the long run because of incomplete or rushed work. If you're seriously considering beginning construction before all plans are complete, remember that changing the building plan during construction is an expensive proposition; instead of erasing a line in a drawing, you may be moving a wall in an actual building.

Depending on the complexity of your project, construction will take anywhere from nine months to two or three years. Among the many difficulties that might plague the project are union problems, climatic conditions that require work stoppages, the contractor's difficulty in performing his job, vandalism, and even repercussions of national or international economic crises. Try to weather this period with good grace, staying in close communication with your architect and doing your utmost to maintain community support.

Products and Decisions for Design Implementation

	Building Program Study	Schematic Design	Design Development	Working Drawings & Construction
Committee Responsibilities	Facilitate the program process: advice from users & committee	Review, guide, and select alternatives of building design and site organization	Review design of spaces for location, size, and form	Review Work Answer Questions Select Contractor
Decisions To Be Made	Image, type, size, quantity, and quality of building spaces	Select design alternative/direction	Approve design for production Approve equipment selection	Review work Questions on construction or design changes Select contractor Approve finished building

Consultants	Specialists as needed. (Arts generalist, architect, etc.)	Architect
		Arts Consultants
		   Theater
		   Museum
		   Acoustic
		Building Engineers:
		   Mechanical
		   Structural
		   Electrical
			Same as Schematic Design
			
			Construction Manager
				Same as Design Development
				
				Clerk of the Works

Outside Approvals	Check with the government agencies for building requirements	Review of schematic design by government agencies	Preliminary permit review Insurance broker Lending institutions Energy expert	Building permits Occupancy permit
Time Line	Small project 2 months Large project 3-6 months	Small project 2 months Large project 3-6 months	Small project 3 months Large project 12-18 months	Small project 10 months Large project 30 months

Interim Products	Memos of program alternatives
	
	Worksheets
		Review direction of alternatives Study:
		   Sketches
		   Plans
		   Models
			Review design decisions made by architect	Review specifications/ Working Drawings
				
				Review payments to contractor

Final Products	Building program workbook	Final schematic:
		   Sketches
		   Plans
		   Models
			Finished design— proceed to production of working drawings	Review of finished building

Cost Estimates	Comparable cost estimates with similar types of projects	Preliminary cost estimates	Project cost estimate *definitive*	Very accurate cost estimate at end of working drawings

The skill and care with which your building program is translated into a design and the architectural drawings are translated into an arts facility depend a great deal on you. Make your needs known, examine all possible alternatives, and take an active part in the design review process. Be sure that you select the best possible contractor for your job and maintain proper field supervision throughout construction. Thorough attention to each detail of the building process will eliminate "surprises" once your doors are open to the public.

I t is never too soon in the planning
process to prepare for opening day.
Long before the doors open, your
committee must consider operational
procedures so that your planned facility
can function optimally. Advance decisions
must be made about:

- Management structure
- The facility manager
- Programming policy
- Operating budgets
- Union negotiations

13. Arts Facility Operations

Without question, the critical issues of operations and management are the ones most often overlooked during planning and design. As a result, many arts facilities that appear beautiful on the outside are operational nightmares on the inside.

Seemingly minor design decisions can make or break the operating budget. Extra dollars needed for utility bills or extra ushers and stagehands means fewer dollars for the programming budget, which affects the overall artistic product.

One way to picture the building in operation is to "walk through" the myriad details of an opening night or the installation of an art exhibit. By imagining how you will cope with union ushers and stagehands, keep the building secure, run the box office, and charge a utilities fee to facility users for a specific event at your facility; you will better be able to foresee problems and figure out how to solve them.

FACILITY MANAGEMENT ISSUES

Deciding on a Management Structure

If yours is a single use facility not tied to public funding, you will probably have a board of directors to which the facility director or manager is responsible. A public facility may be set up as a department of local government, as an administrative board, as a nonprofit corporation, or as a private operation in the hands of a commercial entrepreneur.

If the facility is a **civic department**, or a branch of a civic department, the manager will be directly responsible to the mayor, city manager, city council, or county executive.

The manager's responsibility and authority are clearly established under this system, and his or her degree of independence will hinge on the personalities of local leaders. As a branch department rather than a department in its own right, the facility will not likely be recognized as a separate entity. In some cases, the city appoints an advisory board without specific power to help decide issues relating to an arts facility.

If the facility is governed by an **administrative board** appointed by the mayor, city manager, or city council, the manager usually has more autonomy. The board of directors, commission, or similar body—accountable to the elected official who appointed its members—is responsible for setting policy, hiring the manager, authorizing expenditures, and accounting for revenues and expenditures. Some boards are fiscally independent of the city; others are subject to budget approval by elected officials. The manager is generally permitted to make personnel decisions, subject only to overall policies established by the board.

The current trend in larger cultural facilities is to put facility management in the hands of a **private, nonprofit organization** in order to permit more financial and managerial flexibility within the framework of government support. Although the city still owns the facility, it transfers management to the organization through a long term lease or operating agreement. The management organization may be an existing group, such as the primary arts organization in the facility, a consortium of arts groups, or the local arts council, or the city may set up a brand new organization for this purpose. In some cases, the city retains control over such things as budget approvals and rental rates, while other day-to-day operations fall to the nonprofit corporation.

Private operation means that a commercial entrepreneur under lease or contract to the city manages the facility for a specified fee or system of compensation.

Whatever your arrangement, you should be aware of certain pitfalls in dealing with local government. If possible, avoid using city maintenance personnel because the level of maintenance required by a cultural facility is far greater than that of a typical city building. If your contract with the city stipulates that you must use municipal janitors, be sure to get a detailed list of services to ensure the highest possible level of maintenance. Contracting out for janitorial services may be a good idea, provided that the contract is written to your standards.

Another fact of municipal government is that city auditors are slow to act on contracts and disbursements. A bid process is generally required for public contracts, and the lowest bidder must be awarded the contract. When artistic services are involved—the hiring of a symphony conductor, for example—management needs more flexibility, a matter that must be worked out carefully between the manager and the appropriate municipal body. In a contract disbursement situation, try to keep a measure of control over your work force, even though it is paid with city funds. One positive aspect of a municipal facility is the possibility of having administrative salaries paid in full or in part by the city.

The Board of Directors

Select your board of directors during the early phases of design and construction. Some board members may have served on the planning committee; others will be chosen for their administrative expertise. Members should serve a fixed term, usually three years at the maximum. They will be responsible for establishing policies, raising funds to underwrite these policies, and supervising the work of the manager, who in turn oversees the other personnel. Standing committees will be appointed as needed. Decision making power is usually vested in a smaller executive committee, composed of officers and chairpersons of other working committees, that can gather and vote more swiftly.

The Facility Manager

Ideally, the manager should be hired during or immediately after the feasibility stage to work on a half time basis until the building is under construction. An experienced manager can offer invaluable advice on design, programming, and management that is well worth the part time salary. By hiring the manager early, you can smooth the transition between the design process and the day-to-day workings of the facility.

A brand new arts organization might hire an interim director/consultant to insure that the facility will be suited for whatever programming may occur under the permanent artistic director or museum director. By hiring a consultant with no vested interest in the building, your group is more likely to end up with a flexible space adaptable to a range of artistic programs.

Make sure the manager knows whom to report to and exactly what is expected of him or her before the building opens. You may want the manager to serve as a liaison with the consultant team, as a "watchdog" monitoring the work of the architect, as an arts programming consultant—or as an advisor in all three areas. By the time ground is broken, the manager should have set up an office and begun searching for a staff. The manager should also be meeting with union representatives on labor issues and establishing policy for lease agreements, rentals, box office operations, accounting, and other administrative matters.

The manager must take a leadership role in dealing with the arts groups that use the facility as well as with the staff. To operate a performing arts facility, the manager should have experience in contract negotiations with artists and unions, general knowledge of marketing and promotion, the ability to schedule programs, fundraising and budgeting skills, and tact in dealing with the community. A museum usually has an administrative director who handles personnel and budgeting matters and shares fundraising duties with the museum director.

Setting Management Policy

Certain policy issues must be decided by the manager, together with the executive committee and board of directors before the facility opens. Is a separate, nonprofit organization the best management option? If so, should the organization control only building operations, or should its authority extend to arts programming as well? Any restrictions on the function of the nonprofit organization need to be spelled out clearly. Control of the box office and advertising, for example, may be left in the hands of individual performing groups.

The makeup of the board of directors and staff will hinge on such policy decisions. The manager and present board or planning committee may want to hold roundtable sessions with managers of other facilities to discuss options for management organization, budgeting, and operation policy. Their suggestions may then be incorporated into a system that will accommodate local needs.

Rental Rates

As the primary source of income for a performing arts facility, rentals are crucial to its success. Yet, local groups used to paying little or nothing for makeshift performance space may be priced out of the facility if they are charged the "going rate" that covers operating costs. The building may then go unused when it is not hosting a touring company that can afford the fees.

There are several possible solutions. The local users may be able to find a special source of contributions, such as a hotel tax fund, to make up the difference between the going rate and what they can pay. Another option is to scale rental fees according to user, charging standard, professional rates for performing groups that pay union scale salaries, special rates for local groups that don't pay their performers, and possibly a commercial rate for businesses and conventions.

Rental rates must also be broken down by length of use (morning, evening, or all day) and portions of the facility used (stage only, stage plus shop space, rehearsal spaces, entire facility). Different rates are usually charged for performance and rehearsal time. Rates typically include the services of key personnel necessary for the safe functioning of the theater. Users pay for additional box office and technical personnel or extra ushers at the going rate for the size and location of the facility.

Union Negotiations

Your involvement with unions depends on the type of facility, the program in question, the strength of unions locally, and the type of technical equipment to be used. Owners of a small "alternative" space, for example, will normally be free from union pressure because they would not hire a significant number of union workers on a regular basis.

Initiate informal discussions with local unions early in the planning process and get to know the shop stewards. Figure out which of your events might require specific kinds of union participation. The key point is to establish a fair policy on the number and type of union workers required for each type of event. Remember that union arrangements are subject to negotiation. You can probably work out a deal whereby unions will relinquish authority for performances by amateur companies and allow the employment of a certain number of nonunion workers. In a municipal or county-owned facility, where union participation may be required, it is important to be tough from the outset. Negotiate first and hardest with the Operating Engineers Union, which receives the top rate and sets the benchmark for other union pay scales. When possible, negotiate with the American Federation of Musicians for individual events, since a long term contract may involve paying for expensive services you don't need.

Management of a performing arts facility will also be dealing with unions representing janitors, ushers, stagehands, and carpenters. Try to stagger initial union contracts, so that only one contract comes due each year. Remember that IATSE (International Association of Technicians, Stagehands, and Electricians) honors strikes by other unions; if the garbage union is picketing the building, you may not get union workers for your show.

The number of union workers for "yellow card" events—major touring shows, including Broadway musicals and rock concerts—is determined by Local 1 of IATSE, headquartered in New York. After eight hours, union workers get one and a half times the basic hourly rate; after midnight, they receive three times the basic rate.

If your facility is owned by a university or located in a small town, you may be able to negotiate a more flexible arrangement. Many university or college-owned facilities save money by using student interns or hiring nonunion workers with academic standing. In some instances, technicians and stagehands will become part of a general campus union that covers all workers associated with the university. In smaller communities, where union members may moonlight in addition to their union jobs, management can often obtain more flexible rates and conditions. If you need a crew of six for a specific show, negotiate with the union's local business agent to allow two or three community people or students as part of the crew. Additional union people may then be added later if needed.

Keep in mind that personnel costs may be directly tied to facility design. Will your setup permit one person to run the light and sound booth, or are the two areas widely separated? The number of people needed to raise the stage curtain depends on the sensitivity of the counterweight system; the number of ticket takers depends on the entrance design; and the number of ushers depends on the layout of doorways leading into the auditorium.

DAY-TO-DAY FACILITY OPERATIONS

The following are some key points to keep in mind with regard to security, insurance, box office operations, utility service, life cycle costing, and deficit financing:

Security
Early in the planning process get advice from security firms on the best design for large public assemblies, methods of securing outside doors, ways

to guard the shipping and receiving area, and other specifics. Such advice is usually free because the companies hope to get your service contract. Remember that most facilities require round-the-clock surveillance, either by guards or television monitor systems.

Internal security is essential in both visual and performing arts facilities. In a museum or art center, the major concerns are avoiding damage to the art objects and controlling an outbreak of fire. A well-run checkroom, where patrons are asked to check all parcels and umbrellas, and properly worded signs warning people not to touch the art can help reduce thoughtless damage. Visitors generally respond better to signs that explain the reasons for a "hands off" policy. Uniformed security guards trained to deal courteously with visitors should always be on duty in public areas.

In a performing arts facility, management should know how to deal with traffic control, box office security, and emergency conditions like bomb threats and fire. Work closely with the police department to determine the best arrangements for special events (like rock concerts) that involve extensive traffic control and may pose a major threat to building security. In any theater, the box office area should have special locks and cages and to prevent theft. Technical equipment located in storage areas or backstage must be protected with alarm systems and locks.

Insurance

Whatever type of facility you build, you *must* have insurance. A publicly owned performing arts facility generally needs more insurance than the amount the city agrees to carry, because of the possibility of injury to a performer or audience member.

Make sure your coverage provides for errors and omissions by the board of directors and for auto travel by staff members. Check with an insurance representative early in the design phase about additional safeguards. For example, university facilities rented to community or professional groups will have specific insurance requirements.

You also must develop guidelines for the type and amount of insurance that must be carried by groups renting your facility. Typically, certificates specifying the amount of liability coverage must be presented ten days prior to a performance ($1 million is common for larger events, with an additional $300,000 for damages to the facility). Many facilities prorate insurance costs in the basic rental fee.

Box Office Operations

Your architect will probably have little, if any, knowledge about the actual workings of a box office. Yet, the design of this tiny space deserves a great deal of attention because of the variety of operations handled there. In planning your box office, you must consider how often, when, and by whom it will be used. Typically, there should be room for one or two persons to read seating charts, handle money, call to verify charge account numbers, and possibly use a computer terminal. Easily available ticket storage also must be provided.

In a smaller facility, a full time box office may not be necessary. One group decided to have a secretary sell tickets during the day and to use the box office only at night. Although this arrangement required the racks of tickets, seating charts, money box, and charge machines to be moved back and forth five times a week, it eliminated the cost the hiring someone to staff the box office during the day, when as few as twenty people would be purchasing tickets.

Be sure to talk to managers of other facilities about the design and operation of their box offices before making final decisions. One of the best models can be found in the athletic department of the nearest college or university, where the box office staff regularly deals with large crowds and significant sums of money.

Consult Further Reading for useful references on box office management.

Utility Service

Consult with your local power company about design and emphasize energy efficiency to your architect. The ability to open only a small area of the facility at one time can be an important money-saver. In a visual arts facility, for example, you want visitors to be able to enter a lecture hall without passing thorugh galleries that would have to be lit. In a performing arts facility, you will want to close off the major portion of the building during daytime hours when patrons come only to purchase tickets.

Be certain to obtain the best option for utility service and establish a management program for controlling energy use. (Consult the ACUCAA and IAAM handbooks listed in Further Reading for specific energy program recommendations.) Include a utilities fee as part of your rental agreements, and remember that different users will consume vastly different amounts of energy. Opera performances typically require up to 50 percent more electricity than do other theatrical or musical events, so an opera company should pay a proportionately higher utility bill as part of its rental fee. By using room sensors to monitor energy usage, you will be able to determine the exact amount a specific event consumes.

Life Cycle Costing (Maintenance)

Because maintenance is usually the first item cut from any facility budget, be sure to get top-of-the-line equipment; heating, ventilation and air conditioning systems; and building materials. Cheaper equipment could cost you more in the long run because of expensive repair bills. Make sure that annual maintenance costs are included in early budgeting. In your rental contracts, be certain to clarify the users' responsibility for cleaning up after a performance.

From the day you open the doors, develop a program of cyclical costs and make a schedule for annual facility repairs. Examine similar facilities to see what costs can be expected at certain points in the life of a building or piece of equipment. Generally, maintenance and life cycle costs are light during the first three years of a new facility and increase thereafter.

Operating costs are affected by power consumption, temperature and humidity controls, and lighting maintenance, as well as by wear and tear from constant traffic through the building. In a visual arts facility, use a minimum number of efficient lighting fixtures and maintain them properly to ensure the same quality of light throughout the life of the installation. Keep the lamps clean, so you continue to get maximum illumination for your dollar.

Deficit Financing

Because earned income makes up only a percentage of an arts organization's total budget—50 to 75 percent for performing arts, 15 to 40 percent for visual arts—you will soon become familiar with deficit financing. As early as possible in the planning process, your group should gather detailed information on the cost of running an arts facility. Use the charts in Appendix A to develop your projected budget and determine other sources of income to help balance a negative cash flow. Make sure the capital fund drive includes an endowment campaign of sufficient scope to help offset the projected deficit. Identify potential contributors, both public and private, whose support you can count on.

If the facility is publicly owned, you must convince government officials that the fiscal and cultural benefits of your facility justify ongoing public support. You should also try to allocate as many salaried staff members as possible to the city payroll.

Aggressive marketing techniques that can raise additional revenue are vital for every arts facility in today's economy. For example, you may be able to stipulate a percentage of the gross in a contract with a catering service. But don't give away your liquor license to a franchise if your group may legally sell drinks! You might rent your hall for conferences and meetings to profit groups who can afford to pay top dollar. Retail sales, festivals, and cable and video markets are other options you may want to investigate. If you facility is associated with a university, however, check with the legal and accounting departments before sponsoring a special money raising project to make sure you are not jeopardizing the tax exempt status of the facility, land, and academic programs.

Take special care throughout the planning process, to consider the seemingly subtle design decisions that will affect future operational efficiency.

Early policy decisions that your committee makes regarding who will manage the facility, and the structure for decision-making will determine how well "the show goes on."

Appendix A
Financial Feasibility Worksheets

These worksheets are guides, not blueprints. They are intended as a framework illustrating some of the financial analysis necessary during the facility planning process. Obviously your specific situation will vary from these in details (a long-established organization, for example, will have on hand far more detailed information than these charts outline). Remember that the charts should be adjusted for your situation.

Appendix A is divided into two parts. **Part One** presents operating budget worksheets for both visual arts facilities (pages 189-195) and performing arts facilities (pages 199-204) in five sequential tasks. A five year financial plan summary worksheet concludes Part One.

Part Two presents worksheets for visual arts facilities (pages 196-198) and performing arts facilities (pages 205-207) to calculate costs for capital construction and funding sources for capital construction.

Visual Arts Facility
Part One: Operating Budget Projections

In generating the figures for the feasibility analysis, don't be afraid to guess, using the best available information and common sense. We suggest that you develop a range of high and low numbers as a "ballpark" estimate rather than attempting to pinpoint any specific number.

Task 1. Estimate Annual Ticket Revenues , Visual Arts

Regular Daily Admission Fee

_____ Number weekdays open X
_____ Number of people @
_____ Average ticket price = $

_____ Number weekend days open X
_____ Number of people @
_____ Average ticket price = $

Special Exhibits Admission Fee

_____ Number days X
_____ Number of people per day @
_____ Average ticket price = $

Special Events

Festivals
_____ Number days X
_____ Number of people @
_____ Entrance fee = $

Concerts
_____ Number concerts X
_____ Number of people @
_____ Average ticket price = $

Films
_____ Showings X
_____ Number of people @
_____ Average ticket price = $

Lectures
_____ Number of lectures X
_____ Number of people @
_____ Average ticket price = $

Other $

TOTAL ESTIMATED REVENUE FROM ADMISSIONS $

Task 2. Estimate Educational Activity Revenues , Visual Arts

Educational activities are often a source of revenues for visual arts facilities. If these activities will be included in your programming, complete this task.

Studio Classes

1. _____ Name of class
   _____ Number of sessions offered X
   _____ Number of students @
   _____ Fee per student = $

2. _____ Name of class
   _____ Number of sessions offered X
   _____ Number of students @
   _____ Fee per student = $

(And so on for additional classes) $

Lecture Classes

1. _____ Name of class
   _____ Number of sessions offered X
   _____ Number of students @
   _____ Fee per student = $

2. _____ Name of class
   _____ Number of sessions offered X
   _____ Number of students @
   _____ Fee per student = $

(And so on for additional classes) $

**TOTAL ESTIMATED REVENUE
FROM EDUCATIONAL ACTIVITIES** $

Hints

- Check with other facilities that program similar types of events in order to estimate your attendance, ticket prices, revenues, operational costs, etc.
- Average daily attendance may vary significantly depending on the season or day of the week.

Task 3. Estimate Total Annual Earned Revenues , Visual Arts

Admission Revenues (Task 1)	$
Education Revenues (Task 2)	$

Memberships

_____ Number of individual members @
_____ Annual Membership fee = $

_____ Number of corporate members @
_____ Annual Membership fee = $

Sales Revenues

Gift Shop	$
Restaurant/Concessions	$
Other	$

Rentals

Facility Rentals (to other groups)	$
Art Rentals	$

Parking Fees	$
Investment of Endowment Income	$
Other Earned Income	$
TOTAL ESTIMATED ANNUAL EARNED INCOME	**$**

Hints
- Membership fees are often staggered into categories (member, friend, patron, etc.).
- Check with other facilities and businesses to estimate sales revenues and rental income.
- Parking revenues if applicable, are based on number of car spaces, frequency of use, and hourly rental rate.

Task 4. Estimate Annual Operating Expenses , Visual Arts

Fixed Costs

Salaries and benefits	$
Administration and overhead (phone, office supplies and equipment, postage, travel, etc.)	$
Legal and accounting services	$
Security	$
Maintenance	$
Contract Services (janitorial service and garbage removal)	$
Insurance	$
Debt Service (loan repayment)	$

Variable Costs

Advertising	$
Utilities	$
Repairs	$

Special Exhibition Programming Costs

Exhibits organized by facility (consultants, installation, etc.)	$
Traveling exhibitions (rental fees and installation costs)	$

Special Events Programming Costs

Festivals	$
Films	$
Lectures	$

Educational Expenses (supplies, additional personnel)	$

Acquisitions	$

Other	$

TOTAL ESTIMATED ANNUAL OPERATING EXPENSES	$

Hints:

- Personnel categories are:

1. MANAGEMENT	Director	
	Administrative Director	
	Director of Development	
	Public Relations Director	
	Education/Program Director	
2. SUPPORT	Secretaries/Receptionist	
3. CURATORIAL	Curatorial Staff	
4. TECHNICAL	Exhibition Designer	
	Preparator	
	Registrar	
	Carpenters	
5. MAINTENANCE	Maintenance Foreman and Crew	
	(or contract service)	
6. OTHER	Part time personnel	

- Add 20 percent payroll burden to personnel expenses in order to estimate additional costs for health benefits, insurance, and taxes.

Task 5. Net Operating Position , Visual Arts

Total Earned
Income   **−**   Total Operating
Expenses   **=**   NET
OPERATING
(Task 3)   Expenses   POSITION
          (Task 4)

If Net Operating Position is POSITIVE, go to Task 6. If it is NEGATIVE, do Task 5A.

Task 5A. Estimate Additional Revenue Sources for Operations , Visual Arts

General Public Funding (Annual Support)

City appropriation	$
County appropriation	$
State appropriation	$

Foundation Funding

For special projects	$
For annual operations	$

Corporate Support

For special projects	$
For annual operations	$

Individual Support

Annual fund drive, benefits	$

Other Fundraising Possibilities

1.	$
2.	$
3.	$

Other Rental or Sales Revenue Possibilities

1.	$
2.	$
3.	$

TOTAL CONTRIBUTED INCOME	$

ADJUSTED NET OPERATING POSITION $.
Total earned income (Task 3) plus total
contributed income (Task 5A) minus operating
expenses (Task 4). Net operating position figure
must be zero or greater. If less than zero, list
difference in "unknown."

UNKNOWN	$

Hints
- If "Unknown" category above is a large percentage of the total additional revenue, you must re-examine costs.
- Prioritize funding. How secure is money from each source? How far can it stretch?

Summary Five Year Financial Plan
Projection of Net Operating Position

Fiscal year ending	1983	1984	1985	1986	1987
Earned Income Revenues (Task 3)					
Contributed Income Revenues (Task 5)					
Subtotal A					
Operating Expenses (Task 4)					
Special Programming Costs					
Subtotal B					
Excess (deficit) of Earned Revenues and Contributed Income (A) over Expenses (B)					
Accumulated Surplus (deficit) beginning of fiscal year					
Accumulated Surplus (deficit) end of fiscal year					

Visual Arts Facility
Part Two: Capital Construction Cost Estimates and Funding Sources

Task 6. Estimate Capital Construction Costs, Visual Arts

"Hard" Costs

Site acquisition	$
Site preparation	$
Utility extensions	$
Demolition	$
Building Construction	$
_____ Room type	
_____ Number of square feet, @	
_____ Cost per square foot =	$
_____ Room type	
_____ Number of square feet, @	
_____ Cost per square foot =	$
(and so on for additional rooms)	
Site construction (parking, landscaping, etc.)	$
Equipment	$
Movable furniture	$

"Soft" Costs

Permit fees	$
Real estate and legal fees	$
Architects and building consultant design fees	$
Insurance during construction	$
Interim taxes	$
Construction financing	$
Contingency fund (15 percent or higher of subtotal)	$

TOTAL ESTIMATED CAPITAL CONSTRUCTION COSTS	$
(Use current dollar amounts and note date of estimate)	

Hints

- "Hard" costs include "bricks and mortar" expenses to build the building and the necessary equipment to run the facility. These costs typically make up between 66-75 percent of the total project cost.
- "Soft" costs include such items as design and legal fees, insurance and taxes during construction, and construction financing. These costs typically make up between 25-33 percent of the total project costs.
- At this stage of the planning process, rough "ball park" estimates are close enough, with a margin of error between 20-25 percent of actual costs. Later on, you will make more detailed estimates.

Task 7. Estimate Current Assets on Hand Available for Capital Construction and Potential Funds from Public and Private Sources , Visual Arts

Current assets available for capital construction	$

Local Funding Sources (city or county)

Bond revenues (general obligation, revenue, other)	$
General tax funds (generally a one-time allocation for planning or construction)	$
Special tax funds (% for art, hotel/motel, coal/oil, utility, etc.)	$
Categorical grants	$

State Government Funding Sources

Special programs and grants	$
State arts council grants	$
State historical society	$

Federal Government Funding Sources

Department of Commerce (Economic Development Administration)	$
Department of Energy	$
Department of Housing and Urban Development (Community block grants, urban development action grants)	$
National Endowment for the Arts (planning grants, challenge grants)	$
National Endowment for the Humanities	$
National Trust for Historic Preservation	$
Other programs	$

Private Contributions and Grants

Individual contributions	$
Corporate and business contributions	$
Fundraising events	$
Donated services, materials, and facilities	$
Foundation grants and contributions	$

Private Investment

Insurance and bank loans	$
Special low interest loans	$

Other Funding Sources Specific to Situation (developer's contribution, student fees, matching funds, sale of air rights, etc.)	$

TOTAL DOLLARS AVAILABLE FOR FACILITY CONSTRUCTION Total dollar amount available must be equal or larger than estimated construction budget. If less than equal, list different in "UNKNOWN".	$
UNKNOWN	$

Hints

- See Chapter 3 for a more detailed description of public funding sources.
- See Chapter 4 for a discussion of nontraditional real estate arrangements as potential funding sources.
- Your organization can structure private donations in a way that provides donors with special tax advantages. Get the advice of a top-notch tax lawyer.

Performing Arts Facility
Part One: Operating Budget Projections

When you generate figures, don't be afraid to guess; use the best available information and common sense. Develop a range of high and low numbers as a "ballpark" estimate rather than attempting to pinpoint a specific figure.

Task 1. Estimate Annual Ticket Revenues, Performing Arts

If your organization produces events, you will earn revenue from ticket sales. Prepare a list of events for a typical year. Assign an audience figure and an average ticket price to each event.

1. _____ Name of event
   _____ Length of event in days X
   _____ Estimated audience size @
   _____ Average ticket price = $

2. _____ Name of event
   _____ Length of event in days X
   _____ Estimated audience size @
   _____ Average ticket price = $

(And so on for additional events)

TOTAL ESTIMATED DAYS OF FACILITY USE   /365

TOTAL ESTIMATED ATTENDANCE

TOTAL ESTIMATED TICKET REVENUE $

Hints
- The events list can be taken from:
  1. Existing groups plus additional events sponsored by those groups.
  2. Events sponsored by the facility itself. Check with similar size facilities in nearby communities for more arts programming possibilities.
- Base attendance on your own past attendance figures and/or on audience figures for similar events in other communities.
- Between 200-300 event days/year is an upper average; be careful not to overschedule. Reserve days for rehearsal and maintenance. Be sure your technical staff can handle the estimated load.

Task 2. Estimate Annual Rental Revenues, Performing Arts

If your organization or facility will be presenting touring groups or renting the performance space to other organizations, you will earn rental revenues and possibly a percentage of ticket sales. An event list must be prepared for these rentals in order to estimate this income. Then, determine the number of events and rental price per event.

Rentals to Nonprofit Organizations

_____ Name of organization
_____ Number days they would rent annually @
_____ Rental fees per day = $

_____ Name of organization
_____ Number days they would rent annually @
_____ Rental fees per day = $

(And so on for additional organizations)

Rental to Commercial Ventures

_____ Name of organization
_____ Number days they would rent annually @
_____ Rental fees per day = $

TOTAL ESTIMATED DAYS OF FACILITY USAGE   /365

TOTAL ESTIMATED RENTAL INCOME $

Hints

- Rental rates should be established from existing local rates and those at similar facilities in other communities.
- Rates for nonprofit organizations are generally lower than rates for commercial groups. Rates are usually established at a daily rate and weekly rate.
- Rental rates usually include only the key personnel who are regular members of the staff. Additional box office personnel, ushers, and stage or media technicians would be billed at going rates.

Task 3. Total Annual Earned Revenues, Performing Arts

Ticket Revenue (Task 1)	$

Rental Income (Task 2)
  Nonprofit organizations
  Commercial groups
  % ticket sales in addition to rental (if applicable)
	$
	
	$

Sales Revenue
  Restaurant
  Concessions
  Gift Shop
  Other
	
	$
	$
	$
	$

Parking Fees	$
Educational Revenue	$
Investment or Endowment Income	$
Other Earned Income	$
TOTAL ESTIMATED ANNUAL EARNED INCOME	$

Hints

- A percentage of ticket sales is sometimes charged to outside groups in addition to a flat rental rate.
- Concession income should be based on the estimated annual attendance. Calculate a per person amount ($.50 per person X 500,000 annual attendance = $250,000 concessions revenue).
- Parking fee revenues are based on the number of events, the number of available parking spaces, and the parking charge.

Task 4. Estimate Annual Operating Expenses , Performing Arts

Fixed Costs

Salaries and benefits	$
Administration and overhead (phone, office supplies and equipment, postage, travel, etc.)	$
Legal and accounting services	$
Maintenance	$
Contract Services (janitorial, security)	$
Insurance	$
Debt Service (loan repayment)	$

Variable Costs

Advertising	$
Technical personnel	$
Repairs	$
Utilities	$
Special programming and production costs for facility sponsored events	$
Artists' fees for touring events	$
Other	$

TOTAL ESTIMATED ANNUAL OPERATING EXPENSES $

Hints:

- Personnel categories are:
1. MANAGEMENT	General Manager or Executive Director
	Operations Manager
	Office Manager/Bookkeeper
	Booking/Programming Manager
	Director of Development/Fundraising
	Public Relations Director
2. SUPPORT	Secretaries/Receptionist
3. TECHNICAL	Technical Director/Stage Manager
	Technical Staff
	Building Engineer
4. MAINTENANCE	Maintenance Foreman and Crew (or contract service)
	Security (or contract service)
5. OTHER	Part time personnel (ushers, stage hands)

- Add payroll burden at 20 percent of total salaries to cover taxes, social security, health coverage, and insurance.
- For facility-sponsored events, calculate costs for artists' fees, marketing and promotion, security, additional personnel for box office, and technical and house operations.

Task 5. Net Operating Position , Performing Arts

Total Earned Income (Task 3)	**–**	Total Operating Expenses (Task 4)	**=**	NET OPERATING POSITION

If Net Operating Position is POSITIVE, go to Task 6. If it is NEGATIVE, do Task 5A.

Task 5A. Additional Revenue Sources for Operations

General Public Funding (Annual Support)

City appropriation	$
County appropriation	$
State appropriation	$

Foundation Funding

For special projects	$
For annual operations	$

Corporate Support

For special projects	$
For annual operations	$

Individual Support

Annual fund drive, benefits	$

Other Fundraising Possibilities

1.	$
2.	$
3.	$

Other Rental or Sales Revenue Possibilities

1.	$
2.	$
3.	$

TOTAL CONTRIBUTED INCOME	$

ADJUSTED NET OPERATING POSITION $
Total earned income (Task 3) plus total contributed income (Task 5A) minus operating expenses (Task 4). Net operating position figure must be zero or greater. If less than zero, list difference in "unknown."

UNKNOWN	$

Hints
- If "Unknown" category above is a large percentage of the total additional revenue, you must re-examine costs.
- Prioritize funding. How secure is money from each source? How far can it stretch?

Summary Five Year Financial Plan
Projection of Net Operating Position , Performing Arts

Fiscal year ending	1983	1984	1985	1986	1987
Earned Income Revenues (Task 3)					
Contributed Income Revenues (Task 5)					
Subtotal A					
Operating Expenses (Task 4)					
Special Programming Costs					
Subtotal B					
Excess (deficit) of Earned Revenues and Contributed Income (A) over Expenses (B)					
Accumulated Surplus (deficit) beginning of fiscal year					
Accumulated Surplus (deficit) end of fiscal year					

Performing Arts Facility
Part Two: Capital Construction Cost Estimates and Funding Sources

Task 6. Estimate Capital Construction Costs , Performing Arts

"Hard" Costs

Site acquisition	$
Site preparation	$
Utility extensions	$
Demolition	$
Building Construction	$
_____ Room type,	
_____ Number of square feet, @	
_____ Cost per square foot =	$
_____ Room type,	
_____ Number of square feet, @	
_____ Cost per square foot =	$
(and so on for additional rooms)	
Site construction (parking, landscaping, etc.)	$
Equipment	$
Movable furniture	$

"Soft" Costs

Permit fees	$
Real estate and legal fees	$
Architects and building consultant design fees	$
Insurance during construction	$
Interim taxes	$
Construction financing	$
Contingency fund (15 percent or higher of subtotal)	$

TOTAL ESTIMATED CAPITAL CONSTRUCTION COSTS	$
(Use current dollar amounts and note date of estimate)	

Hints
- "Hard" costs include "bricks and mortar" expenses to build the building and the necessary equipment to run the facility. These costs typically make up between 66-75 percent of the total project cost.
- "Soft" costs include such items as design and legal fees, insurance and taxes during construction, and construction financing. These costs typically make up between 25-33 percent of the total project costs.
- At this stage of the planning process, rough "ball park" estimates are close enough, with a margin of error between 20-25 percent of actual costs. Later on, you will make more detailed estimates.

Task 7. Estimate Current Assets on Hand Available for Capital Construction and Potential Funds from Public and Private Sources, Performing Arts

Current assets available for capital construction	$

Local Funding Sources (city or county)

Bond revenues (general obligation, revenue, other)	$
General tax funds (generally a one-time allocation for planning or construction)	$
Special tax funds (% for art, hotel/motel, coal/oil, utility, etc.)	$
Categorical grants	$

State Government Funding Sources

Special programs and grants	$
State arts council grants	$
State historical society	$

Federal Government Funding Sources

Department of Commerce (Economic Development Administration)	$
Department of Energy	$
Department of Housing and Urban Development (Community block grants, urban development action grants)	$
National Endowment for the Arts (planning grants, challenge grants)	$
National Endowment for the Humanities	$
National Trust for Historic Preservation	$
Other programs	$

Private Contributions and Grants

Individual contributions	$
Corporate and business contributions	$
Fundraising events	$
Donated services, materials, and facilities	$
Foundation grants and contributions	$

Private Investment

Insurance and bank loans	$
Special low interest loans	$

Other Funding Sources Specific to Situation (developer's contribution, student fees, matching funds, sale of air rights, etc.)	$

TOTAL DOLLARS AVAILABLE FOR FACILITY CONSTRUCTION Total dollar amount available must be equal or larger than estimated construction budget. If less than equal, list different in "UNKNOWN".	$
UNKNOWN	$

Hints

- See Chapter 3 for a more detailed description of public funding sources.
- See Chapter 4 for a discussion of nontraditional real estate arrangements as potential funding sources.
- Your organization can structure private donations in a way that provides donors with special tax advantages. Get the advice of a top-notch tax lawyer.

Appendix B
Design Competitions

One method for selecting an architect and developing alternative design schemes for a project is to hold a design competition. It will produce a wider variety of design solutions than any other method. And it will generate ideas in a way that publicizes and celebrates the event of creating an arts facility. However, a competition should not be a means of trying to save design costs or of moving the project through on an accelerated schedule.

Types of Competitions

There are five basic types of competitions: open, prequalified, invited, staged, and the on-site charette. The choice depends on the complexity of the project and the sponsors' objectives.

- **Open** competitions are, as the name implies, open to all qualified competitors. While a competition of this type is good for gathering the widest possible range of participants, it is not recommended for projects that involve specific expertise or highly technical knowledge. Open competitions require the greatest amount of time (as long as a year) because they must be widely advertised in the professional media.
- **Prequalified** competitions require the initial presentation of qualifications and credentials. Competitors are interviewed and their portfolios are reviewed. Eligible applicants will then enter the design phase of the competition.
- **Invited** competitions involve a roster of competitors drawn up by the competition advisor on the basis of research and the advice of local or state design arts societies. Those who qualify tend to come from the ranks of established designers or designer teams.
- **Staged** competitions combine the qualities of open and invited classifications. The first step is an open call for design entries. From this group, a smaller number of competitors are selected for further consideration. Step one finalists' qualifications may then be reviewed

or the finalists may be asked to develop the ideas they presented for the project during the first round. In the latter case, competitors are compensated for their work at the going professional rate.

- An **on-site charette** involves a roster of potential competitors who are chosen on the basis of a review of their qualifications and experience. Each competitor develops his or her alternative scheme on the site. The advantage of this type of competition is the guiding concept of equal time, circumstances, exposure and access to information.

The Order of Events

Most competitions are run according to a predetermined order of events:

1. **Preliminary planning.** Competition goals are set; professional advisor is appointed; advisory board is organized.
2. **Competition planning.** Program and rules are developed; project budget is designed; awards and prizes are determined; awards jury is selected; procedures are developed for the documentation and handling of projects and awards.
3. **Competition initiation.** Public announcement of the competition; receipt of applications and fees; program is mailed to competitors.
4. **Design stage.** Preparation of design submissions by competitors; selection of winner by design jury.
5. **Awards jury proceedings.** Examination of design submissions by professional advisor; selection of winner by jury.
6. **Announcements.** Awarding of prizes and contracts; announcement and publication of competition results.
7. **Follow-up.** Return of submissions to competitors; winners are contacted; project is implemented.

Cost, Time and Organization

There is a cost factor in running a competition. It is not a way of getting free design work. Typically, the cost of the competition is less than one percent of the construction budget. Competitions can run from six weeks to as long as a year, depending on the size, nature and complexity of the project.

Select a capable advisor to plan, organize and manage all steps of the campaign. The advisor should be an individual or design firm with previous competition experience, knowledge of the design process, and an ability to mediate divergent interests.

An advisory board of up to seven people may be selected either in lieu of or in addition to the professional advisor. Boards are especially useful in competitions run by public agencies. For projects involving broad public support, a range of abilities should be represented on the board, including at least one local design arts professional.

To get the best results from the architects working on the competition, make sure that all the political, economic, and program issues are clearly defined prior to the opening of the competition. It is not the architect's task to solve these issues. That is why the planning group should already have established the building program and feasibility criteria. The architect will specify the image of the facility, but the committee must know what kind of programs will be held in it. If no clear sense of direction is specified by the client, the competition will yield a variety of disparate directions rather than true alternatives based on one central idea of the purpose of the facility.

The competition program implies certain contractual agreements between the sponsor, professional advisor and awards jury and the competitors. The contract must clearly state the objectives of the competition, rules for eligibility and the sponsor's commitment to the results of the competition. Specific elements of the program include:

- Deadline
- Schedule of events
- Mode of design presentations
- Role and responsibility of professional advisor, jury and sponsor
- Amount of money to be awarded
- Terms of employment for the winner (if applicable)
- Ownership and use of the entries

The Design Arts Program of the National Endowment for Arts can give you further advice on holding a design competition and provide handbooks and other materials that fully explain the procedures involved in the process.

Appendix C
Building Codes

Building codes govern the use of a building and provide minimum standards to protect public safety, health and welfare. Responsibility for formulating and adopting building codes falls to the states, although it is sometimes delegated to local communities. Building codes address not only structural considerations but also fire, safety, plumbing, and electrical utilities. There is no uniform building code in use throughout the U.S. (A legal fire escape in New York, for example, will not pass the California code.) In the broad geographical area for which this handbook is intended, building codes vary widely. Therefore, when you are first analyzing the physical requirements of your art form, you will need to consult the local building permit department to see what code they use.

There are four basic codes a municipality can follow.

1. National Building Code (NBC)
2. Uniform Building Code (UBC)
3. Basic Building Code (BOCA)
4. City or state code

The first three codes are updated yearly. Cities in close proximity all may use one of these codes, but they may have adopted variants from different years that do not agree on all points.

Many cities, towns and states develop their own codes; these may be adaptations of the four basic codes or they may be special codes dealing with unique situations within the area covered by the code. The ultimate source of interpretation for your community is your building department. You should always obtain department opinions and decisions in writing.

Familiarity with the following terms and chapters of the building code will be helpful in understanding code requirements.

Access stairs. Stairs between two floors which do not meet requirements for an exit.

Occupancy rating. The code section that outlines specific activities permitted in your facility as well as the number of people allowed in the building at one time. *Certificate of Occupancy* is the document issued by the building department authorizing the use of a space by a certain number of people for specified activities.

Corridor. An enclosed public passageway providing access from rooms or spaces to an exit.

Dead load. The weight of all permanent materials, equipment and construction supported by a building, including its own weight.

Exit. Means of egress from the interior of a building to an open exterior space described in the building codes. Examples of exits that come under code restrictions are: exterior door openings; stairs or ramps; exit passageways; horizontal exits; interior stairs; exterior stairs; fire escapes.

Exit Passageway. A horizontal extension of stairs or ramps, or a passage leading from a yard or court to an open exterior space.

Fire isolation. Isolation involves:
1. Use of a fire barrier between the auditorium and the stage
2. Automatic and/or human sensing of fire and closing of all doors
3. Required venting at the roof by automatically opening smoke hatches and automatically operated sprinklers (located at the grid level in a theater).

Fire resistance rating. A rating, given in hours, that indicates the amount of time a wall, floor or ceiling must remain intact during a fire. In a theater the means of egress must conform to the rating required for theater use.

Fire-retardant. Describes materials that have been pressure-impregnated with chemicals to reduce combustibility.

Flameproof. Describes materials that have been externally treated with chemicals to reduce combustibility.

Insurance. If your area does not have a strict code, you may want to check with your insurance company to see what kind of building standards it uses as a base for its premium structure.

Live load. The weight of all occupants, materials and equipment likely to be moved or relocated in a building in addition to the dead load. Live load is rated in pounds per square foot.

Means of egress. The path of exit. This can include any combination of doors, stairwells, and passageways.

Occupancy. The type of activity for which a building or space is used and/or the number of persons using a space. In a theater space this includes audience, actors, and employees. In a museum each gallery will have an occupant load.

Zoning approvals and building permits.

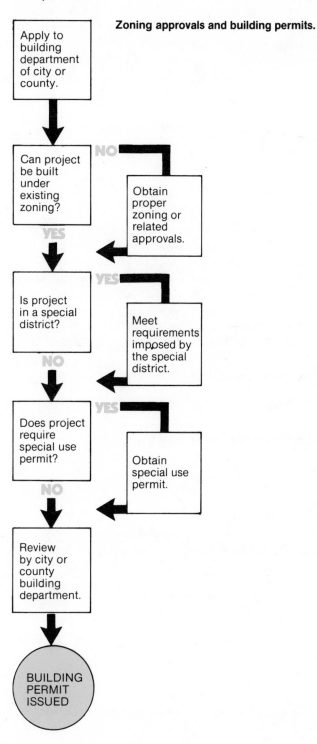

Appendix D
Case Study List

T he following arts facility construction and renovation projects were
visited by the CITYWEST team in order to gather background
information for this book. During the planning stage of your project,
additional information from relevant case study examples (those similar in
scope to your project, or located nearby) may provide specific hints of
indications of problems that may occur along the way.

Each facility is listed under the generic type that seems most
applicable to the details of the project. Location, a brief description of the
project, and a contact person are provided.

GENERIC FACILITY TYPES

Facilities Devoted Exclusively to the Arts

Single Purpose Performing Arts Facility
- May be built by a single arts organization or as a public project.

Multidisciplinary Performing Arts Facility
- Typically a civic project initiated by arts or civic groups.
- May incorporate some gallery space for visual arts exhibits.

Visual Arts Facility
- May be built as a public project or by a single organization.

Community or Neighborhood Cultural Center
- Serves local needs for visual and performing arts activities and is a focal
  point for local gatherings.

Arts Facilities Combined with Nonarts Uses

Convention or Civic Center Model
- Combines convention and/or meeting function with space for performing arts.
- Built by city or county; supported by civic funds.

Elementary/Secondary School Facility
- Space shared by school and community for meetings and arts use.
- Typically an auditorium, cafeteria or gymnasium.

College/University Facility
- Generally a theater or other cultural facility jointly used by college/university and community.

Combined Commercial/Cultural Uses (Mixed Use)
- Private developer includes cultural spaces, often by public agency mandate, within the commercial center.

Cultural Plan or Cultural District Model
- Cultural uses organized into a central area to create stimulating urban environment.
- Usually integrated with other urban uses: commercial, office, housing, or a convention complex.

Combined Social Service/Cultural Use
- Typically found in rapidly growing communities and smaller towns with limited resources.
- Combines health care, library, administrative offices, meeting rooms, and spaces for the arts.

THE CASE STUDIES

Facilities Devoted Exclusively to the Arts

Single Purpose Performing Arts Facility

Seattle, Washington: Bagley Wright Theatre at Seattle Center
(Producing Company), Seattle Repertory Theatre
Home of Seattle Repertory Theatre, 860 seat theater with proscenium stage and additional performance space seating 170.

> Marnie Andrews, Public Relations Director
> 155 Mercer Street
> Seattle, WA 98109
> (206) 447-2210

Salt Lake City, Utah: Salt Lake County Center for the Arts
New symphony hall seating 2,800, art center/gallery and renovated Capitol
Theatre, 1945 seat home of opera and dance companies. Built by county
with Bicentennial funds.
> Steven H. Horton, Director
> Fine Arts Division, Capitol Theatre
> 50 West 200 South
> Salt Lake City, Utah 84101
> (801) 521-6060

Cheyenne, Wyoming: Cheyenne Little Theater Players, Inc.
Community theater group owns two facilities, a new theater and a renovated
movie theater. One seats 260 and the other accommodates 155 for dinner
theater.
> Bill Barton, President (or Tina St. Clair, Board Member)
> P.O. Box 1086
> Cheyenne, WY 82003
> Theatre (weekdays 9-12) (307) 638-6543

Multidisciplinary Performing Arts Facility

Billings, Montana: Fox Theater
Planning group worked to save a 1500 seat historic movie theater for
presenting and sponsoring organization.
> Ian Elliot, Manager of Facility and Managing Director
> Fox Committee for the Performing Arts
> 302 N. Broadway
> Billings, MT 59101
> (406) 259-7400

Boulder, Colorado: Boulder Center for the Arts Plan
Arts bond issue for a $7.9 million complex (two renovated buildings and a
new theater) failed in 1980 for a combination of reasons. Only the Boulder
Center for the Visual Arts was upgraded.
> Marcelee Gralapp, Director (general information)
> Boulder Public Library
> P.O. Drawer H
> Boulder, CO 80306
> (303) 441-3100
> Karen Hodge (arts center information)
> Boulder Center for the Visual Arts
> 1750 13th Street
> Boulder, CO 80302
> (303) 443-2122

Colorado Springs, Colorado: Pikes Peak Center

After four unsuccessful attempts, the bond campaign for an 1800 seat theater for Colorado Springs' Symphony was successful because of good timing and a well-managed publicity campaign. (Seating capacity can be increased slightly for larger function, i.e., Broadway show.)

> Beatrice Vradenburg, Manager
> Colorado Symphony
> P.O. Box 1692
> Colorado Springs, CO 80901
> (303) 633-4611

Aurora, Colorado: Arts Center

Proposed center, including a 500 seat theater, areas for public meetings, studio arts and visual arts display, was defeated in the bond issue vote. Now planning to open the Aurora Fox Arts Center with 250 seats in 1984.

> Alice Lee Schimming
> Cultural Arts Administrator
> 13655 E. Alameda
> Aurora, CO 80012
> (303) 344-1776

Carbondale, Colorado: Performing Arts Center

Cultural center desired for town with population of 2200; insufficient performing spaces at present, but summer arts festival attracts 8000 people yearly.

> Gayla Duckowitz, Executive Director
> Carbondale Council on the Arts & Humanities
> P.O. Box 174
> Carbondale, CO 81623
> (303) 963-1680

Cheyenne, Wyoming: Cheyenne Civic Center

Performing arts theater for touring shows and local productions, constructed in 1980. Seats 1500.

> Bob Stewart, Managing Director
> 2101 O'Neil Avenue
> Cheyenne, WY 82001
> (307) 637-6364

Denver, Colorado: Denver Center for the Performing Arts

Within four square blocks the center contains a theater complex with 3 theaters and 1 cinema, concert hall, auditorium theater and 7 story parking facility. One management entity acts as umbrella for facility management and operations.

> Jan Steinhauser, Director of Public Relations
> Denver Center for Performing Arts
> 1245 Champa Street
> Denver, CO 80204
> (303) 893-4000

McMinnville, Oregon: Gallery Players Theater
Two hundred seventy-five seat theater and dance classroom for longstanding
theater group.
> Ted Desel, Chairman of Theatre Department
> Linfield College
> McMinnville, OR 97128-9989
> (503) 472-4121

Flagstaff, Arizona: Coconino Center for the Arts
Lecture hall and meeting rooms serving the city. When combined a 212 seat
amphitheater is formed.
> Hank Chaikin, Director
> Coconino Center for the Arts
> c/o Coconino County Courthouse
> N. Fort Falley Road, Highway 180
> Flagstaff, AZ 86001
> (602) 774-5011

Olympia, Washington: The Washington Center
Renovation of vaudeville theatre currently in the design-development stage.
Construction planned early 1985 with seating to be approximately 1000.
> (Mr.) Lynn Schrader, Project Coordinator
> P.O. Box 202
> Olympia, WA 98507
> (206) 753-8585

Phoenix, Arizona: Central Phoenix Theater Study Project
Extensive feasibility study for a downtown repertory theater to be called the
Herberger Theater. Funds are available but project is still in the planning
stage. No estimated date of opening yet.
> Deborah Whitehurst, Museum/Special Projects Coordinator
> Arizona Commission on the Arts
> 2024 N. 7th Street, Suite 201
> Phoenix, AZ 85006
> (602) 255-5882

Portland, Oregon: Portland Center for Performing Arts
Restoration of 2750 seat movie theater for symphony and theater and
construction of a 1400 seat new theater plus small "black box" facility.
Renovation has begun for three spaces within center: Arlene Schnitzer
Concert Hall, estimated to open fall 1984 and seating 2750; flexible theater
seating up to 900; and a showcase theater space for 450 which is to feature
local groups. The latter two spaces should open by late 1986.
> Robert Scanlan, Finance Chairman
> 1300 SW Fifth, Suite 2600
> Portland, OR 97201
> (503) 221-4845

Salem, Oregon: Elsinore Theater
A local arts group conducted a feasibility study for renovation of a 1200 seat movie theater. The bond was rejected in 1981. There is now an agreement to use the theater 18 days a year. Seating is 1340.

> Bob Stevens, Board Member
> 461 High Street
> Salem, OR 97301
> (503) 399-5519

Oakley, Idaho: Howells Opera House
A "road show" theater undergoing slow process of renovation by local arts council in this small town. When completed in 1985, seating will be 350.

> Kent Severe, President
> Oakley Valley Arts Council
> P.O. Box 176
> Oakley, ID 83346
> (208) 678-2242

Santa Fe, New Mexico: Armory for the Arts
Old National Guard armory renovated in several stages for visual and performing arts. The 350 seat theater houses the Santa Fe Festival Theatre each summer and other events during the year.

> Ian Rosenkranz, Director
> 1050 Old Pecos Trail
> Santa Fe, NM 87501
> (505) 988-1886

Tacoma, Washington: Pantages Theater
Vaudeville/movie house seating 1174, renovated in 1981 for the local and touring symphony, opera and theater.

> Sue Saltmarsh, Assistant Manager
> 901 Broadway
> Tacoma, WA 98402
> (206) 591-5890

Yakima, Washington: The Capitol Theatre
Fire-damaged vaudeville/movie house renovated into a 1527 seat theater presenting primarily touring events.

> Eli Ashley
> P.O. Box 102
> Yakima, WA 98907
> (509) 575-6267

Visual Arts Facility

Aspen , Colorado: Aspen Center for the Visual Arts

Visual arts facility in renovated historic building.
> Laurel H. Jones, Director
> 590 N. Mill Street
> Aspen, CO 81611
> (303) 925-8050

Billings, Montana: Yellowstone Arts Center

Important western art center moved into the old city jail ten years ago.
> Donna Forbes, Director
> 401 N. 27th Street
> Billings, MT 59101
> (406) 259-1869

Mesa, Arizona: Museum for Youth

Currently occupying temporary site near future location under renovation in order to build a base of support. Estimated opening 1984.
> Barbara Meyerson, Director
> Bonnie Lewis, Director of Education
> P.O. Box 77
> Mesa, AZ 85201
> (602) 967-3757

Miles City, Montana: Custer County Art Center

Old city waterworks converted to visual arts center with galleries and studio spaces.
> Julia Cook, Executive Director
> P.O. Box 1284
> Miles City, MT 59301
> (406) 232-0635

Park City, Utah: Kimball Art Center

Excellent renovation of garage, primarily for visual arts exhibits and workshops.
> Alan Seko, Director of Public Relations and Education
> P.O. Box 1478
> Park City, UT 84060
> (801) 649-8882

Seattle, Washington: Daybreak Star Art Center

Traditional and contemporary Indian art gallery combined with a community center which can seat 250.
> Bernie Whitebear, Director
> United Indians of All Tribes Foundation
> P.O. Box 99253
> Seattle, WA 98199
> (206) 285-4425

Portland, Oregon: Portland Center for the Visual Arts

Alternative gallery space with sophisticated contemporary exhibitions and active lecture/event program.

> Donna Milrany, Executive Director
> 117 NW Fifth Avenue
> Portland, OR 97209
> (503) 222-7107

Portland, Oregon: Oregon School of Arts and Crafts

Four buildings on former orchard property house extensive class, sales and exhibition space.

> Mary Greeley, Interim Director
> 8245 SW Barnes Road
> Portland, OR 97225
> (503) 297-5544

Elko, Nevada: Northeastern Nevada Museum

Regional museum for arts, science and history. New addition includes gallery and small 100 seat theater.

> Howard Hickson, Director
> P.O. Box 2250
> Elko, NV 89801
> (702) 738-3418

Seattle, Washington: and/or

Multidisciplinary, avant-garde art center with library, music and video departments. Also houses 175 seat performance hall and 100 seat lecture hall.

> Anne Focke, Director
> 915 E. Pine, Room 420
> Seattle, WA 98122
> (206) 324-5869

Community or Neighborhood Cultural Center

Roseburg, Oregon: Umpqua Valley Arts Center

Former veterans' hospital leased by city to local art association. Exhibits and studio art classes.

> Douglas Beauchamp, Director
> P.O. Box 1542
> Roseburg, OR 97470
> (503) 672-2532

Salem, Oregon: Bush Barn Art Center

Barn converted into a visual arts center located in a city park.

> Doris Helen Nelson, Executive Director
> 600 Mission Street, SE
> Salem, OR 97302
> (503) 581-0100

Arvada, Colorado: Arvada Center for the Arts and Humanities

Community performing and visual art center owned by city and run by separate city agency. Theater seats 502 (including 2 wheelchair spaces).

> Frank Jacobsen, Executive Director
> 6901 Wadsworth Blvd.
> Arvada, CO 80003
> (303) 431-3080

Preston, Idaho: Oneida State Academy

A former academy saved from demolition and partially restored. Serves as a community art center seating 250.

> Scott Beckstead, Secretary of the Board
> Friends of the Academy
> 30 East First South
> Preston, ID 83263
> (208) 852-2527

Ogden, Utah: Union Station

Railroad station renovated for use as community arts center. Rooms are used for community performing arts productions, local gatherings and a collection of guns and cars.

> Mrs. Kenneth (Teddy) Griffith, Director
> 2501 Wall Avenue
> Ogden, UT 84401
> (801) 399-8582

Arts Facility Combined With Nonarts Use

Convention or Civic Center Model

Casper, Wyoming: Casper Event Center

Large arena seating 10,000 now open. Plans for incorporating performing arts facilities.

> Jim Walczak, Director
> Box 140
> Casper, WY 82602
> (307) 577-0967

Elko, Nevada: Elko Convention and Visitor's Authority

Facility combines a 923 seat theater for local theatrical productions with convention facilities.

> Mary Jean Buffington, Director of Sales and Marketing
> 700 Festival Way
> Elko, NV 89801
> (702) 738-4091

Eugene, Oregon: The Hult Center for the Performing Arts
Completed in 1982, the Center contains a large hall seating 2450, a 500 seat
theater, a two story convention center and a parking structure.
>Richard C. Reynolds, Executive Director
>One Eugene Center
>Eugene, OR 97401
>(503) 687-5087

Farmington, New Mexico: Farmington Civic Center
Combines 1200 seat performing arts space with convention exhibit halls and
community meeting needs.
>Paul Abe, Director
>P.O. Box 900
>Farmington, NM 87499
>(505) 327-7701

Scottsdale, Arizona: Scottsdale Center for the Arts
City owned center with galleries, convention spaces, 882 seat theater and
165 seat cinema.
>Ronald F. Caya, Director
>7383 Scottsdale Mall
>Scottsdale, AZ 85251
>(602) 994-2301

Mesa, Arizona: Centennial Hall and Amphitheater
Cultural complex includes convention facility with performing arts spaces.
Centennial Hall seats 1890 and an outdoor amphitheater has space for 3800.
>Jack Cummins, Director
>P.O. Box 1466
>Mesa, AZ 85201-0904
>(602) 834-2178

Vancouver, Washington: Performing Arts and Convention Center Study
Many feasibility studies done for major downtown convention project
planned with two theaters and visual arts facility.
>Eric Hovee, Economic Development Manager
>City of Vancouver
>P.O. Box 1995
>Vancouver, WA 98668
>(206) 696-8216

Elementary/Secondary School Facility

Hardin, Montana: Hardin Junior High School
Performing arts facility used jointly by school and community with seating
for 700.
>Gary Fulkee
>700 Terry Avenue
>Hardin, MT 59034
>(406) 665-1408

Longmont, Colorado: Vance Brand Auditorium
Cooperation between the city and school district led to the creation of a
finely-designed 1459 seat auditorium to accommodate touring groups.
> Joanna Ramsey, Manager
> 600 E. Mountain View
> Longmont, CO 80501
> (303) 651-0123

Joseph City, Arizona: Joseph City Schools Auditorium
High school performing arts facility, seats 650.
> Dr. Joseph Ball
> Superintendent of Schools
> P.O. Box 8
> Joseph City, AZ 86032
> (602) 288-3307

College/University Facility

Boise, Idaho: Morrison Center for the Performing Arts
A 2030 seat multipurpose auditorium. Will open February 1984. To be used
jointly by university and community.
> Frank Heise, Director of Operations
> Morrison Center, Boise State University
> 1910 University Drive
> Boise, ID 83725
> (208) 385-1609

Prescott, Arizona: Yavapai County Cultural Needs and Resources Study
Planning study to determine county arts plan and need for a new theater.
> Elizabeth Ruffner, Chair
> Planning Committee
> 1403 Baranca Drive
> Prescott, AZ 86301
> (602) 445-5644

Tempe, Arizona: Gammage Center for the Performing Arts
Excellent performing arts facility, part of university yet also serving local
community.
> Miriam Boegel, Assistant Vice President
> ASU Public Events
> Gammage Center, Room 105
> Arizona State University
> Tempe, AZ 85287
> (602) 965-3445

Tsaile, Arizona: Ned A. Hatathli Center Museum at Navajo Community College

Museum collects and preserves cultural artifacts of Native American origin.

> Janice Hillis, Director
> Ned A. Hatathli Center Museum
> Navajo Community College
> Tsaile, AZ 86556
> (602) 724-3311, Ext. 156

Combined Commercial/Cultural Uses (Mixed Use)

Bellevue, Washington: Bellevue Art Museum

Original facility was razed to make way for a shopping center. The museum moved into third floor of new shopping center. Reduced rental granted in return for offering cultural "plus" to mixed use development. First museum in U.S. to locate above shopping mall arcade.

> John Olbrantz, Director
> 301 Bellevue Square
> Bellevue, WA 98004
> (206) 454-3322

Evanston, Wyoming: Human Services Complex

Arts center to be incorporated along with health care, recreation center, senior center, library.

> George Ives
> 350 Vinta View Drive, Suite 201
> Evanston, WY 82930
> (307) 789-7194

Reno, Nevada: Sierra Arts Center

The Sierra Arts Foundation has been acting as a developer of its own visual and performing arts center since 1979. Lease payments from an office building located on SAF property will be used as a building endowment for the arts center construction. This is being done in concert with Reno's center city redevelopment plans which include new retail shops, street improvements, parking garage, and a new Harrah's auto museum.

> Carol Mousel, Executive Director
> Sierra Arts Foundation
> P.O. Box 2814
> Reno, NV 89505
> (702) 329-1324

San Francisco, California: Yerba Buena Center
Joint use mandated in land disposition agreement between city and
developer. Cultural component to be integrated into retail and office use.
Intensive artist and community involvement in the planning process for
development of the 50,000 square foot cultural center. Proposed opening
1985.

> Mrs. Cathy Pickering, Senior Administrative Assistant
> Yerba Buena Center Project
> 939 Ellis
> San Francisco, CA 94109
> (415) 771-8800, Ext. 280

Los Angeles, California: Museum of Contemporary Art
Community Redevelopment Agency project in Bunker Hill area (six million
square feet) includes provision for construction of an art museum, with
capital funding to come from the developer.

> Sherri Gelding, Administrator
> 414 Boyd Street
> Los Angeles, CA 90013
> (213) 621-2766

San Luis, Colorado: San Luis Museum Cultural and Commercial Center
Retail/cultural uses (theater, library and offices) within low income rural area.

> Juanita Gurlue, Director
> P.O. Box 619
> San Luis, CO 81152
> (303) 672-3611

Seattle, Washington: Seattle Art Museum
Key parcel of downtown land jointly developed by city, developer and
museum. The city agreed to acquire property, relocate businesses, build
parking garages and deal with utility and traffic issues. The developer
acquired air rights from the city for rental space and would share the cost of
public circulation systems and site work. The museum also will lease air
rights from the city for relocation and expansion of its operations. Project
stalled due to problems in working out compromises among the three
parties. Negotiations will continue at least through 1984.

> Arnold Jolles, Director
> Seattle Art Museum
> Volunteer Park
> Seattle, WA 98112
> (206) 447-4787

Cultural Plan or Cultural District Model

Missoula, Montana: Riverfront Corridor Study and Design Competition

A small town pooled its resources—university, commercial real estate interests and the arts community—and developed a plan for revitalizing the riverfront, incorporating arts facilities, open space and other projects. Not yet feasible but cooperation continues.

> William Coffee, Chairman
> City Spirit Facilities Committee
> 115 W. Front Street
> Missoula, MT 59802
> (406) 542-2744

Los Angeles, California: American Film Institute

Group received bank loans and grants from two foundations to buy vacant campus with three buildings on 8.6 acres. Warner Communications Building has gallery space and Mark Goodson Theater seats 135. Plans are underway to build an additional 400 seat theater.

> Emily Robertson, Campus Facilities Coordinator
> 2021 N. Western Avenue
> Los Angeles, CA 90027
> (213) 856-7622

Combined Social Services/Cultural Use

Wright, Wyoming: Latigo Hills Mall

New construction with community room, library and 120 seat auditorium in ARCO company town.

> Walt Wierzbick, Coordinator for Commercial Properties
> P.O. Box 574
> Wright, WY 82732
> (307) 464-0049

San Ildefonso, New Mexico: Pueblo Museum

Small tribal museum built six years ago with EDA money; serves 400 member tribe.

> Gary Roybal, Museum Director
> San Ildefonso Pueblo
> Rt. 5 Box 315-A
> Santa Fe, NM 87501
> (505) 455-2424

Seattle, Washington: Good Shepherd Center

Former girls' home purchased and managed by Historical Seattle; houses arts and social service groups providing classes and offices.

> Steve Ruden, Manager
> 4649 Sunnyside North
> Seattle, WA 98103
> (206) 632-5281

Appendix E
Technical Assistance
& Consultant Resources

Arts Agencies

Your State Arts Agency
Each state has an arts agency with offices at the state capital. This valuable resource is staffed with people with expertise in a wide variety of areas. When you call, ask to speak to the staff person responsible for community arts development.

Your Regional Arts Organization
Regional organizations are associations of state arts agencies in the same geographic area. These organizations undertake and coordinate activities that the individual states cannot tackle, such as performing and visual touring programs, workshops, conferences, publications and special projects.

Affiliated State Arts Agencies of the Upper Midwest
528 Hennepin Avenue, Suite 302
Minneapolis, Minnesota 55403
(612) 341-0755
Serves MI, IA, ND, SD, WI

Consortium for Pacific Arts and Cultures
P.O. Box 50225
Honolulu, Hawaii 96850
(808) 524-7120
Serves Guam, American Samoa and the Northern Marianas Islands

Great Lakes Arts Alliance
11424 Bellflower Road
Cleveland, Ohio 44106
(216) 229-1098
Serves IL, IN, MI, OH

Mid-America Arts Alliance
20 West Ninth Street, Suite 550
Kansas City, Missouri 64105
(816) 421-1388
Serves AR, KS, NB, OK, MO (TX is an associate member)

Mid-Atlantic States Arts Consortium
11 East Chase Street, Suite 7-B
Baltimore, Maryland 21202
(301) 685-1400
Serves DE, DC, MD, NJ, NY, PA, VA, WV

New England Foundation for the Arts
25 Mount Auburn Street
Cambridge, Massachusetts 02138
(617) 492-2914
Serves MA, CT, NH, VT, ME, RI

Southern Arts Federation
1401 Peachtree Street, NE, Suite 122
Atlanta, Georgia 30309
(404) 874-7244
Serves AL, FL, GA, TN, NC, SC, MS, KY, LA

Western States Arts Foundation
141 East Palace Avenue
Santa Fe, New Mexico 87501
(505) 988-1166
Serves AZ, CO, ID, MT, NV, NM, OR, UT, WA, WY

National Endowment for the Arts
1100 Pennsylvania NW
Washington, D.C. 20506
(202) 682-5400 (Information Office)

The federal agency's support includes grants, information and technical services. Contact NEA for the name of the Regional Representative in your area for assistance in identifying the appropriate program for your organizational needs. The representative will provide information and assistance at no charge to individuals, arts organizations and other interested people.

Several NEA programs are of specific interest to the facility planning committee:

Design Arts Program promotes excellence in the design fields through technical assistance, grants and publications. The Design Arts Program funds feasibility studies, design competitions and design research.

Visual Arts Program promotes "art in public places" and the integration of the visual arts into building design.

Museum Program provides assistance to existing museums in the forms of grants to hire visiting specialists.

Other Arts Agencies

Advisory Council on Historic Preservation
1100 Pennsylvania Avenue, NW
The Old Post Office Building, Room 809
Washington, D.C. 20004
(202) 786-0503
Information, publications and advisory services.

Affiliate Artists Inc.
155 West 68th Street
New York, New York 10023
(212) 580-2000
A nonprofit organization organizing with corporate sponsors, artists residencies for communities.

American Arts Alliance
424 C Street, NE
Washington, D.C. 20002
(202) 544-3900
Nonprofit organization of national arts service organizations with aim of monitoring and influencing governmental actions impacting on the arts.

American Association of Museums (AAM)
1055 Thomas Jefferson Street, NW, Suite 428
Washington, D.C. 20007
(202) 338-5300
Membership organization represents the museum on a national level. Principal programs: museum accreditation, annual meeting, publications, training programs.

American Council for the Arts
570 Seventh Avenue
New York, New York 10018
(212) 354-6655
National organization that serves all art forms by addressing needs that cut across all disciplines, and serves as an advocate for all the arts nationally. Principal programs: conferences, technical assistance, publications and advocacy.

American Symphony Orchestra League
633 E Street, NW
Washington, D.C. 20004
(202) 628-0099
Represents the interests and need of American symphony orchestras; assists in the development of new symphony orchestras. Principal programs: conferences, publications, consultancies.

The Art Museum Association of America
(formerly the Western Association of Art Museums)
270 Sutter Street
San Francisco, California 94108
(415) 392-9222
Only national organization devoted to needs of art museums and visual art centers. Services include publications, an extensive touring program and consultant referral services.

Arts and Business Council
130 East 40 Street
New York, New York 10016
(212) 683-5555
Nonprofit organization serves as a liaison between the arts and business. Principal programs: corporate volunteer consultancies, seminars, publications.

Arts and Special Constituencies Project
1419 27th Street, NW
Washington, D.C. 20007
(202) 965-3306
National center for information on architectural and programmatic accessibility to the arts for the handicapped.

Association of Artist-Run Galleries
152 Wooster Street
New York, New York 10012
(212) 226-3107
Clearinghouse for information on starting a gallery, exhibitions and festivals.

Association of Hispanic Arts
200 East 87 Street
New York, New York 10028
(212) 369-7054
Nonprofit organization disseminates information on Hispanic arts activities and provides Hispanic arts groups with technical assistance.

Business Committee for the Arts
1775 Broadway, Suite 510
New York, New York 10019
(212) 664-0600
Encourages corporate support and involvement in the arts through counseling of corporations and arts organizations, conferences, and publications.

Canadian Museums Association
280 Metcalfe, Suite 202
Ottawa, Ontario, Canada K2P 1R7
(613) 223-5653
Book sales list with more than 300 titles, bibliography of more than 10,000 items and correspondence courses.

Center for Arts Information
625 Broadway
New York, New York 10012
(212) 677-7548
Serves as a clearing house for information on the arts. Reference services and publications.

Clearinghouse for Technical Assistance
294 Washington Street, Suite 501
Boston, Massachusetts 02108
(617) 426-2606
Provides information on publications and services.

Educational Facilities Laboratories/Academy for Educational Development
680 Fifth Avenue
New York, New York 10019
(212) 397-0040
Established to guide and encourage constructive change in education and other "people-serving" institutions. Conducts research, provides public services and disseminates information.

The Foundation Center
888 Seventh Avenue
New York, New York 10019
(800) 424-9836 (toll free)
(212) 975-1120
National service organization providing coordinated information on foundation giving with eighty libraries nationwide participating. Principal programs: free library service, computer services, training sessions, publications.

Foundation for the Extension and Developmet of the American Professional Theatre (FEDAPT)
165 West 46 Street
New York, New York 10036
(212) 869-9690
Nonprofit organization interested in the development of managerial capabilities of staff in professionally oriented theater and dance companies. Services include training sessions, management consultancies and publications.

The Grantsmanship Center
1031 S. Grand Avenue
Los Angeles, California 90015
(213) 749-4721
Nonprofit educational institution assisting nonprofit groups and governmental organizations with information on grants. Services include newsletter, publications and workshops.

Museums Collaborative
15 Grammercy Park South
New York, New York 10003
(212) 674-0030
Nonprofit organization encouraging the joint use of resources by museums, zoos, botanical gardens, and historical societies. Contact for information on publications and services.

National Assembly of Local Arts Agencies
1785 Massachusetts Avenue, 7 NW, Suite 413
Washington, D.C. 20036
(202) 483-8670
Publishes *Technical Assistance: A Guide for Local Arts Agencies* (1980, 48 pp., $5.00), an excellent resource book.

National Assembly of State Arts Agencies (NASAA)
1010 Vermont Avenue, NW
Washington, D.C. 20005
(202) 347-6352
Membership organization represents the needs of state arts agencies providing a forum and information clearinghouse.

National Trust for Historic Preservation
1785 Massachusetts Avenue, NW
Washington, D.C. 20036
(202) 673-4000
Office consultation and professional advice on preservation problems; file of preservation consultants; grants and loans; publications.

Opera America
633 E Street, NW
Washington, D.C. 20004
(202) 347-9262
Opera company membership organization assists in developing resident professional opera companies and in the improvement of the quality of operatic presentations. Principal programs: management training seminars, community education workshops, consultancies, publications.

Opportunity Resources for the Arts
1501 Broadway
New York, New York 10036
(212) 575-1688
Nonprofit organization acting as a placement service for arts organizations seeking professional personnel. Contact for advice on conducting a personnel search.

Partners for Livable Places
1429 21st Street, NW
Washington, D.C. 20036
(202) 887-5990
A nonprofit coalition of organizations, municipalities, corporations and individuals dedicated to improving the quality of life in the nation's communities. Services include handbooks, technical assistance, workshops and conferences.

Public Interest Public Relations
225 West 34th, Suite 1500
New York, New York 10001
(212) 736-5050
Provides nonprofit public interest and cultural organizations with counseling and skills in public relations and programs in support of fundraising efforts.

Publishing Center for Cultural Resources
625 Broadway
New York, New York 10012
(212) 260-2010
Assists nonprofit cultural and educational organizations in achieving well-planned, economical publications through production assistance consultancies.

TAG Foundation Ltd.
(Technical Assistance Group)
200 Park Avenue South
New York, New York 10003
(212) 777-8210
Nonprofit organization provides for performing arts groups a full range of technical and management services.

Theatre Communications Group
355 Lexington Avenue
New York, New York 10017
(212) 697-5230
National organization of member theaters serves as communications network for the profession. Principal programs: seminars and workshops, audience development consultancies, member information services, publications.

Theatre Development Fund
1501 Broadway
New York, New York 10036
(212) 221-0885
Nonprofit organization working to expand the audience for nonprofit and commercial theater, music, and dance. Provides advice and assistance for audience development and marketing.

Trust for Public Land
82 Second Street
San Francisco, California 94105
(415) 495-4014
Provides information and training to nonprofit groups seeking to acquire and preserve land for public use.

United Nations Educational, Scientific and Cultural Organization (UNESCO)
UNIPUB (UNESCO Publications Center)
205 E. 42nd Street
New York, New York 10017
(212) 916-1650
International selection of publications on museums.

Urban Land Institute
1090 Vermont Avenue, NW, Suite 300
Washington, D.C. 20005
(202) 289-8500
Encourages effective land use planning and development through educational seminars and publications.

Volunteer Lawyers for the Arts
1560 Broadway, Suite 711
New York, New York 10036
(212) 575-1150
With national offices in New York City and regional offices throughout the country, provides legal service through volunteer lawyers to artists and nonprofit organizations. Principal programs: legal assistance, workshops, publications, legislative research and consultation.

VOLUNTEER: The National Center for Citizen Involvement
1111 N. 19th Street, Suite 500
Arlington, VA 22209
(703) 276-0542
Resource center dedicated to citizen volunteer efforts, offers a wide range of expertise in volunteer management and citizen involvement.

The following organizations provide touring visual arts exhibitions. Information on requirements and fees is available on request. There are also corporate, regional association, and state traveling exhibitions. For information on these, contact your state arts council.

American Federation of Arts
41 East 65th Street
New York, New York 10021
(212) 988-7700

American Institute of Graphic Arts
1059 Third Avenue
New York, New York 10021
(212) 752-0813

The Art Museum Association of America
(formerly the Western Association of Art Museums)
270 Sutter Street
San Francisco, California 94108
(415) 392-9222

Museum of Modern Art
c/o Richard Palmer, Exhibitions Program
11 West 53rd Street
New York, New York 10019
(212) 708-9656

Extension Service (for films and slides)
National Gallery of Art
Washington, D.C. 20506
(202) 842-6263

Smithsonian Institution Traveling Exhibition Service
The Arts and Industry Building, Room 2170
Washington, D.C. 20560
(202) 357-3168

Professional Organizations

Acoustical Society of America
335 East 45th Street
New York, New York 10017
(212) 661-9404, Ext. 564
Professional organization, membership directly available.

Actors' Equity Association
165 West 46th
New York, New York 10036
(212) 869-8530
Labor union for professional stage actors and stage managers. Regional offices in Chicago, Los Angeles and San Francisco.

American Association of Fund-Raising Counsel, Inc.
25 W. 43rd Street
New York, New York 10036
(212) 354-5799
Membership organization provides information and referrals.

American Institute of Architects
1735 New York Avenue, NW
Washington, D.C. 20006
(202) 626-7300
National professional organization with 250 chapters and state organizations. Publications, design assistance teams.

American Institute of Graphic Arts
1059 3rd Avenue
New York, New York 10021
(212) 752-0813
National professional organizations with some local and state chapters; publications and a yearly graphic design annual.

American Planning Association
1776 Massachusetts Avenue, NW
Washington, D.C. 20036
(202) 872-0611
National professional organization provides publications and technical assistance.

American Society of Interior Designers
1430 Broadway, 22nd Floor
New York, New York 10018
(212) 944-9220
National professional organization provides publications and membership mailing lists.

American Society of Landscape Architects
1753 Connecticut Avenue, NW
Washington, D.C. 20009
(202) 466-7730
National professional organization with state chapters provides publications
and referral service.

American Theatre Association
1010 Wisconsin Avenue, NW, Suite 630
Washington, D.C. 20007
(202) 342-7530
Nonprofit membership association comprised of individuals and
organizations affiliated with noncommercial theater.

Artists' Equity Association
1725 K Street, NW, Suite 1003
Washington, D.C. 20006
(202) 628-9633
National advocacy organization for visual artists. Referrals and publication.

Association of College, University and Community
Arts Administrators (ACUCAA)
6225 University Avenue
Madison, WI 53705
(608) 233-7400
Membership organization, assists and coordinates the efforts of college,
university, and community personnel responsible for the presentation of
cultural events. Principal programs: seminars, publications, employment
referral.

International Association of Auditorium Managers
500 North Michigan Avenue, Suite 1400
Chicago, Illinois 60611
(312) 661-1700
Provides information on consultants; publications include the monthly
Auditorium News; Directory, published annually; and *Industry Profile Survey,*
a reference guide to descriptions and statistics on public assembly facilities.

League of Historic American Theatre, Inc.
c/o The National Theatre
1312 E. Street, NW
Washington, D.C. 20004
(202) 289-1494
Membership organization providing publications and consultant referrals.

League of Resident Theatres (LORT)
1984 address — changes annually:
c/o Peter Culman
Artistic Director of Center Stage
700 N. Calvert Street
Baltimore, Maryland 21202
(301) 685-3200
Membership organization of regional theater administrative directors.

U.S. Institute for Theatre Technology
330 West 42nd Street, #1702
New York, New York 10036
(212) 563-5551
Provides publications on theater administration, architecture, engineering and performing arts legislation. *Theatre Design & Technology,* published quarterly. Consultant recommendations.

Further Reading

Please consider the prices listed in this bibliography as approximate. These costs fluctuate continually.

GENERAL OVERVIEW: BUILDINGS FOR THE ARTS AND THE FACILITY DEVELOPMENT PLANNING PROCESS

Arnott, Brian. *A Facility Development Workbook: A Planning Guide for the Development of Buildings to Accommodate Non-profit Arts Activities.* Ontario Ministry of Culture and Recreation (Queens Park, Toronto, Ontario M7A2R9, Canada), 1978. 30 pp. (FREE)

Arnott, Brian. *A Facility Design Workbook: A Guide to The Design Process for Arts Facilities.* Ontario Ministry of Culture and Recreation. (in progress) Educational Facilities Laboratories/Council of Educational Facilities.

Educational Facilities Laboratories/Council of Educational Facilities. *Community Planning Assistance Kit.* Columbus, Ohio. C.E.F.P., 1980. Available from C.E.F.P., 29 West Woodruff, Columbus, Ohio 43210. A set of charts, booklets and planning assistance materials intended to help community groups plan together for all types of community services. *New Places for the Arts: A Scrapbook.* 1976. 76 pp. ($5.00) *New Places for the Arts: Book Two.* 1978. 57 pp. ($3.00) New York: Educational Facilities Laboratories. (680 Fifth Avenue, New York, New York, 10019). Catalogs of facilities built in the 1970's. Includes photographs, statistics, costs and consultants employed.

Golden, Joseph. *Olympus on Main Street: A Process for Planning a Community Arts Facility.* Syracuse, New York. Syracuse University Press, 1980. 220 pp. ($9.95) Based on personal experience of author, book covers initial planning, feasibility, design programming and management.

Mayer, Martin. *Bricks, Mortar and the Performing Arts.* Report of the Twentieth Century Fund Task Force on Performing Arts Centers. New York. The Twentieth Century Fund, 1970. 99 pp. ($7.00) Early guide to performing arts facility development process. Discusses motives, facility types and building costs.

National Endowment for the Arts Grant Recognition Program. *Design Arts 2: Places and Spaces for the Arts.* New York. Municipal Art Society of New York, 1981. 112 pp.

Stewart, H. Michael. *American Architecture for the Arts.* Dallas. Handel & Sons Publishing, Inc., 1978. 233 pp. 160 photographs of arts centers and theaters built or restored in the last twenty five years. Data on architects, building statistics, costs, funding sources and contact persons.

Young, Edgar B. *Lincoln Center: The Building of an Institution.* New York. New York University Press, 1980. 334 pp. ($24.95) Good overview of Center's development from 1955-1970; early planning, design and construction, and capital financing are covered.

Architectural Record. Published monthly by McGraw-Hill. Offices at 1221 Avenue of the Americas, New York, New York 10020.
Progressive Architecture. Published monthly by Reinhold Publishing. Offices at P.O. Box 95759, Cleveland, Ohio 44101. Over the years, virtually every significant arts facility built in the United States has been documented in these magazines. The·magazines are generally found in large libraries. Consult the *Art Index* for citations.

THE PERFORMING ARTS FACILITY

References for Developing Design Standards

Alberta Culture Facility Development Branch. *The Theatre Handbook: An Introduction to Planning and Design of Performing Arts Facilities.* Edmonton: Alberta Culture (Facility Development Branch, 12th floor, CN Tower, 10004 104 Avenue, Edmonton T5J0K5) 1979. 120 pp. (FREE) An excellent handbook. Presents design guidelines for performing arts facilities.

American Theatre Planning Board. *Theatre Check List: A Guide to the Planning and Construction of Proscenium and Open Stage Theatres.* Middletown, CT: Wesleyan University Press, 1969. 71 pp. (out of print)

Armstrong, Leslie and Morgan, Roger. *Space for Dance: An Architectural Guide for Dance and Performing Arts Facilities.* Commissioned by the Design Arts Program and the Dance Program of the National Endowment for the Arts. Available through the National Endowment for the Arts, Design Arts Program. (in progress)

Arts and Special Constituencies Project. *504 and the Performing Arts.* 1979. 31 pp. (FREE) Describes 1973 federal legislation requiring that facilities and programs be accessible to the handicapped. Available from Special Constituencies Project, 1419 27th Street, NW, Washington, D.C. 20007.

Association of British Theatre Technicians. Roderick Ham, editor. *Theatre Planning.* Toronto. University of Toronto Press, 1972. 292 pp. A handbook for architects and other building professionals.

Burris-Meyer, Harold and Cole, Edward C. *Theatres and Auditoriums.* 2nd edition. Huntington, New York. Robert E. Krieger Publishing Company, 1975. 470 pp. ($38.50)

Department of the Army. *Design Guide for Music and Drama Centers* (DG 1110.3.120). Issues by Engineering Division, Military Programs Directorate, Office of the Chief of Engineers, U.S. Army; 1982. Excellent resource. Consultants for the project: Hardy Holzman Pfeiffer Associates; Jules Fisher & Paul Marantz, Inc.; Jaffe Acoustics, Inc. Limited number of copies available from the OCE Publications Depot, 890 Pickett Street, Alexandria, Virginia 22304.

Egan, M. David. *Concepts in Architectural Acoustics.* New York. McGraw-Hill, 1972 ($28.95)

Izenour, George C. *Theatre Design.* New York. McGraw-Hill, 1977. 631 pp. ($195.00)

Joseph, Stephen, editor. *Actor and Architect.* Manchester. University of Manchester,1964. Important comments by Tyrone Guthrie and others on owner/architect relationships.

Other References
Foundation for the Extension and Development of the American Professional Theatre. *Investigation Guidelines for Setting Up a Not-for-Profit Tax-Exempt Regional Theatre,* New York. Foundation for the Extension and Development of the American Professional Theatre, 1979. ($15.00)

THE VISUAL ARTS FACILITY

References for Developing Design Standards
Arts and Special Constituencies Project. *504 and the Visual Arts.* 1979. 31 pp. (FREE) Describes 1973 federal legislation requiring that facilities and programs be accessible to the handicapped. Available from Special Constituencies Project, 1419 27th Street, NW, Washington, D.C. 20007.

Brawne, Michael. *The Museum Interior: Temporary & Permanent Display Techniques.* New York. Architectural Book Publishing Company, 1982. 159 pp. ($33.95) A useful handbook on interior elements with 330 illustrations.

Department of the Army. *Design Guide Arts and Crafts Centers.* (DG 1110-3-124). Issued by Engineering Division, Military Construction Directorate, Office of the Chief of Engineers, Department of the Army; August 1976. 65 pp. Limited number of copies available from OCE Publications Depot, 890 South Pickett Street, Alexandria, Virginia 22304. One of the only books to cover detailed design guidelines for studio art spaces.

Harrison, Raymond O. *The Technical Requirements of Small Museums.* Ottawa: Canadian Museums Association, 1977. 27 pp.

Hilberry, John. *Museum Facilities Design Checklist: A Convenient Guide for the Museum Professional.* 1980. 14 pp. (pamphlet). *Museum Storage Design Checklist: An Outline Guide for the Museum Professional.* 1981. 21 pp. (pamphlet) Can be ordered from John Hilberry & Associates, Inc., 1455 Centre Street, Detroit, Michigan 48226.

Illuminating Engineering Society. *Lighting of Art Galleries and Museums.* Technical Report, No. 14. London. Illuminating Engineering Society, 1970.

Levy, Howard and Roso-Molloy, Lynn. *Beginning a Community Museum.* New York. New York Foundation for the Arts and the New York State Council on the Arts, 1975. 84 pp. ($3.00) Available from Publishing Center for Cultural Resources, 625 Broadway, New York, New York 10012. Guidelines for starting a small museum with a limited budget and staff.

Lewis, Ralph H. *Manual for Museums.* Washington, D.C. National Park Service, 1976. 412 pp. ($6.50) (U.S. Printing Office Stock No. 024-005-00643-5). Technical information for all types of museums on the care of museum collections, the preparation of museum records, exhibit maintenance.

Royal Ontario Museum, Communications Design Team. *Communicating with the Museum Visitor: Guidelines for Planning.* Toronto. Royal Ontario Museum, 1976. 518 pp. ($65.00, non-members) Available from Canadian Museums Association Booksale Programme, 331 Copper Street, Suite 400, Ottawa, Ontario K2P0G5. Excellent, one of a kind publication. Mandatory reading for planning an exhibition facility.

In Search of the Black Box: A Report on the Proceedings of a Workshop on Micro-Climates Held at the Royal Ontario Museum, February, 1978. Toronto, Ontario. ROM, 1979. 99 pp. ($16.00) Available from Canadian Museums Association. Detailed information describing the design of light and humidity/temperature systems in a large museum. Excellent bibliography.

Tillotson, Robert G.; Menkes, Diana D., editors. *Museum Security/La Securite dans les Musees.* Paris. International Council on Museums with American Association of Museums, 1977. 256 pp. ($15.00) Available from American Association of Museums, 1055 Thomas Jefferson Street, NE, Washington, D.C. 20007.

White, Ken. *Bookstore Planning & Design*. New York. McGraw-Hill, 1982. 181 pp. ($39.50).

Witteborg, Lothar. *Good Show! A Practical Guide for Temporary Exhibitions*. Washington. Smithsonian Institution, 1981. 169 pp. ($17.50) Available from Smithsonian Institution Press, P.O. Box 1759, Washington, D.C. 20560. Mandatory reading for any group planning for a visual arts facility. Chapters on advance planning of your space for an exhibit, preparation, installing the exhibit, security and resources.

Other References

American Association of Museums. *Museums: Their New Audience*. Washington, D.C. AAM, 1972. ($.75)

Professional Standards for Museum Accreditation: The Handbook of the Accreditation Program of the American Association of Museums, 1978. 79 pp. ($6.50) AAM, 1055 Thomas Jefferson Street, NE, Suite 428, Washington, D.C. 20007.

Brawne, Michael. *The New Museum*. New York. Praeger Publishers, 1965. (out of print)

Council on Museums and Education in the Visual Arts. *The Art Museum as Educator: A Collection of Studies as Guides to Practice and Policy*. Berkeley. University of California Press, 1978.

Educational Facilities Laboratories. *Hands-On Museums: Partners in Learning*. New York. EFL, 1976.

Hendon, William S. *Analyzing an Art Museum*. New York. Praeger Publishers, 1979. 263 pp. ($27.95) Careful and thorough analysis of an existing museum's programming and operations, useful in understanding how a museum works.

Hudson, Kenneth. *Museums for the 1980's: A Survey of World Trends*. Prepared for UNESCO, Paris. London. Macmillan, 1977. For information contact UNESCO Publications Center, 801 Third Avenue, New York, New York 10022.

Searing, Helen. *New Art Museums in America*. New York. Whitney Museum of American Art, 1982. A well written and illustrated catalog to accompany an exhibit of seven art museums in the planning or construction stage.

SPECIAL CASES: RENOVATIONS, SCHOOLS AND COMBINED USES

Educational Facilities Laboratories. *Community School Centers*. New York. EFL, 1979. 141 pp. ($5.00) Best source of information on this topic. Book covers planning, management and design of community school centers. These centers may include arts facilities, libraries, health clinics, elementary or secondary schools, swimming pools and other recreation facilities, day care centers, senior citizen services or other social agencies. Excellent resource bibliography.

Reusing Railroad Stations, Book Two. New York. EFL, 1975.

Reusing Space for the Arts: A Planning Assistance Kit. New York. EFL, 1981.

The Arts and Surplus School Space. New York. EFL, 1981. Case studies demonstrate ways in which school buildings have been reused as facilities for the arts.

Elder, Eldon. *Will It Make a Theatre: A Guide to Finding, Renovating, Financing, Bringing Up-to-Code, the Non-Traditional Performance Space.* New York. O.O.B.A. (Off Off-Broadway Alliance) 1979. 206 pp. ($8.00) Available from Drama Book Specialists, 150 West 52nd Street, 4th Floor, New York, New York 10019. This excellent book will help any group thinking about renovating a visual or performing facility.

Friedman, Daniel and Valerio, Joseph. *America's Movie Palaces: Renaissance and Reuse.* New York: Educational Facilities Laboratories, 1982. 128 pp. ($11.00) Available from EFL, 680 Fifth Avenue, New York, New York 10019. (Attention: Publications).

Museums and Adaptive Use, A special issue of *Museum News,* the journal of the American Association of Museums. September, 1980, Volume 59, Number 1. 104 pp. ($3.25) Available from A.A.M., 1055 Thomas Jefferson Street, NE, Washington, D.C. 20007.

Parrot, Charles A. *Access to Historic Buildings for the Disabled.* Washington D.C. Heritage Conservation and Recreation Services. 1980. HCRS Publication No. 46. (FREE)

Urban Land Institute. *Adaptive Use: Development, Economics, Process and Profiles.* Washington, D.C. Urban Land Institute, 1978.

U.S. Department of Transportation. *Recycling Historic Railroad Stations: A Citizens' Manual.* Washington, D.C.: U.S. Government Printing Office (GPO# 050-000-00143-1), 1978.

FUNDING, REAL ESTATE AND COMMUNITY SUPPORT

Baumol, William J., and Bowen, William G. *Performing Arts: The Economic Dilemma. A Study of Problems Common to Theater, Opera, Music and Dance.* New York. Twentieth Century Fund, 1966. 581 pp. ($35.00) Comprehensive economic analysis of all financial problems of professional performing arts organizations in the United States.

Brownrigg, W. Grant. *Corporate Fundraising: A Practical Plan of Action.* New York. American Council for the Arts, 1978. 74 pp. ($12.50) Description of a seven phase plan for fundraising.

Coe, Linda C.; Denney, Rebecca; and Rogers, Anne. *Cultural Directory II: Federal Funds and Services for the Arts and Humanities.* Prepared for the Federal Council on the Arts and the Humanities. Washington, D.C. Smithsonian Institution Press, 1980. 256 pp. ($7.75)

Coe, Linda C. *Funding Sources for Cultural Facilities: Private and Federal Support for Capital Projects.* Revised edition. Prepared for the Design Arts Program, National Endowment for the Arts, 1980. 72 pp. (FREE)

National Endowment for the Arts Research Division. No. 6 *Economic Impact of Arts and Cultural Institutions: A Model for Assessment and a Case Study in Baltimore.* 1977. 96 pp. ($2.50)

Urban Innovations Group. *The Arts in the Economic Life of the City.* New York. American Council for the Arts, 1979. 150 pp. ($14.95) Available from A.C.A., 570 Seventh Avenue, New York, New York 10018.

Urban Land Institute. *Adaptive Use: Development, Economics, Process and Profiles.* Washington, D.C. Urban Land Institute, 1978.

U.S. Office of Management and Budget. *Catalog of Federal Domestic Assistance.* Washington, D.C. Government Printing Office, published and updated semi-annually. ($20.00) A complete listing of all federal programs to aid state and local governments and nonprofit organizations. Write: OMB, Executive Office Building, 17th & Pennsylvania Avenue, Washington, D.C. 20006.

White, Virginia P. *Grants for the Arts.* New York. Plenum Press, 1980. 350 pp. ($19.50) Available from Plenum Publishing Corporation, 227 West 17th Street, New York, New York 10011.

PLANNING FOR MANAGEMENT AND OPERATIONS OF THE ARTS FACILITY

Organizing the Planning Group or Board of Directors

Adizes, Ichak. *The Unique Character of Performing Arts Organizations and the Functioning of Their Board of Directors.* Los Angeles: University of California, Los Angeles, Graduate School of Management, 1971. 14 pp. ($1.50)

Internal Revenue Service. *How to Apply for Recognition of Exemption for an Organization.* Publication number 557. Call your nearest IRS office for this pamphlet. Also ask for forms SS-4, 1023, 990 and 5768. (FREE)

Naumer, Helmuth. *Of Mutual Respect and Other Things.* Washington, D.C. American Association of Museums, 1977. 31 pp. ($2.75) On trusteeship responsibilities and nature of director/trustee relationships.

Weber, Joseph. *Managing the Board of Directors.* New York. The Greater New York Fund, Inc., 1975. 21 pp. ($1.25) Guidelines for organizing, recruiting and orienting board members.

Programming and Presenting Performing Arts

Arnott, Brian. *A Program Development Workbook: A Planning Guide for the Development of Performing Arts Programs for Non-profit Arts Facilities.* Ontario Ministry of Culture and Recreation, 1979. 40 pp. (FREE)

Association of College, University and Community Arts Administrators. *ACUCAA Handbook: Presenting the Performing Arts.* Madison, Wisconsin. ACUCAA, 1977. 490 pp. ($60.00) (Free with new membership from ACUCAA, P.O. Box 2137, Madison, WI 53701.)

Barrell, M. Kay. *The Technical Production Handbook: A Guide for Sponsors of Performing Arts Companies on Tour.* Santa Fe. Western States Arts Foundation, 1977. 31 pp. ($3.00)

Wolf, Thomas. *Presenting Performances: A Handbook for Sponsors.* Second edition. Cambridge, MA. New England Foundation for the Arts, 1977. 160 pp. ($3.95) Thoroughly readable book with excellent information for the arts organization interested in presenting touring groups.

Performing Arts Facility Management

Beck, Kirsten. *How to Run a Small Box Office.* New York. Off Off-Broadway Alliance, 1980. 71 pp. ($14.95) Available from Drama Book Specialists (Publishers) 150 W. 52nd Street, New York, New York 10019.

Foundation for the Extension and Development of the American Professional Theatre (FEDAPT). *Box Office Guidelines.* 1974. 44 pp. ($3.75) Available from FEDAPT, 165 W. 46th Street, Suite 310, New York, New York 10036.

Gruver, Elbert A. *The Stage Manager's Handbook.* New York. Drama Book Specialists, 1972. ($7.95)

Jewell, Don. *Public Assembly Facilities: Planning and Management.* New York. John Wiley & Sons, 1978. 195 pp. ($22.50) Written for convention facilities, topics covered include equipment, rates and policies, spaces for exhibition concession, admissions and box office.

Langley, Stephen. *Theatre Management in America: Principle and Practice.* Revised Edition. New York. Drama Book Specialists (Publishers), 1980. 490 pp. ($17.95) Available from Drama Books, 150 West 52nd Street, New York, New York, 10019.

Performing Arts Audience Development

MacIntyre, Kate. *Sold Out: A Publicity and Marketing Guide.* New York. Theatre Develoment Fund, 1980. 48 pp. ($5.00)

Morison, Bradley G., and Fliehr, Kay. *In Search of an Audience: How an Audience Was Found for the Tyrone Guthrie Theatre.* New York. Pitman Publishing Corporation, 1968. 230 pp. (out-of-print)

National Endowment for the Arts. Research Division. No. 9 *Audience Studies of the Performing Arts and Museums: A Critical Review.* 1978. 106 pp. ($3.00) No. 11 *Conditions and Needs of the Professional American Theatre.* 1980. 144 pp. ($4.50)

Newman, Danny. *Subscribe Now! Building Arts Audiences Through Dynamic Subscription Promotion.* New York. Theatre Communications Group, 1977. 304 pp. ($7.95)

Visual Arts Programming and Facility Management

Lee, Sherman, editor. *On Understanding Art Museums.* Englewood Cliffs, New Jersey. Prentice-Hall, 1975. 212 pp. ($9.94) Eight specialists discuss aims, tasks, problems, and future of art museums, covering such areas as the international market, nature of governing boards and accountability to public.

Meyer, Karl E. *The Art Museum: Power, Money, Ethics.* A Twentieth Century Fund Report. New York. William Morrow and Company, 1979. 352 pp. ($15.00) A critique of art museums. Appraises role of trustees, financial conditions, acquisition costs, "blockbuster" exhibitions and professionalism of staffs.

National Endowment for the Arts. *Museums USA: Art, History, Science and Others.* Research conducted by the National Research Center of the Arts. Washington, D.C. Government Printing Office, 1974. 203 pp. ($4.00) Survey of 1,821 museums, covers every major aspect of museum operations.

Zeyler Myer, Rebecca. *Gallery Management.* Syracuse, New York. Syracuse University Press, 1976. (Cloth-bound $11.95, paperback $5.95)

Other References

Coe, Linda and Stephen, Benedict. *Arts Management: An Annotated Bibliography.* New York. Center for Arts Information, 1980.

Western States Arts Foundation

The Western States Arts Foundation is dedicated to a vision of the West as a national center for the performing, literary, and visual arts. The Foundation strives to make national quality in the arts available to the people of the West and to promote the best of the region to the rest of the nation.

Success in the mission is due to the collaborative nature of the Foundation, established in 1974 by the state arts agencies of Arizona, Colorado, Idaho, Montana, Nevada, New Mexico, Oregon, Utah, Washington, and Wyoming. By bringing together the artistic resources and professional expertise of these states, and working in partnership with regional corporations and the National Endowment for the Arts, the Foundation is addressing a variety of important cultural needs and opportunities in the West.

The research on the region's existing cultural facilities which has resulted in *Building for the Arts* is an example of the Foundation's programs supported by the member states for the mutual benefit of their constituents and others around the country. Additional activities range from the touring of 48 quality performing arts companies to the publication of *Architectural Crafts,* a critically acclaimed book featuring the handcrafted work of 108 Western artisans. The Foundation's efforts assist artists and writers in reaching national markets through the Western States Exhibition Series and the Western States Book Awards, provide management training to volunteers and staffs of arts organizations, develop approaches for the use of microcomputers in the arts, and annually bring performances in music, dance, and theater to over 400,000 people in 78 Western cities of all sizes.

For more information about regional arts activities in the West contact the Western States Arts Foundation, 141 East Palace Avenue, Santa Fe, New Mexico, 87501, (505) 988-1166.

To learn more about the arts programs and services in the individual Western states, contact the appropriate arts agency as listed.

Arizona Commission on the Arts
2024 North 7th Street
Phoenix, Arizona 85006
(602) 255-5882

**Colorado Council on the Arts
and Humanities**
770 Pennsylvania Street
Denver, Colorado 80203
(303) 866-2617

Idaho Commission on the Arts
c/o Statehouse Mail
Boise, Idaho 83720
(208) 334-2119

Montana Arts Council
1280 South 3rd Street, West
Missoula, Montana 59801
(406) 543-8286

Nevada State Council on the Arts
329 Flint Street
Reno, Nevada 89501
(702) 789-0225

New Mexico Arts Division
224 East Palace Avenue
Santa Fe, New Mexico 87501
(505) 827-6490

Oregon Arts Commission
835 Summer Street, NE
Salem, Oregon 97301
(503) 378-3625

Utah Arts Council
617 E. South Temple Street
Salt Lake City, Utah 84102
(801) 533-5895

Washington State Arts Commission
9th & Columbia Bldg. - MS: GH-11
Olympia, Washington 98504
(206) 753-3860

Wyoming Council on the Arts
Capitol Complex
Cheyenne, Wyoming 82002
(307) 777-7742

CITYWEST

CITYWEST, Inc. is an urban design and architectural consulting firm specializing in the cultural, aesthetic and economic development of Western cities. Their philosophical approach integrates design with finance, policy and implementation concerns. Recent cultural projects include: The Cultural Plan for Yerba Buena Center in San Francisco; Aspen Center for the Performing Arts; and the Central Phoenix Theater Study. The authors are founders and principals of the firm, which is based in Los Angeles.

Catherine R. Brown is an urban designer with a Bachelor of Landscape Architecture from Louisiana State University. She also holds a Masters of Landscape Architecture and Urban Design from Harvard University's Graduate School of Design. Ms. Brown, author of several articles on landscape architectural history and theory, teaches in Los Angeles and has served on the faculties of Morgan State University and Tulane University.

William B. Fleissig is an architect and urban designer specializing in implementation strategies and public finance. He holds a Bachelor of Arts from the University of Pennsylvania, a Bachelor of Architecture (Urban Design) from City College of New York, and a Masters of Public Administration from Harvard's Kennedy School of Government. Mr. Fleissig currently teaches at U.C.L.A. and U.S.C. and is Director of Urban Affairs at University of Southern California's School of Architecture.

William Rees Morrish is an architect and urban designer. He holds a Bachelor of Architecture degree from University of California, Berkeley and a Masters of Architecture and Urban Design from Harvard University's Graduate School of Design. Currently teaching architectural design and graphics at University of Southern California, Mr. Morrish has also served on the faculties of Morgan State University, Tulane University and UC Berkeley.

Index

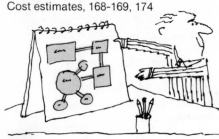

D

E

F

G

N

National Assembly of Local Arts
  Agencies, 233
National Assembly of State Arts
  Agencies (NASAA), 233
National Endowment for the Arts, 23,
  24, 28, 51, 68, 229
National Information Systems Project
  (NISP), 69
National Trust for Historic
  Preservation, 233
Nevada
  Elko. Civic Auditorium and
    Convention Center, 31, 222
  Northeastern Nevada Museum, 221
  Reno. Sierra Arts Center, 225
New England Foundation for the Arts,
  229
New Mexico.
  Farmington. Farmington Civic
    Center, 223
  San Ildefonso. Pueblo Museum, 227
  Santa Fe. Armory for the Arts, 219
New York (City)
  Museum of Modern Art, 28-29, 46,
    236
  Whitney Museum of American Art,
    45
New York (State)
  Onondaga County Civic Center, 31
Nonprofit status, 10

O

Offices, staff, 129-131, 144-145
Olympus on Main Street, 15, 31, 69,
  112
Opera America, 233
Operating Engineers Union, 181
Operating policy, 82, 178-185
Opportunity Resources for the Arts,
  234
Opportunity vs need, 6, 8
Oregon
  Eugene. Hult Center for the
    Performing Arts, 30, 223
  McMinnville. Gallery Players
    Theater, 218
  Portland. Civic Auditorium, 21
  Oregon School of Arts and Crafts,
    221

Portland Center for Performing Arts,
  20, 218
Portland Center for the Visual Arts,
  221
Roseburg. Umpqua Valley Arts
  Center, 22, 221
Salem. Bush Barn Art Center, 221
Elsinore Theater, 219

P

Parking, 155
Partners for Livable Places, 234
Percentage for Art Ordinance, 27
Performance space, 97-111
Performers, facilities for, 119-121
Performing arts facility
  administrative areas, 129-130
  audience seating area, 112-119
  facilities for performers, 119-121
  functional diagram, 130-131
  house design principals, 115-119
  production preparation, 121-123
  public areas, 127-129
  sample feasibility study, 68-74
  specific stage requirements
  chamber music, 111
  choral music, 111
  dance, 106
  drama, 104
  musicals, 108
  opera, 107
  orchestral music, 109-111
  stage types, 98-101
  storage, 121-123
  technical facilities, 124-126
Petitions, 21
Planning committee, 54, 64-65, 80-81
  checklist, 10-12
  composition of, 8-9, 18, 35
  funding, 9
  organizing, 9
  outreach, 13
  publicity, 15
  purpose, 2, 10
  records, 9
  reorganization of, 81
Planning process, 10-22
Production preparation areas, 121-124

Project goals, 80
  budget, 81
  difficulties, 17-18, 79-80
  evaluation of, 78-83
Property
  donated, 42
  government, 42
  leasing, 41
  optioning, 41-42, 81
  purchase, 40-41
  rental, 41
  sale/leaseback, 43
  tax arrears, 42-43
  see also Location
Public
  areas, 127-129, 133-138
  coatroom, 129
  restrooms, 128, 136
  See also Audience
Public Interest Public Relations, 234
Public relations, 21-22, 82
Public workshop, 14
Publishing Center for Cultural
  Resources, 234

R

Real estate, 35-47
Redevelopment agencies, 25
Rehabilitation Act of 1973, 127
Remodeling, 160-162
Renovation, 36-37, 83, 89, 153-160
Rental rates, 181, 185
Request for Proposal (RFP), 52, 55, 56, 68
Request for Qualifications (RFQ), 52
Research
  buildings, 36, 156-157
  inventory, 10-12
  other facilities, 13
  sites, 36-39
Restaurant See Food and beverage
  service
*Reusing Space for the Arts: A
  Planning Assistance Kit*, 37
Revenue sharing, 27, 30
Rouse Company, 45

S

Sculpture garden, 142
Seating See Audience
Security, 148-151, 182-183
  electronic, 148-149
  guards, 149
  sculpture garden, 142
  Smithsonian Institution Traveling
    Exhibition Service Security
    Requirements, 149-151
Sale/leaseback See Property
Seed money, 23-25
Services-in-kind, 25-26
Shipping and receiving, 122, 142-143
Shopping Centers See Mixed use
Sightlines, 115-117, 154
Signs, 134-135, 153
Site See Location
Site planning, 164
Smithsonian Institution Traveling
  Exhibition Service (SITES), 149-
  151, 236
Sound systems, 125-126
Southern Arts Federation, 229
Stage
  parts of, 101-103
  requirements, 101-111
  size, 102, 105-111, 154
  types of, 98-100
Storage areas, 123-124, 143-144
Storefront buildings, renovation of,
  159
Strategy
  financial, 33-34
  implementation of, 18-20
  memos, 19
Studios for teaching See Classrooms
Subcommittees, 81-83
Support
  community, 8, 17-22, 29
  financial, 17, 23-34
  government, 7-8, 17, 20-22, 29
  physical, 17
  political, 17, 20-22

T

TAG Foundation Ltd. (Technical
　Assistance Group), 234
Tax
　credits, 33
　laws, 33
　money, 27
　tax-exempt status, 10
Technical facilities
　performing arts, 124-126
　visual arts, 142-144
Telephone survey form, 69-71
Temperature and humidity, 147-148
Temporary exhibits, 22
Theater See Performing arts facility
Theatre Communications Group, 235
Theatre Development Fund, 235
Trust for Cultural Resources, 46
Trust for Public Land, 235

U

Unions, 181-182
United Nations Educational, Scientific
　and Cultural Organization
　(UNESCO), 235
U. S. Institute for Theatre Technology
　(USITT), 51, 239
Urban Land Institute, 235
Utah
　Ogden. Union Station, 222
　Park City. Kimball Art Center, 220
　Salt Lake City. Salt Lake County
　　Center for the Arts, 216
Utilities, 184

V

Visual arts facility
　administrative support, 144-145
　educational spaces, 145-147
　exhibition spaces, 136-142
　fire protection, 151
　functional diagram, 152
　public support spaces, 133-136
　sample feasibility study, 66-68
　security, 148-150

technical support areas, 142-144
temperature and humidity control,
　147-148
Volunteer Lawyers for the Arts, 235
VOLUNTEER: The National Center
　for Citizen Involvement, 15, 236
Volunteers, 8-9, 17-18, 21, 25, 32

W

Warehouses, renovation of, 159
Washington, DC. National Gallery of
　Art, 236
Washington (State)
　Bellevue. Bellevue Art Museum, 31,
　　45, 225
　Olympia. The Washington Center, 218
　Seattle. And/Or, 221
　Bagley Wright Theatre, 215
　Daybreak Star Art Center, 220
　Good Shepherd Center, 7, 227
　Seattle Art Museum, 30, 226
　Tacoma. Pantages Theater, 219
　Vancouver. Performing Arts and
　　Convention Center Study, 223
　Yakima. Capitol Theater, 30, 219
Western Association of Art Museums
　See Art Museum Association of
　America
Western States Arts Foundation, 51,
　229, 250-251
Will It Make A Theater ?, 37
Wyoming
　Casper. Casper Event Center, 222
　Cheyenne. Cheyenne Civic Center, 217
　Cheyenne Little Theater Players, 32, 216
　Evanston. Human Services
　　Complex, 225
　Wright. Latigo Hills Mall, 227

Z

Zoning, 37, 164, 170